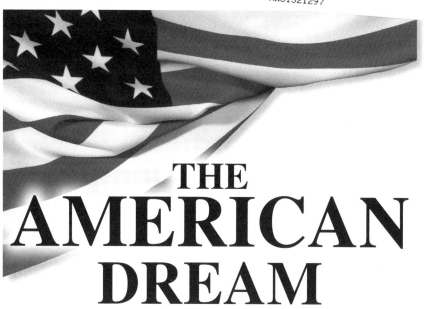

THE AMERICAN DREAM

The Rags to Roses Story of
BOB WARHURST
and the Founding of
MERRIFIELD GARDEN CENTER

SHARON AND SAL RUIBAL

Copyright© 2014 by Merrifield Garden Center, Merrifield, Virginia

All rights reserved. No part of this book may be reproduced or transmitted in any form or by any means, electronic or mechanical, including photocopying, recording, or any information storage or retrieval system, without permission in writing from the author and publisher.

For information, please contact: Merrifield Garden Center
PO Box 848, Merrifield, Virginia 22116 or info@mgcmail.com.

Printed in the United States of America

ISBN: 978-0-9862505-0-7
ISBN: 978-0-692-32443-1

CONTENTS

Preface iv

Introduction viii

Acknowledgments x

Chapter One - Make Every Day Count 1

Chapter Two - No Challenge Too Big 15

Chapter Three - Becoming Bob Warhurst 28

Chapter Four - Anything To Make Money 49

Chapter Five - Turning Trash Into Cash 62

Chapter Six - Bob and Buddy's Garden Center 79

Chapter Seven - Flying High 98

Chapter Eight - Fun In The Sun 117

Chapter Nine - A Sixth Sense 138

Chapter Ten - The Plant Whisperer 150

Chapter Eleven - Showtime 165

Chapter Twelve - George Washington Was Here 180

Chapter Fourteen - Superstitious Nature 204

Chapter Fifteen - Still Standing Strong 216

Chapter Sixteen - Family Is Everything 240

PREFACE

By Bob Warhurst

Thank you for reading my book, "The American Dream." Although various titles were considered for this book about my life, this title was ultimately chosen because I feel that it accurately captures what my journey was all about. I was fortunate enough to be born in a country where regardless of where I may have started out in life, the possibilities of what I could achieve were endless so long as I was willing to work hard to create my own opportunities.

The American Dream is not about how much money you make, what title you earn or what possessions you might collect along the way. To me, it's about having the ability to choose your own path and have the chance to fulfill your dreams. It's about working hard and having the freedom to do whatever you feel gives you the best chance to make a better life for you and your family. I chose my path and I couldn't have enjoyed it more.

But I didn't walk my path alone. For me to be able to achieve what I have in my life has required the love, support and assistance of so many others. There are too many people that have helped me along the way to possibly thank here, but I would like to acknowledge a special few who have meant so much to me. And for me that thanks starts with my family.

First and foremost, I would like to thank my beautiful wife of 57 years, Billie Jean. You have not only been a loving and supportive partner from the very beginning, but you have always been the most wonderful person I have ever known. You are my rock and without a doubt, the best thing that has ever happened to me. Nothing I have achieved in my life could have been possible without you.

I would also like to thank our five children—Debbie, Rob, Larry,

Donny and Kevin—and all of your families, including spouses and our 11 grandchildren, who have meant so much to us and helped me accomplish the things that I have. Owning and operating a family business would not have been possible without the hard work and sacrifices that you all have made. Every one of you have contributed in so many ways to our success, and I am grateful that you chose to follow me on this amazing journey.

And speaking of family, I would be remiss if I didn't mention my mother and father—Claude and Mary Warhurst—and my seven siblings—Charles, Lee, Jim, Margene, Tracy, Jane and Carl—who have all meant so much to me. Daddy and Mother taught me and my brothers and sisters so much while we were growing up in Alabama. We didn't have much, but they raised us with the core values that were needed to sustain a happy and healthy life, regardless of what material possessions we might attain.

It has been more than 50 years since Daddy passed and almost 29 years since we lost our mother, but the lessons they taught us have stayed with me throughout my entire life. Four of my siblings have passed on, and each one of them worked with me and for me at one point or another. But no matter where we were or what we were doing, our family always looked after each other, even though time and distance often kept us from seeing each other as much as we would have liked. I would especially like to thank my older brother Lee, who helped me on my journey from Alabama to Virginia, and my youngest brother Carl, who has been with me and helped me for so many years.

I would also like to thank my dear friend and business partner Buddy Williams, his wife Doris, and their three children—Wanda, Hal and Kim—whose hard work and dedication helped make our shared dream of Merrifield Garden Center a reality. It has been an honor and a privilege to work with each of you through the years. We worked hard every day to provide outstanding quality, selection and service to our customers and had a lot of fun doing it.

And in doing so, we were able to offer our customers something beautiful and lasting. I am tremendously proud of that legacy and couldn't have done it without all of you.

I would like to thank all of the people—past and present—who have worked at Merrifield Garden Center and helped make it the company that it has been for all these years. The Williamses and I are so proud of all of you and appreciate your contributions in building one of the largest independent garden centers in the country. We are especially thankful for all of those who have continued to work there for so long, including many who have been there for decades.

And I would like to thank all of our customers who have supported Merrifield Garden Center. Our entire Merrifield family is honored to serve you every day and appreciates your patronage more than you'll ever know. Because for us it wasn't just a job, but a labor of love that afforded us the opportunity to do something fun and special. Needless to say, Merrifield Garden Center would not be possible without our valued customers who have supported us, and for that we thank you.

And last but not least, I would like to thank Sharon Ruibal and her husband Sal for putting my life story into words. I may be the one who lived through it and witnessed it all happening in real time, but it was your job to take 75 years of experiences and put them into words. And I think you have done a great job of taking input from me and so many others to piece the whole story together.

I hope readers enjoy this story about my life. It has been a wonderful journey and I am so thankful to have lived it my way and on my own terms. I have certainly made my share of mistakes along the way, but I have no complaints. I have lived a happy and fulfilling life. I have achieved The American Dream!

So thank you again for buying my book. In doing so, you will also be doing a good deed, for a portion of the proceeds from the sale of each copy will be donated to the American Cancer Society. Hopefully one day some bright young man or woman might follow his or her own dream and pursue a career in science and medicine and finally find a cure for that disease, which has affected so many.

>Thank you and happy gardening!
>Bob Warhurst

INTRODUCTION

America has given birth to a thousand rags-to-riches stories, thanks to the freedoms that we enjoy. Our culture and heritage have made it possible for the lowliest of our citizens to rise above the circumstances of their impoverished beginnings to attain great power and wealth.

This is the American dream. But few of these stories can match the ascension of Bob Warhurst, a common man with an uncommon drive, not only to make money but to make the world a more beautiful place.

If you have spent any time in Washington, D.C., or the surrounding suburbs of Virginia and Maryland, you have seen his work. Merrifield Garden Center, founded by Bob and his friend and business partner Buddy Williams in 1971, is one of the largest independent garden centers in the nation. There is scarcely a neighborhood in the area that hasn't been beautified with the Merrifield touch. From the leafy estates of U.S. Supreme Court justices and U.S. senators to the lush, flowering gardens in swanky Georgetown to multitudes of others from all walks of life, Bob's work is literally growing all around us.

Bob Warhurst and the Merrifield team have created an abundance of beauty and elegance, including his own seven-acre estate built on historic Hope Parke in Fairfax, Virginia, where George Washington was once a frequent guest. Bob did this despite beginnings so harsh and barren that one cringes at the thought of a child not only enduring them but also carrying his family on his small, bent back.

Bob's sense of history is also reflected in his work. Merrifield Garden Center has expanded west from the outskirts of Washington D.C., along U.S. Route 29, the road that Thomas Jefferson followed north by horse from his home in Monticello to the U.S. Capitol for his second presidential inauguration in 1805.

Today, Bob Warhurst is a quietly powerful man in a city built on raw power. He harnesses modern tools with the same astute vision he had when scratching out a living in dirt poor Alabama during the rebuilding years immediately following the Great Depression. The same hands that were once bloodied picking cotton and catching frogs to put meat on the family dinner table now dance on the virtual keys of an iPad as he manages millions of dollars on the world's stock exchanges.

Told to the best of his recollection, Bob's evolution from back roads ragamuffin to trash collector to captain of commerce was not always pretty and the odds were stacked against him, but that is also the history of this great nation. What we all can learn from Bob Warhurst is that the human spirit is indomitable and resilient, and that doing the right thing is the only thing to do.

This is also an inspiring story of family and how unconditional love, dogged determination and tireless work can overcome a lack of formal education and inherited wealth. It also is a story of how Bob and his family stayed united in the face of a world that sometimes valued chicanery over honesty and financial connections over family ties.

The Bob Warhurst story is a tale of America as it used to be and should be today. Inclusion is a big part of The Merrifield Way, with immigrant employees learning English working next to American workers, including Bob, learning Spanish. Customer service is at the center of all that happens, a philosophy that didn't come from business school but from the heart of a man who never met a stranger.

After reading about Bob Warhurst and his incredible life story, you'll count him as a friend, too.

ACKNOWLEDGMENTS AND THANKS

This is Bob Warhurst's book, a chronicle of his amazing life as he remembers it. The events and actions described are from his own memory and the recollections of his family, friends and others who were present at various times in his life. It was an honor for us to write this book.

The Warhurst family, especially Kevin Warhurst, who took on the Herculean task of making sure that this book was not only accurate but also represented the lifelong values of his father and mother.

The Williams family and Merrifield Garden Center employees who gave lengthy interviews about their jobs and their personal histories with Bob Warhurst.

Michie Shaw, editor and proofreader. We were lucky to have the collaborative skills of a professional with an eagle eye and a sharp pencil on our team.

Suzani Pavone, cover and layout designer. This artist captured the look and feel of Bob's life with her artistic touches that reflect his life and rise to greatness.

Fran Bindon, Trish Tharp and Judy Taylor, manuscript reviewers. A writer's best friend is a first reader with great taste in literature and narrative style, as well as big-picture sensibility honed by a lifetime of reading books.

Franklin County Archives in Russellville, Alabama, for historical research. An extraordinary resource for fact-checking big and small. No other archive in the world could tell us when Bob's childhood neighborhood got electric power. Other great resources include the "History of the Boll Weevil in Alabama, 1910-2007," the Franklin County Chamber of Commerce in Russellville, Alabama, and the Alabama Department of Archives and History in Montgomery, Alabama.

Collector Sector for the "Flying Lady" story. "Hope Park and the Hope Park Mill" by Martin Petersilia and Russell Wright, a treasure chest of facts great and small about George Washington and his family. For the story about Nettie and her pig, we are indebted to "The Civil War in Fairfax County: Civilians and Soldiers" by Charles V. Mauro.

"This was Vienna, Virginia" by Connie Pendleton Stuntz and Mayo Sturdevant Stuntz. A wonderful history book about the neighborhood where Bob and Billie Jean and Buddy and Doris raised their children.

CHAPTER ONE

MAKE EVERY DAY COUNT

It was a chilly, late autumn afternoon in Russellville, Alabama, in 1950. Before he headed out to work on the railroad for the week, Claude Rea pulled aside his 12-year-old son to give him an important assignment.

He told Bobby that winter was coming and he needed to slaughter the hog that the family kept behind the house. The meat was needed to provide food throughout the long, dark days ahead.

With wide eyes, Bobby looked up at his father and pleaded, "Daddy, I don't know how to do it."

As he quickly walked out the door to head to the train station, Claude turned and said in a grave voice, "You'll figure it out."

The next day, young Bobby walked in the woods, trying to summon the courage and strength to accomplish his father's command. He sat down on a frost-rimmed tree stump and started to think up a plan to kill the hog, which as a farm animal destined for the supper plate, had no name, making its inevitable demise less personal.

At 200 pounds, the filthy, grunting beast was twice as big as Bobby, who remembered that his older brother Lee had a 22-caliber rifle. That would do for the killing, but the slaughtering would be difficult. He had to find a way to scald the corpulent beast to remove its wiry hairs.

Bobby began hacking away at the hard Alabama dirt and soon had a hole deep enough to hold the carcass. He transformed an old and rusting 55-gallon metal drum into a cooking pot, placing it at a 45-degree angle to make it easier to drag the hog into the drum. He carefully stacked firewood beneath the rickety apparatus, which he would use to boil the water.

Bobby tied a rope around the hog's snout ring and coerced the waddling animal to make its last living steps toward the makeshift abattoir. He carefully took aim at the hog, the rifle barrel pointed between the animal's squinting eyes. His small finger curled around the trigger and, after a sharp pop and a whiff of gunpowder smoke, the hog was dead.

Then Bobby pulled out a large kitchen knife and carefully slit the hog's fatty throat, the blood spilling onto the cold dirt in thick ribbons of red. As the water in the drum began to boil, the hog was unceremoniously slipped into its first and only hot bath.

Bobby's wits got him that far, but he needed some hands-on expertise to turn the 200-pound corpse into food for his family. He convinced 22-year-old neighbor Stratt Barnes to help him butcher the hog in exchange for a portion of the meat.

The hog was laid out on a rough wooden bench. Barnes took a big swing with his axe and broke the hog's breast bone. With a hand saw, he opened the beast lengthwise. They tied a rope around the hog's legs and threw the line over a branch and yanked the animal off the ground.

They cleaned out the carcass with buckets of water from the nearby stream and began removing the inedible organs and other unusable parts. The hog was quickly divided into a collection of bacon, chops, ham and other random pieces that would later be ground to make pork sausage. To keep the raw meat from spoiling, Bobby stacked the meat in a wooden box and covered the layers with coarse salt from a 50-pound bag.

SLAUGHTERING THE HOG WAS A CHALLENGE beyond what anyone could reasonably expect from a child, even one as hard-willed as Bobby.

Born on December 8, 1938, Robert Paul Rea's early years in Alabama were not idyllic. The Great Depression that began in 1929 and lasted until 1939 was the worst economic downturn in the history of the industrialized world. Alabama's industrial center, Birmingham, was considered the hardest hit city in the nation, with employment in the crucial iron and steel industries falling from 100,000 to only 15,000. Away from the cities, cotton farming had not recovered from the boll weevil infestation that began in 1910. One of the few growing businesses was the production and distribution of illegal "moonshine" whiskey. It would take almost a full decade and World War II to revive the nation's economy.

But young Bobby's quick mind and strong back provided for the family, a theme that would be repeated many times over in his life and propel him from a hardscrabble life in rural Russellville to booming post-war Washington, D.C., where he would become both a prosperous business executive and notable "Plant Whisperer" whose work is on display at the homes of U.S. presidents, U.S. senators, U.S. Supreme Court justices and multitudes of others from all walks of life.

The road to prosperity would be long and difficult.

Bob was the fourth of eight children born to Claude Lee Warhurst and Mary (Flippo) Warhurst in Russellville, a farming town in Franklin County in northwest Alabama near the Tennessee and Mississippi borders. Russellville had a population of 5,510 in the 1940 census and now has a population of 9,830.

Claude never really knew his father, William Jefferson Warhurst. The relationship between William Jefferson and Claude's mother Vardie Rea ruffled some feathers in her family. As the story goes, the Reas were not thrilled that the 24-year-old William Jefferson Warhurst courted their 15-year-old daughter. It's unclear if they knew at the time that he was a divorcee. The Reas eventually ran William Jefferson Warhurst out of town and, as family rumor has it, he joined a traveling circus as a high-wire walker.

Claude remained in Russellville with his mother's side of the family. The name Warhurst was so distasteful to the Reas that they changed Claude's surname to Rea. When he got married and had children of his own, Claude gave them the last name Rea out of respect for the family. So young Bob became known as Bobby Rea, a name that was on his birth certificate and one he would keep until he made his way to Virginia in 1955, when the Warhurst name was once again revived.

Mary was born and raised in Lawrenceburg, Tennessee, but her family moved about 60 miles south to Russellville when her father got work at a saw mill. On their first date, Claude and Mary were part of a double date, but he was with another girl and Mary was with one of Claude's friends. Midway through the date, Claude discovered that he was attracted to Mary. He pulled his friend aside and asked if they could switch girls. The friend said yes and the rest is Rea family history.

For little Bobby Rea, life started out a bit strange. At one point, he almost "became" a girl. After beginning his family with three sons —Charles, Lee and Jim—Claude was hoping for his first daughter. But along came Bobby. Not to be totally denied, Claude refused to cut Bobby's gorgeous blonde hair, letting it grow long, all the way down to his shoulders. Bobby was even dressed in girl's clothing for awhile. Bob doesn't remember those days, but now says, "I saw photos of me dressed in a gown. Daddy wanted a girl so bad that he tried to make one out of me. I don't know what he was thinking."

But Bobby always knew his goal was to become a successful man. "Life is such a gift," he now says. "You have to make every day count. You don't get a second chance at that day. My earliest memories are thinking of ways to better myself. I didn't like people going through life just getting by. I had a feeling that I had to follow my destiny."

FOR THE FIRST FEW YEARS OF BOBBY'S LIFE, the Reas were tenant farmers at The Old Pace Place, a 100-acre farm about five miles north of Russellville. A majority of the farms in Alabama at that time were operated by tenants, not landowners. The family grew vegetables, raised chickens for meat and eggs, as well as hogs for bacon and sausage and cows for milk. The Reas owned about 15 Jersey and Holstein cattle, two big draft horses for plowing the fields, along with some goats, ducks and guinea hens. They had no electricity, indoor plumbing or street lights near their house. Money was tight, but an honor system was created to keep food on the table of Russellville's working poor. "People paid on credit," recalled Helen Bendall Berry, whose father owned Bendall Grocery. "When you got paid, you came into the store and squared up. People grew watermelons, cotton and corn. When the crops came in, they had money. They owed the doctor. There was no health insurance. You bartered or traded or owed. They were hard-working people. It was the honor system, and sometimes people couldn't pay back."

Joyce Poss Swinney, who grew up during those difficult years, remembered that "it was uncommon to eat meat. But everyone seemed to have a hog. You did anything you could to keep from spending money. You never threw away anything. You could always find a use for something." In those tough times, women made clothing out of feed sacks. But these weren't just plain cotton bags, because the textile mills knew that women used them for clothing and other household items. The bags were decorated with floral prints and other designs that disguised their original purpose. In those days, even packaging had to work two jobs. "We didn't know what the rest of the world was like," Helen remembered. "We didn't even know what Birmingham (the largest city in Alabama) looked like."

The children called Claude "Daddy" and Mary "Mother." Claude insisted on that title for her. Perhaps it was because at 15 he found out that the girl he thought was his sister was really his mother and that the woman he thought was his mother was really his grandmother. In those days, it was common for a mother to raise her young, unwed daughter's child to shield her from judgmental eyes.

Claude's wife Mary was a kind and gentle soul with unflagging patience. An attractive woman with a slim figure, Mary was a hard worker who had her hands full with the children and the demands of the house but was seldom seen without a smile. "She was the most wonderful person," said Jane Von Pingel, Bob's youngest sister. "If something terrible was happening, she'd say one sentence to make it all better."

Bob marvels at how his mother could take nothing and make something of it, a valuable skill during those lean years. Sometimes the children feared they'd go to bed with an empty stomach, but he says "Mother was always able to pull out of a hat something to eat. We threw nothing away. We might only have had a can of pineapple and some leftover biscuits in the house. Mother would add a little mayonnaise and make pineapple sandwiches. I still make myself pineapple sandwiches all the time."

Many struggling farm owners were offered federal subsidies, so the need for tenants to provide income waned, forcing many renters off the farms. Even in those circumstances, Bob remembers a wonderful childhood. "We didn't have anything," he says. "We barely had enough to eat. But as long as you have enough food to survive, that's really all you need to be happy."

Mary taught her children to dream big, a habit she kept herself. She wrote songs and sang throughout the day. "She sent songs to the Grand Ole Opry and Elvis," said Bob's sister Margene Scruggs. "It was like seven dollars if they kept it. They were probably country songs. Love songs." Claude, too, was perpetually happy despite the troubled times and financial hardships. And Claude wasn't afraid to show his affection for his wife, showering her with kisses. He was fond of saying, "I wish I married her in the morning. I wasted all day."

Most folks in the Russellville area could not afford a telephone, which was considered a luxury at the time. Radios and especially television sets were rare. Community social life was centered around small country churches, where a preacher led congregations of 35 to 50 people. The church was where the latest news and town gossip were exchanged. Many local businesses closed early on Wednesday afternoons so churchgoers could attend the popular Wednesday evening prayer services.

On Sunday mornings, the Rea family would often attend the Church of Christ in Russellville, but the worship didn't stop there. Not a day went by that Claude and Mary didn't read the Bible. "They were both Godly people," Bob's sister Jane said. "My mother always said people should thank God, no matter what type of shape they're in, even if you could only move a finger." Claude and Mary made it a priority to instill right and wrong in their children. No stealing. No lying. No cheating. And no exceptions. "If we did," Jane said, "we'd be skinned alive."

Despite the hardships and scarcity of work, Claude was able to find a job with the Southern Railroad Company, where he used his construction skills to build and repair railroad stations. But that meant spending most of his time away from the family he loved. On Sunday afternoons, after a big family meal, he would hitch a ride of about 20 miles to Tuscumbia, Alabama, where he would catch the train and work down the line until Friday night, when he would make the trip back to Russellville. Unfortunately, railroad work could be unsteady. "If they didn't have any work, they'd lay him off," Bob recalls. "Two, three months at a time. And the most he ever made was 60 cents an hour, and if he got a raise, it was just two or three cents."

During their father's absences, Bob's older brothers, Charles and Lee, did the hard work around the farm, with the bigger and stronger Charles hitching up the family horses to plow the fields and the smaller Lee feeding the livestock and helping his mother around the house. "We didn't have no time to be boys," Lee recalled. "Me and my brother were working while the other boys in town were hunting and fishing and playing baseball."

CLAUDE WAS TALL AND LEAN with a flat belly and the strength of an ox. He had a well-deserved reputation as a compassionate man who was always ready to assist those in need. Family and friends say "he never knew a stranger." He was talkative and good-hearted, almost to a fault. When he built a fence, a casket, an addition to a house or whatever else the townspeople needed, they would ask how much money they owed him. Claude was famous for saying, "You don't owe me a thing."

"Daddy was a good man and a hard worker," Bob says. "He was talented as a Mason and a 32nd degree Shriner. He was a simple man. Never had a car or knew how to drive one. He liked to dress up but didn't have but one suit. He was full of life."

Claude was a proud man who never accepted public assistance or handouts of any kind, even though many people in Russellville were on welfare or received commodities periodically. He used to always say, "We may not have much, but I can tell you one thing, we ain't never going to be on welfare."

That pride often made things more difficult for his family, who were forced to do without. But that was just Claude's way.

"When I was born, it was the Great Depression," Bob says. "As far as Daddy was concerned, there was no Depression. Daddy would give away everything. He'd say 'Go and help so and so but don't take anything for it.' I remember one day I stopped by the people's house who lived a few doors down from us and I saw that they had no food in the house and no money to buy food. I went home and told Daddy and he reached into his pocket and grabbed the last two dollars he had and told me to give it to them. That's the kind of man he was. We never faulted Daddy for it, but we knew we needed money as much as everyone else did."

Sometimes the family had a little hope to cling to. There was big talk of a family gold mine in Ireland that would someday be inherited and lift them from their hard-knock existence. "For years, we thought we'd get money from it," Bob recalls. "Business people and lawyers would come and talk to Daddy about it. Nothing ever came of it."

Bobby realized his family was poor when they didn't get anything for Christmas. "It made me sad," he says now. "I would dream of having a red wagon or a pony." Bobby knew those dreams, like the dreams of millions of other kids in those rough times, had little chance of coming true. But dreams were free, and he had plenty of them along with a strong sense of self-confidence. Much of that came from Claude, who told his young children that, despite their current position in life—no electricity, no running water, no car and sometimes fried frog and squirrel meat for dinner—he had high expectations of them. "Look son, you're a Warhurst," Claude told them. "You can do anything you want. We can do stuff regular men can't do. When you're walking, swing your arms with pride." It was curious that Claude used the name Warhurst. Perhaps he gave his children the surname Rea to appease his mother's family, but in his heart he thought of his children as Warhursts.

That family pride was severely tested one day when the usual daily menu of eggs, sausage and biscuits for breakfast and pole green beans and boiled potatoes for supper dwindled to mere scraps. "One day, I saw that Mother looked worried," said Lee, who was just nine at the time. "I asked her what was wrong."

With a sorrowful look, Lee's mother confessed to her young son that the family cupboard was nearly empty, something she could not tell her proud husband. "I used the last drop of flour and the last drop of Crisco," she said.

Lee thought for a moment and then jumped into action, pulling fresh corn from the family garden and walking to the city, where he started knocking on people's doors. Within 30 minutes, all the corn was sold. Lee returned home with a sack of flour over his shoulder, a can of Crisco under his arm and 35 cents in his damp palm.

"Daddy was as nice of a man as there ever was," Lee said. "But he wasn't a money maker. He wanted to help people. He needed to change. We needed money. I had to take things into my own hands. We had youngsters, Jim and Bob. My mother counted on me."

It was not long before Lee had set up a small dairy business selling milk, hen's eggs, duck eggs and turkey eggs. All his earnings went to their mother for groceries. While their father was pleased, he still let his big heart do the talking. "One thing I ask you," he told Lee, "don't charge the widows."

Lee was stunned, as widows were the biggest segment of his customers, telling his mother, "I'm selling it to them cheaper than what they get it for at the store. They have money to go to the picture show, but we don't."

"It's your business," she replied. "I'm not going to tell you how to run it."

That was the only time Lee disobeyed his father. From then on, the widows paid just like everyone else.

When Bobby was a few years older, the family moved into the "city." Claude told young Lee to sell most of their Jersey and Holstein cattle and two or three goats to raise the $60 needed to buy the one-acre parcel of land at the corner of Marlin Street and Harrison Avenue in Russellville. Not yet a teenager, Lee already had the business smarts to negotiate with Marvin Terry, a local man who bought cattle for Hester's Sale Barn.

At their new place, Claude and Charles took a cross-cut saw and cut down several oak trees on the property. They cut the trees into sections, loaded them on their wagon and took them to a saw mill, where the trees were cut into boards to make their home. They paid a standard fee, providing the saw mill operators several trees in exchange for the service. It took Claude and Charles just six weeks to build their two-bedroom home, which included one bedroom for Claude and Mary and another for the four strapping boys to share. An outhouse was built about 65 feet out their back door. When it got full, they would simply dig another hole. For toilet paper, they tore pages out of the Sears catalog.

Like most country folk in those hard times, the Rea family got along without many of the comforts we now take for granted. Their simple home was furnished with mismatched, hand-me-down furniture, wood worn smooth from hands calloused by the handles of hoes and shovels. Bob's small bed had a thin, time-worn mattress made of feathers. "It wasn't very comfortable," he recalls. "You would sink down to the springs. But we didn't know any better. We thought everybody had the same thing." Without a television or radio, Bob recalls "you went to bed when it got dark."

Smoking was an inexpensive pastime. Smokers rolled up their own cigarettes with thin papers and a pinch of tobacco from a muslin pouch tied with a yellow string or a rectangular tin can that fit in a back pocket. Claude rolled his own Prince Albert cigarettes. One night, Claude tucked Bobby into bed while smoking. After Claude left the room, Bobby cried out. Some ashes had fallen and the bed was on fire. Claude rushed back in the room and put out the flames.

One of Bobby's daily chores was supplying the family with fresh water. Every morning he filled two 1-gallon buckets from a 4-foot wide, shallow spring that had emerged in a grassy field 150 yards from their house. Even in the blazing heat of an Alabama summer, the water was refreshing and satisfying, with no chemical taste. Often, Bobby lingered at the spring to catch frogs for supper. "I'd skin them and mother would put them in a bowl on top of the ice box, until we were ready to fry them," Bob recalls. "Even though they were dead, those suckers would kick and splash water out of the bowl. I thought it was the funniest thing."

When it came to bathing, the Reas didn't have the luxury of a bathtub or a shower. Instead, they scrubbed themselves under the light of a kerosene lamp with a bar of soap and wet rags, similar to a sponge bath. "We'd wash our faces and feet every day," Bob says now about those days. "The rest of our bodies we'd only wash when they were dirty." Washing clothes by hand for her husband and four sons was a Herculean task that took an entire day. Every Tuesday Bobby's mother would boil the family's clothes in a big, old pot over a fire outdoors and work out the dirt with a scrub board. When the shirts, slacks and socks were cleaned to her satisfaction, she hung them on a clothesline to dry.

Because they sold most of their livestock to buy the new home site, they had fewer animals to tend than at The Old Pace Place. But they still had a cow for milk, two work horses and chickens for eggs and meat for Sunday supper and holidays. They also kept one hog a year, which they would slaughter in the fall. For the family, beef was a rarity, but they grew nearly every vegetable imaginable. Served both fresh and canned, vegetables were the staple of their diet.

MONEY WAS IMPORTANT TO BOBBY because at a young age he saw that commerce was how the world worked. When he was four, Bobby wanted a nickel to treat himself to candy and ice cream. So he sat in the ditch next to the dusty, dirt road near his Uncle Ode Rea's house and waited for hours for his uncle to come by. Uncle Ode was retired and had a little money. But the response was not what Bobby hoped for. "Go on, boy!" Ode said. "You don't need no nickel."

Mortified, Bobby vowed "I'll never ask anyone for money again." That moment set Bobby Warhurst on a path he's still walking today.

Over the next three years, the family continued to grow with the birth of Margene. Charles entered the Army and fought in World War II. Lee left home to find his own way in life. And the family's paltry earnings were stretched to the breaking point once again.

Although he was just seven—much too young to have to be a man—Bobby knew it was time for him to contribute to the family's finances. Finding jobs was still difficult for grown men, but Bobby was determined. "The reason I went to work was to make a little money for the family and myself," Bob says about those days. "It was such a struggle. I didn't like the feeling of having no money.

We desperately needed groceries. And I wanted us to be a little like everyone else. You want the things they have. You want to be able to go to the picture show, to buy a pair of tennis shoes. I always had hand-me-downs from my older brothers. I wore tattered work boots held together with hog nose rings. I was embarrassed. I wanted to be normal like other people. I wanted things, and I was willing to work for them."

Not far from the family's home was the Hendrix Grocery Store, a far cry from today's mega-markets, but still a world of wonder for a young man with big hopes. It was a small, but unique country market with shelves of canned goods and coolers full of delectable cheese and a variety of fresh ham, bologna and chicken, which would be cut to order with a meat cleaver on a big round, wooden block. Fifty-pound bags of flour and sugar lined an aisle. A big metal drink box, filled with water and powered by a condenser, was packed with ice-cold bottles of RC Cola, Dr. Pepper, Nehi Orange and Pepsi. And there were stalks of bananas with ripe fruit for customers to peel off, which added to the exotic nature of the corner store.

The store was owned by Miss Annie Mae Hendrix, a devout Christian, and Sid, her cattle dealer husband. Bob knew Miss Annie Mae from his visits to buy food for his family and was fascinated with her glamorous style and attitude. But he wasn't intimidated by her looks, which remind him even today of Elizabeth Taylor.

At the age of seven, Bobby summoned up the courage to ask her for a job. She smiled a big smile and in a kind voice explained that he was too young to work. But Bobby didn't take no for an answer. He showed up the next day and began working for free to show his worth. He stocked shelves, swept the floors, carried out trash, delivered goods to customers on his bicycle and even helped Miss Annie Mae put on her shoes.

"I was big for my age," he recalls. "I was seven but I looked nine and felt like nine. I could lift a 50-pound feed bag with no trouble.

I was strong and fast. I ran everywhere. I knew I could be an asset."

A couple of weeks later, Bobby had won over Miss Annie Mae and was hired for 50 cents a week. That's equivalent to about $6.50 today. It was Miss Annie Mae who gave Bob his first glimpse of what it takes to manage a business, the value of hard work, taking care of customers and doing what the boss asks you to do with a smile.

"He was always smiling," recalled Barbara Stanley, Miss Annie Mae's youngest daughter. "That's how I remember him. You never saw him misbehave or be mean to anyone. My mother loved him. She thought of him as a son."

Looking back, Bob fondly remembers Miss Annie Mae as a sharp businesswoman. "Hard, but nice," he says. "She had dark hair, a nice figure and stylish clothes. She would stand behind the counter in her bare feet and call out, 'Bobby Rea, come put my shoes on.' After two weeks, she couldn't do without me. That 50 cents was huge. It was the cat's meow."

In the decades to come, that cat would learn to roar.

CHAPTER TWO

NO CHALLENGE TOO BIG

Bobby wasn't always an angel. Sometimes the pressure of his high ambitions and heavy workload were too much for the young man. One morning his father gave him money to buy paint at the store.

On his way to fulfilling his duty, Bobby passed the movie theater and saw that it was showing a cowboy movie that he had been hoping to see. Torn between his mission and his passion, he succumbed to temptation, bought a ticket and slipped into the cool shadows of the darkened theater.

As the movie came to an end, Bobby realized that the paint money was spent and he had to go home and face his father. Paralyzed with fear about what his father would do, he decided to stay at the theater and hunkered down in his seat, oblivious to the movie because his young mind was occupied by the thought of what was in store for him when he got home. As one movie after another reeled on and on, his fears deepened. He spent all day inside the theater.

Finally, it closed and he had to face the grim reality of going home. In the late night darkness, his trepidation increased step by step. He carefully tiptoed up the front steps and tried to turn the doorknob. It would not budge.

First, he knocked gently, hoping his mother would hear it first and let him in.

There was no answer. He knocked a bit louder. No response. He thought about sleeping on the porch, but just as he was about to lie down, the door whooshed open and his father's dark figure filled the doorway.

"I'll deal with you in the morning," was his father's stern greeting.

Even in his own bed, Bobby had trouble sleeping. His eyes had barely closed when he felt his father's coarse hand on his shoulder, shaking him to consciousness.

"Fetch me a switch," he commanded, "so I can whip you."

Trying to delay the inevitable, Bobby wandered about the yard looking for the right implement. He settled on a huge branch that was so heavy he could only drag it to the front porch.

Bobby steeled himself for punishment, but the only sound was his father laughing hard and deep at the enormous piece of wood that was almost as big as the boy and far too heavy to use as a switch. His father was so amused that Bobby was granted a reprieve and was taught a lesson he would remember for the rest of his life.

AS HE MADE THE TRANSITION FROM BOY to young man, Bobby's outlook on the world expanded, and he began to define his life as a series of challenges to be met head on. There was now another mouth to feed in the family with the birth of brother Claude and Bobby gladly took on whatever his father asked him to do while also working at the Hendrix Grocery Store.

"Daddy thought Bob could do anything," said Jane Von Pingel, Bobby's youngest sister. "He'd say, 'Weed this, fix that hole in the roof' or whatever. Bob's shoulders kept getting wider and wider. Bob could do anything he put his mind to. That's the determination he had. He mastered everything he tried to do and always acted a lot older than his age."

In the front yard of Bobby's childhood home was a huge oak tree that was as wide as he could spread his arms. The ancient tree was more than a 100 years old. There was a small patch of green grass in the front yard and the giant tree's thick roots snaked across the bare dirt yard before diving deep underground in search of water.

One day, one of the neighborhood mothers was trying to grab her son, who was about seven years old, so she could cut his long, flowing brown hair. Every time she tried to catch him, he managed to squirm away and escape.

Bobby, who was big for his age, had a plan. He caught the slippery little boy with his strong arms and tied him to the big oak tree with a rope. His prey subdued, Bobby took a pair of his mother's sharp sewing scissors to the boy's bushy hair. The mother was happy, Bobby was proud and only the boy was frowning.

One thing Bobby didn't care for was picking cotton, a community effort in the days before agriculture became mechanized. Schools even closed to allow students to work in the fields. "Your hands would be bloody picking cotton," he says. "You had to wear rags on your hands because we didn't have gloves. We were paid for what we picked."

Bobby was much more interested in working his family's large vegetable garden, where he tilled the red Alabama soil; planted seeds for pole beans, green beans and turnips; hand-pulled thousands of weeds; and then harvested the bounty that nurtured his family. "I always had a love of plants," he says now. "You can't help but fall in love with plants. They're a miracle of life. They're such a wonderful thing." Bobby supplemented the vegetables by hunting squirrels and rabbits, shooting them with Lee's .22 rifle, skinning them and cutting the carcasses into meat. He also had the job of selecting chickens that would be fried for family meals, catching the oldest and slowest free-ranging birds, then quickly wringing their necks. "I could actually take two chickens—one in each hand—and wring both their necks at the same time," Bob recalls.

Although he was taking care of all kinds of chores around the house and working at the Hendrix Grocery Store to help support the family, Bobby felt like he wasn't acquiring as many skills as he'd like. "You just can't learn enough at a grocery store," he said. So Bobby picked up a second job with J.C. Steinecipher, the local plumber. Mr. Steinecipher paid Bobby $1 a day, much more than he could make for Miss Hendrix.

Bobby was now becoming more conscious of his personal hygiene. Not satisfied by just a cursory scrubbing with a rag and bucket of water, he used his newly acquired plumbing skills to rig up his own 7-foot shower behind some thick shrubs near the house. Digging deep into the soil, he located the city water line leading to the spigot on their property. He inserted a T-pipe in the water line to direct water to his shower and completed the job with a shower head.

Although he had tattered clothes, Bobby still liked them to be clean and pressed. "I liked a nice crease in my jeans and shirt," he says. "I liked to be neat." The laundry routine in those days included sprinkling freshly washed clothes with a solution of powdered starch and water. The clothes would be put on a clothesline until dry, and then would get another sprinkle of water when they were ironed. To heat the heavy clothes iron, Bobby built a fire in the wood stove. "(Bobby) was a prankster," said Jane, Bobby's sister. "My Daddy liked starch in his pants. One time, Bob put so much starch in them, they were standing up by themselves!"

Bobby's independent streak also led him to build a tiny house for himself out of discarded wood from a local mill. Any bent nail he could find laying about was quickly transformed into a straight one with his hammer. The 8' x 6' hut had no windows, but he built a sturdy door with a chain that locked from the inside. He would read comic books by the light of a kerosene lamp while reclining on a handmade bunk, nestled deep in a pine-straw mattress. In his rough fortress, he read tales of kings and soldiers, strong men who traveled far and wide in search of their destinies.

"He's pretty much always been his own independent person," said Margene Scruggs, Bob's sister. "He liked doing his own thing. He was always on the go, and you'd have to catch him on the fly."

The Reas eventually got a small radio and Bobby would sometimes listen to the thrilling adventures of "The Lone Ranger" and "The Shadow." On Saturday nights, he could pick up a crackling signal from WCKY in Cincinnati, Ohio, and listen to country music.

In 1951, Bob's mother was 43 years old when she delivered fraternal twins Jane and Carl. With Mary weakened by her ordeal and Claude away working for the railroad, the family was under extreme pressure to provide even the barest essentials of care for all the children. Bobby's many outside jobs helped keep the family from a domestic disaster.

"They was real poor," said Emma Jean Colburn, Bobby's cousin who lived in nearby Spruce Pine, Alabama. "(My mother and I) would go up every week and bring them groceries and canned goods, and help what we could. Margene's hair would be matted up. I had to wash it and brush it. She'd be so happy. The babies wet the floor. They had diapers, but not like today. We got the house cleaned up and cooked for them. We washed all the dirty dishes. I had to boil a fire and heat the water to wash all the dishes. They didn't have nothin' but potatoes to fry. I didn't get a bite they were so hungry."

The Reas eventually were able to afford electricity, but it was only 110 amperes, enough to power a light bulb but not an electric stove. All of the family's cooking was done on a wood stove. Not only was it inconvenient to have to light a fire for every meal, but the house would get blazing hot in the summer. The Reas, of course, had no air conditioning, so they just had to open some windows and make the best of it.

One night Claude came home with a shiny, new electric stove in his wagon. Because the Reas couldn't afford to get the house properly wired, the stove collected dust for years while the family tried to raise the cash to get upgraded to 220 amperes service. One day, Bobby asked Truman Jackson, an electrician who regularly stopped at the Hendrix Grocery Store, how much it would cost to get their house wired for 220 service to power the stove. He told him $60. So Bobby saved his money until he could hire Mr. Jackson. When the big day arrived, his mother was ecstatic. She couldn't believe she could now cook all her meals by just turning on a switch.

DESPITE BOBBY'S THIRST FOR KNOWLEDGE, he wasn't quite as enthusiastic about school, mostly because it wasn't a priority in his family. The children were expected to do chores and work to help support the family, and school took them away from earning money. Because he was born in December, Bobby started school at Russellville Grammar School later than his peers. A knee injury caused him to miss so much school he was held back a grade. Brother Jim accidentally hit Bobby in the knee with a garden hoe, opening a 6-inch wound. Without money to visit the doctor, Bobby picked out the small broken bones in his knee with tweezers. Bobby was homebound for months, and eventually the injury healed itself, although later in life that knee was surgically replaced.

Older brothers Charles and Lee rarely attended school. Jim, who was four years older than Bobby, quit school in fifth grade. Because of his size and maturity, Bobby was assigned extra responsibilities at school. In third grade, he was given the task of keeping the classroom warm by feeding the wood stove. When he reached sixth grade, he was captain of the safety patrol and was responsible for the safety of fellow students coming and going to school.

"I was a leader, but not in grades," he says. "I worked so much. I didn't have time to study. That's where my problem was. Mother had no education. Daddy didn't either, I'm sure."

But Miss Myrtle Reed, his fifth-grade teacher, saw the fire inside his belly, telling Bobby's mother, "You'll never have to worry about Bobby. He'll always be fine."

Bobby enjoyed sports, but didn't have much time to participate. Because his family was struggling financially, he had no tennis shoes, only weathered work boots. In the sixth grade, Bobby desperately wanted to win a one-mile running race that was being held on the street in front of school. He thought he would be better off with his father's Sunday shoes than his own well-worn work boots. Claude wore a size 12, two-and-a-half sizes larger than Bobby's shoes. To make them fit, Bobby stuffed newspaper into the toe box of the shoes. "But I won," he says now with pride. "If I had a regular pair of tennis shoes like everyone else, I would've won by an even bigger margin."

Bobby and best friend Bobby Woodruff played sandlot baseball together. "He was a big, strong, healthy American boy," recalled Bobby Woodruff like it was yesterday. "He'd throw the ball so hard it'd burn your hand. When he hit the ball, the cover would nearly come off it." Bobby Rea played one season of junior varsity football at Russellville High School when he was in the seventh grade. He was able to do that because the school included grades seven through 12. He had soft hands to go with his formidable size and speed, so the coaches made him a tight end.

CHRISTMAS FOR THE REAS was not an opulent affair. Bobby would go into the woods and cut down a six-foot cedar tree and place it on an X-shaped wooden base in the living room. At the time, trees weren't watered indoors and only lasted a few days. There were no lights, but some festive touches included paper chains and popcorn garlands strung by hand with needle and thread. There were no presents under the tree on Christmas morning, but the kids would visit their Aunt Lela and Uncle Howard Willis, who both worked and had no children. They would give each of the kids one practical gift of socks, gloves or underpants. They would share thick slices of their mother's four-layer chocolate and coconut cakes, which they ate with pinto beans, green beans and chicken. "Christmas was just another day," Bob says. "The big thing was the cakes. A turkey was out of the question."

Television was rare, so the most popular form of entertainment for local teenagers on Saturday nights was congregating downtown in old pick-up trucks or cars and watching people go by. If you were lucky, you had money to frequent one of two local movie theaters. Saturday was Bobby's time to splurge. The rest of his paycheck went to his mother for groceries.

The Lyric was old and cost only 15 cents for a movie. In 1949, The Roxy opened and, for the princely sum of 40 cents, kids could escape Alabama and ride with Roy Rogers in the Wild West. Going to the movies was an opportunity for confident Bobby to strut in front of the local girls, wearing his father's black suit, button-down shirt and dashing white scarf. He would splash on some of his father's Old Spice cologne and he was ready for action. But the theater was also a place where he learned about the harder side of life. At that time in Alabama, Blacks did not share in all of society. Blacks and Whites had their own schools and separate drinking fountains, and the train station had separate waiting rooms.

The Roxy's balcony was divided: one section for Whites and another for Blacks. Blacks were not permitted to sit in lower sections. Bobby favored the balcony. "It was a good place to kiss and hold hands," he said. The movies also gave Bobby a chance to build his personal skills. "I didn't have to pay because I made friends with the manager," he recalls. When the manager needed a break, Bobby would collect tickets for him. "I made sure to let my friends in for free," Bobby said. After the movies, Bobby would join the young adults in their 20s and 30s who danced the night away to country music records at the American Legion. Bobby had plenty of rhythm and enjoyed spinning the girls around as his white scarf flashed.

Bobby didn't indulge in the bad habits of that period. Although he grew up in a dry county, finding liquor was about as difficult as finding a dusty road. There was no shortage of bootleggers peddling the throat-burning White Lightning. "I've never been much for alcohol," Bob says now. "I saw many men who drank and smoked away their paychecks and destroyed their families. Everybody was smoking. People used to smoke as soon as they finished their dinner. They'd put out their cigarettes in the leftover food on their plates. I wasn't smart enough not to smoke. It looked like so much fun. I tried it off and on for two or three years. But every time I tried, I thought, 'Wow, what's going on?' I would feel faint. I just didn't like the feeling."

At home, his mother would be waiting up for him after the dances. "I'd tell her how much fun I had," he recalls. "Mother loved hearing the stories. She and Daddy never went anywhere except for groceries on Saturdays."

Like most teenagers, Bobby hit a point in life when he wanted to drive a car. His parents never drove a car, so there was no family vehicle to use. Bobby bought a 1936 Ford for $60. He went to the junkyard and found a license plate for it. He was too young to have a driver's license, but as with most obstacles in his life, he didn't let that stop him. "I saw older kids in neat cars," he says. "I wanted a car, too. I made it happen by work."

When the Ford's engine blew out a year later, Bobby bought Billy the Horse with a $50 IOU. The five-year-old roan quarter horse came with a saddle, bridle and instant charisma. "It was a real luxury to own a horse," Bobby recalls. "Most kids didn't have one. The cheerleaders all wanted a ride. When I bought that horse, I was a big dog!" Billy's tenure as a social icebreaker extended to the local track, where the gelding won a few races.

But as much as Bobby enjoyed riding Billy around town, he wanted another car. So he sold the horse for $40, which went toward purchasing a 1947 Chevy two-door hatchback for $300. "I would pick Daddy up at the train station on Friday nights and then drive him back there on Sunday afternoons," Bobby says.

At 15, Bobby could now see how the world operated, how things got done and what the rewards could be. Russellville, Alabama was quickly becoming too small for his great ambition. His natural confidence was boosted with the knowledge that, as a young boy, he had already accomplished more than many grown men. His gaze was northward, toward Washington, D.C., and the quickly growing Virginia suburbs across the wide Potomac River. Older brother Lee now lived there. Bobby didn't really know him. Lee broke away from Russellville to follow his destiny while Bobby was still a young boy.

Years earlier, Bob's oldest brother Charles had joined the U.S. Army during World War II. It was a ticket out of Russellville, and a chance to make a few bucks and have some adventure. In 1945, Lee signed up. After passing his examination, he was given 30 days to get his affairs in order before going to boot camp. One day, while hanging out at City Lake, the beautiful reservoir just outside of Russellville, Lee recalled a man coming up to him and delivering the big news: "We just dropped a bomb on Japan and the war is over!"

Lee was stationed for two years on Honshu Island in Japan. He was discharged the same week as Charles, who came back home to Alabama with two Purple Hearts, a steel plate in his head and a stump where the middle finger of his right hand used to be. Charles asked Lee, who had good business sense, about his work prospects. Lee said "there ain't no jobs here" and that he was moving to Northern Virginia to find work. Lee knew the Washington, D.C., area before he joined the military. He had made several trips to the nation's capital to pursue Norma Jane Mansfield, a blonde beauty who had left her home in Alabama to live with family in Bethesda, Maryland, and go to college. Twice Lee had presented Miss Norma with a sparkling diamond engagement ring and twice she accepted it, only to mail it back at her parents' insistence. To marry their daughter and work in the family's hardware store required a high school diploma.

"No time for that!" said Lee, who seldom set foot inside a schoolhouse.

Charles decided to accompany Lee, and they boarded a Greyhound the next day. Lee brought the engagement ring, but when he arrived at his destination the next day, he opted not to call on Miss Norma. "I didn't want to be hit up about school again," he said.

Once in Virginia, Lee needed to figure out what he was going to do for a living in a region that was bustling with a post-war economic boom. He browsed through the thick section of help-wanted ads in The Washington Post. Because he lacked formal education, Lee figured he would learn to be a carpenter, painter, plumber or electrician. What caught his eye was that bricklayers made about a dollar an hour more than the other trades. For Lee, it was a no-brainer. He would become a bricklayer. Lee tossed away the newspaper and walked down the street about five or six blocks to inquire about a bricklaying job. He was hired on the spot by Gene Cannon, who taught him the time-honored art of laying brick.

In 1947, Lee married Ivy Saintmayer. Their marriage lasted 25 years. They had no children together, but Ivy had two children from a previous marriage—a son Jennings Webb and a daughter Virginia Webb. Lee treated them like his own.

About two years into his job, Lee was asked to build the foundation of a friend's home. He made more money building that foundation over the weekend than he had working an entire week on his regular job. "I figured I might as well be working for myself," Lee said. "When you work for someone else, you quit at four o'clock. There's another five hours of daylight." In 1949, Lee started his own contracting business.

After finishing the seventh grade, young Bobby took a train to Northern Virginia to visit Lee. Since his father worked the rails, Bobby was able to get a free pass. Bobby didn't know anything about bricklaying, but he had the smarts, strength and boundless energy to impress his big brother. "Bob caught on real fast," Lee said. "He was an excellent employee. He did whatever you wanted him to do and gave you no lip."

Bobby's main responsibility was hauling a hod, a three-sided box that held about 10 to 12 bricks, on his shoulder from the brick pile to the workers. He watched closely as Lee and the others did the actual bricklaying. In his spare time, he devoted himself to learning the craft. There wasn't any time for sightseeing, but Bobby recalls being awed at the size of the buildings, impressed with the stylish clothing and amazed that everyone seemed to own a television set.

When the summer was over, Lee tried to convince Bobby to stay, but Bobby thought he needed to get back to Russellville to help out at home and go back to school. Before he left, Lee took Bobby to an upscale men's store and bought him a brown, fringed suede jacket for the whopping sum of $65. That's equivalent to about $575 in today's dollars. It was the first piece of new clothing that Bobby ever had. "I loved the boy," Lee said later. "He was so nice and such a hard worker. I thought of him as a son. I wanted to do everything I could for him."

Later that month, Bobby entered the eighth grade at Russellville High School. But it wasn't the same. The trip had changed him. He couldn't stop thinking about going back to Virginia, which had so much to offer compared to Alabama. Jobs were plentiful, and there was good money to be made. Although he had a full schedule with his chores, two jobs and school, Bobby always made time to practice laying bricks in their backyard. "Every single brick had to be perfect," he says, "or I took it down and started over."

Bobby thought he could learn more in the real world than in textbooks. Although he wouldn't have minded going to high school and hanging out with his friends, he felt the deck was stacked in favor of going to work and earning money, especially since wages in Virginia were about twice the prevailing rate in Alabama. At the time, Bobby was courting the principal's daughter, Gretchen Williams. "Me—poor as a church mouse, holes in my shoes, holding hands with the principal's daughter," Bob says now.

Dating Gretchen wasn't enough of an incentive to stay.

"It was so poor in Alabama," he says. "It was so hard for our family. I was strong and young. My heart was set on coming to Virginia and making money. I just didn't have time for school."

Bobby began to see that there was a big world out there, far beyond Alabama, a world where the challenges were harder, but the rewards sweeter. Russellville had now become too small for the young man willing to take on the world.

CHAPTER THREE

BECOMING BOB WARHURST

On January 4, 1955—less than a month after he turned 16—young Bobby Rea stepped on the train leaving tiny Russellville, but the person who stepped off the platform in the Washington, D.C., suburbs was a man named Bob Warhurst. Changing his name was the first of his many tasks. He gave himself little time to take in the monumental sights and sounds of nearby Washington, D.C., that was overflowing with newcomers attracted by the growth of the federal government after World War II and the Korean War.

Older brother Jim brought Bob to his modest apartment in Arlington, Virginia, where he ate dinner, went to bed and woke up the next day prepared to work as a bricklayer for his other brother, Lee. There was no time for sightseeing, shopping or musing about the great changes occurring in American society. Work was what he knew, what he wanted and what motivated him.

Lee gave him the choice of working as a laborer for $1.50 an hour or making just 75 cents an hour to learn the trade as an apprentice bricklayer. Bob's previous instinct would have been to take the $1.50 an hour as a bird-in-hand laborer, but this time he thought about it and chose the lower-paying training job to learn a skill that might pay him more in the future. Bob dedicated himself to learning his new craft. During breaks, he would practice building walls, which he would then tear down.

"With everything in life, I have a theory," Bob says. "If someone else can do it, why not me? I have another theory. If you're going to do it, why not be the best? I wanted to do it better and faster than anyone else."

In no time, Bob acquired the knowledge and skills to master the job. Lee rewarded him with a 25-cent raise. Bob's fast but thorough work caused older brother Charles to tell him to slow down, as his speed and dexterity were making the other workers look slow.

"Bob worked fast, worked hard and came to please," said Lee, a perfectionist who had no tolerance for sloppy work or idle chatter. "Without a doubt, he was the best employee I ever had."

Bob's specialty became corners and chimneys, tricky work that some others didn't want to tackle. With their tough-to-fit joints and need for precision, every one of Bob's chimneys earned him a $5 bonus from Lee.

Lee's bricklaying crew built houses, churches and even some commercial buildings in Arlington, Alexandria and other locations around Fairfax County. All of these brick buildings still stand today—except for a Gino's restaurant that was torn down to build a CVS drug store—and look as strong as when the Warhurst boys constructed them more than 50 years ago.

Bob and his brothers, Charles and Jim, were so proud of their skills that they often referred to themselves as "burnt clay artists." But their art was hard, back-breaking work. After toiling all day with bricks, cinder block and mortar, Lee and Bob went home to shower and eat supper. Then they returned to the job site and moved the equipment and tools to the next day's project. By the time they moved the mixer, water barrel, scaffolding and hoses, the day would have turned to night. "It was a long day," Bob recalls. "We'd do it regularly." Working together created a strong bond—especially between Lee and Bob—that was rock solid throughout their lives.

But Bob, whose personal philosophy is that he has never met a stranger, wasn't all work and no play. His favorite "toy" was a fast car. In the spring of 1955, Bob was driving a 1949 Ford that he purchased for a couple hundred dollars from a used-car lot and decided to start a car club to organize his newfound hot-rod buddies. On a lark, he bought a "Ladies" bathroom sign from a hardware store and attached it with two pieces of wire to the bottom of the rear bumper of his car. The club members were in on the fun name. From then on, they were known as "The Ladies Club."

Other racing enthusiasts heard about the club and asked if they could join. At stop lights, it wasn't unusual for someone to pull up next to Bob and ask, "Hey Bob, can I join your club?" "Yup, give me your name and $10," he would answer. To meet the initiation fee, the new member would then hand over a wad of crumbled bills to Lee through the passenger side window.

Bob's love of cars began with his 1936 Ford but reached a new high in October 1955 when he spent nearly $3,000 for a top-of-the-line 1956 model Chevrolet Bel Air convertible, perhaps the most desired model to come out of Detroit that fall. The black-and-white Bel Air was equipped with a powerful engine. Chevy engineers made the model even more impressive by lengthening the car body by 4 inches with a special grille and rear fins. Now, nearly 60 years later, the Hagerty Price Guide says a comparable model is worth $53,036.

Because he was only 16 at the time, Bob needed his 21-year-old brother Jim to buy the car under his name. After pulling out of the showroom floor, trouble started. Bob's new car's engine sputtered and stalled when idling at stop lights, so Bob decided to "blow out" the carburetor on Shirley Highway, one of the first major highways on the Virginia side of the Potomac River, designed to funnel government workers to Washington, D.C. "It was kind of a dumb thing to do," Bob says now. "We just needed to make some adjustments. I should have known better. But I was just so excited to have a brand new car."

That maneuver shot the Chevy and the brothers to around 100 miles per hour on the highway, which soon caught the attention of the local police. The boys pulled into the parking lot of a Hot Shoppes drive-in and were quickly surrounded by four or five Arlington County police cars. "They thought we stole the car and were headed south," Bob says. Bob and Jim were escorted to the Arlington

County Courthouse. Three days later, Bob went before a judge, who promptly suspended Bob's license for 30 days. So the shiny new car sat in front of Bob's residence, which was the attic of Lee's in-laws on North Danville Street in Arlington off Wilson Boulevard. Bob had moved there after a year of sharing an apartment with Jim.

Bob tried to make the best of the situation by sitting in the car with the motor running, listening to the radio. He soon got bored with that routine and decided to take action. "A month is a long time when you have a brand new car and only drove it one day," Bob remembers. "After about 12 days, I thought, 'This isn't good. I needed the car to get to work.'"

On the next rainy day—he couldn't miss a work day—Bob walked down the street to the courthouse to see if he could meet with the judge. Bob was contrite, and politely explained that he was only trying to adjust the carburetor and besides, he needed the car to get to work.

"It's very difficult for me to get to work," Bob recalls telling the judge. "My brother Lee has to pick me up. I'd like to ask if I could please have my license back."

The judge thought about it for a long minute, then opened a drawer in his desk and pulled out Bob's precious license.

"I was very grateful," Bob remembers. "I ran the half mile home, jumped in that car and took off."

With his Chevrolet Bel Air convertible back in business, Bob's interest in driving fast cars continued to grow. But after his speeding ticket, he realized now more than ever that his need for speed required a legal outlet. About eight months after he started "The Ladies Club," Bob changed the name of the club to "The Southern Ramblers." Bob made a deal with Al Gore—owner of a Manassas, Virginia auto race track, not the future U.S. vice president—to allow The Southern Ramblers to race at the track on off days. At the height of the club's popularity, membership stood at about 250 members. It was a fun group that made a habit of duckpin bowling at Pla-Mor

Lanes in Arlington after their Wednesday night meetings. Similar to traditional tenpin bowling, duckpin bowling is famous for its smaller pins and balls with no finger holes.

On the track, Bob was greased lightning with a 1957 Ford Fairlane that he acquired from a used car dealer and rebuilt into what was then called a "hot rod," a souped-up car with a big engine that made a lot of noise and went very fast. The car was originally gray and white, but he had it painted black.

With the '57 Ford, Bob even won the Maryland State Championship for drag racing one year in the late 1950s at the Aquasco Speedway. "I really liked that car," Bob says. "I remember I found $60 under the back seat. It was in an envelope." Bob's secret to success was removing his car's exhaust system before a race, as the street-required muffler and tailpipes limited performance. He also took off the hood ornament and emblems. And he made sure the car was firing on all cylinders by replacing the ignition points and spark plugs. Bob could coax his Ford to almost 100 mph over the quarter-mile strip.

One time, Bob's victory was challenged by a competitor who insisted, "It's not natural for a Ford to be that fast."

Bob just smiled. He knew that any protest had to be backed up with a $500 fee that would be awarded to him if the protest was overturned.

"I'm so glad you protested me," Bob crowed. "I'm going to have $500 when it's over, and I need the money to buy gas to get home."

An official later told Bob that the protest had been dropped. "In car racing back then, you won trophies," Bob recalls. "You didn't win money. But it was so exhilarating to look back and see the guy behind you."

AFTER WORK, BOB WOULD REGULARLY VISIT People's Drug Store in Clarendon, Virginia. The gregarious Bob became friends with Essie Russo, who usually worked behind the soda counter where he chowed down on hamburgers and cherry Cokes.

Essie was impressed with Bob and wanted him to meet her daughters.

One rainy day, Bob gave Essie a ride home in his sharp Chevy Bel Air so she wouldn't have to wait for the bus. Essie lived in a small, one-bedroom apartment on North Troy Street in Arlington with daughters Joann, 17, and Billie Jean, 14, and son Jack, five.

Bob didn't meet the daughters that day, but in one of those small moments that starts a chain of significant events, Essie left her umbrella in Bob's car. He told her he would return it when it was convenient for her. A few days later, she told him to come over. Because there were two daughters, Bob brought along one of his friends. Bob and Billie Jean were instantly attracted to each other.

"I liked what I saw," he recalls. "She was so pretty and innocent." Billie Jean remembered thinking, "He was cute and very easy to talk to."

The young couple quickly found out that they had much in common. Both were country kids with steadfast values who worked hard and lived a simple life.

"From that time on, they were inseparable," said Joann (Allgood) Ferguson, Billie Jean's sister. But Joann and Bob's friend didn't have the same result. They didn't click, and their first date was their only date.

Billie Jean was born August 21, 1942, in Elkin, North Carolina, a small town in the rolling hills south of the Virginia border. The fictional town of Mayberry in the popular "The Andy Griffith Show" was set in this area, not far from Pilot Mountain, called Mount Pilot in the TV series.

Elkin, which bills itself as "the best small town in America," is also home of the famous Chatham Manufacturing Company, recognized around the world for its fine wool blankets. Billie Jean's maternal grandparents, Diana and Thurman Eldridge, worked at the textile mill. Billie Jean's mother, Essie, was 15 when she married Herman O'Dell Allgood, who was in his late 20s. After about five years of marriage, two daughters and another child on the way, Essie filed for divorce.

"He wasn't very nice to her," Billie Jean said. "He had a drinking problem that she didn't know about. Grandma made her leave him because he could get physical."

During the divorce proceedings, the judge decided to split up the children, awarding oldest daughter Joann to her father and second daughter Nancy to Essie.

"We were distributed like you distribute furniture after a divorce," said Nancy (Allgood) Zwack, Billie Jean's sister. While she was getting ready to give birth to Billie Jean, Essie sent Nancy to live with Essie's sister Louise. The arrangement became permanent. In the summer, Joann, Nancy and Billie Jean would spend a week together at their grandmother's house. When you visited, "you didn't sit and watch TV," Billie Jean said. "You worked."

Grandma Eldridge was known for her wonderful rose garden and other bright blooming flowers. She also tended a large vegetable garden that fed the family. She canned green beans, pickles, squash and nearly every other type of vegetable. The girls learned their homemaking skills there, too. They were taught how to clean a house and cook delicious, hearty meals—two things Billie Jean is known for.

"One thing I learned from my grandmother was how to work," Billie Jean said. "Mother always had me helping her, too. She was always cleaning. I'd say, 'It's not dirty yet!'"

When she was in fifth grade, Billie Jean and her mother Essie moved to New York City. That's where Essie met and married her second husband, Jack Russo. Essie and Jack had a son, Jack Russo, Jr. When Jack, Sr., died, Essie moved to Arlington, Virginia, with Billie Jean and Jack, Jr., at the encouragement of her brother, Thurman Eldridge, who was living there with his family. Billie Jean was upset about the move, preferring to stay in Brooklyn with her friends. "We'd be playing on the streets and a car would come around the corner and everyone would yell, 'Run!'"

In fact, after the move, Billie Jean pestered her mother about returning to Brooklyn. Finally, Essie took her daughter back for a visit. Her memories of fun and games in Brooklyn were quickly replaced with the reality of urban grit and grime, trash-filled streets and ragged bums.

"On the cab ride from Penn Station, you saw all the dirt and trash and bums on the street," Billie Jean recalled. "I thought our neighborhood in Brooklyn was nice until we moved to Virginia, where it was so nice and green. All of a sudden I didn't like Brooklyn anymore. I apologized to Mother. Then I was satisfied." Once they returned to Virginia, oldest daughter Joann moved in with Essie, Billie Jean and Jack, Jr.

DURING THEIR COURTSHIP, BOB AND BILLIE JEAN spent a great amount of time in Clarendon, which is about two miles as the crow flies across the Potomac River to Washington, D.C. As Northern Virginia's retail hub, Clarendon was a popular place to hang out. At the time, there were no big shopping malls and the iconic Washington Beltway highway had not been built.

One of their favorite places was the famous Tops Drive Inn, located at the corner of Arlington Boulevard and Glebe Road in suburban Arlington. Tops was well known for its plethora of specialty sandwiches, the most popular being the "Sir Loiner," a double stack of freshly ground sirloin steak, and the "Jim Dandy," a mouthwatering combination of Hawaiian-baked ham, Swiss cheese, sliced tomato, shredded lettuce and secret sauce on Grecian bread. It was a typical "Happy Days" type of joint where a female "car hop" waitress came to the customer's car, took the order and returned with the hot food in a matter of minutes.

Bob and Billie Jean liked to drive around in Bob's big Chevy convertible, listening to music on the radio. Elvis Presley was the big star in those days and his hit song "Love Me Tender" was their favorite.

"We were soul mates from the time we met," Billie Jean said. "I'm usually shy with someone new, but we just talked and talked." Billie Jean gave Bob a black-and-white photo of herself and wrote this on the back:

My Dearest,

Please don't let my age make you believe that I don't love you because I do. I only know what is in my heart. But I can't tell you how much I really love you."

Love You Always,

Billie

It is a promise that she has kept every day.

Five months after they met, Bob asked Billie Jean to marry him.

"She's the perfect person," Bob says. "She's as honest as the day is long. She never swears. If she is going to say the word 'damn' she spells it out."

Bob popped the question as they were driving back from the Lee Highway Drive-In in Merrifield, Virginia. Billie Jean was eager, but she figured her mother would be a tough sell, even though she thought the world of Bob.

She was right.

"My mother shouted, 'No! You're too young!'" Billie Jean recalled.

Essie was so upset about the proposed nuptials that she threatened to send Billie Jean to Elkin. But Essie's mother wisely advised her that "you might as well let her get married, otherwise they'll just run off."

There were other obstacles, too. At 14, Billie Jean was not allowed under Virginia Commonwealth law to marry. But the young couple researched a bit and discovered that Maryland had more lenient laws. Bob bought an engagement ring for his fiancée from Roger's Jewelry in Clarendon. "The diamond was really, really small," he says. "It wasn't a carat. A carat would never happen. You had to look really close to see the diamond."

Bob, a true pragmatist who was always thinking about work, picked January for their wedding because it was a slow time in the construction business. On the snowy Wednesday of January 16, 1957, Bob and Billie Jean exchanged vows and rings at Rockville Baptist Church. Bob paid the preacher with two $20 bills. The couple looked resplendent, with Billie Jean in an immaculate white, square-neck A-line dress and Bob standing tall in his black suit with a button-down white shirt.

"I can't believe I came all the way from Alabama to Washington, D.C., when I was 16 and found the perfect woman," Bob says. "Now that's talent."

Billie Jean's sister Joann was maid of honor and Bob's brother Lee was best man. Essie, Lee's wife Ivy and Joann's boyfriend were in attendance. Bob's parents were not able to attend the impromptu ceremony, but Billie Jean had met the couple months earlier. "They were wonderful people," she recalled. "I loved them right from the start. They were down home country people."

After the wedding, Billie Jean's uncle, Thurman Eldridge, treated them to dinner at Mr. Lee's Chinese Restaurant in Clarendon. Raised on simple country food, this was Bob's introduction to Chinese cuisine. He greatly enjoyed it and for the past 57 years, the two of them have celebrated their anniversary with Chinese food.

"They were so young," Billie Jean's sister Nancy said. "I never thought they'd still be married after all these years. He was a country boy. He had nothing. She was just a kid. She wasn't going to finish school."

Billie Jean moved into Bob's efficiency apartment in Arlington, but it wasn't a sumptuous love nest. The couch folded out into a bed and the bathroom was located upstairs and was shared with other tenants. It was suitable for a bachelor who worked long hours but not for a married couple. A few months later, they upgraded to a small apartment at Fillmore Gardens on South Walter Reed Drive in Arlington. To help make ends meet, Billie Jean found a job folding sweaters at Lerner's, a popular women's clothing store in Clarendon. Joann worked there, too. They would not let anyone know they were sisters, though, because company rules forbid family members from working together.

Now that he was married, Bob took on several odd jobs to make extra money. He posted a notice at Louis Watts' hardware store in Tyson's Corner that said he was available to work. One day Louis told Bob he had a job for him: cleaning out the chicken coops on his 20-acre chicken farm in nearby Oakton, Virginia. Being a country boy, Bob knew his way around a chicken coop, a place that provided fresh eggs and an occasional bird in the oven. But this job turned out to be a nightmare. Knee deep in manure, Bob tried to shovel out the chicken coops but the ammonia smell gagged and sickened him, forcing him off the job. "It was awful," Bob recalls. "I barely made it home. I called him and said, 'I can't finish the job. You don't owe me anything.'" Billie Jean said Bob was sick for two days from it.

In the winter of 1958, Bob worked at Hajoca, a plumbing, heating and industrial supplies company that was founded 100 years earlier in Philadelphia and was a pioneer in the indoor plumbing industry. One of Bob's friends found him a job at Hajoca's Rosslyn, Virginia, branch. Bob filled orders for customers and quickly became familiar with the business. "I learned all about plumbing, sinks, bathtubs, copper pipe, galvanized and copper fittings, commodes," Bob recalls. It was an education he would use many times later in his life. But when warm weather arrived in March, Bob left Hajoca and went back to laying brick.

Bob and his older brother Jim had been raising about 60 hogs in Nokesville, just outside Fairfax County, to peddle at sale barns.

Those hogs probably ate better than many people in those days because Bob and Jim made arrangements with several upscale restaurants in Arlington to put their scraps in wood barrels. Every day after work, Bob and Jim would pick up the barrels. "The restaurant owners got to liking us and sometimes we got a plate," Bob recalls. But Bob eventually gave his share of the business to Jim. "I realized this wasn't a good idea," Bob says. "I don't remember making much money and it was taking a lot of time. (Billie Jean) was pregnant."

On April 11, 1958, Bob and Billie Jean became parents. That's when a tiny girl they named Deborah Lee was born at the Columbia Hospital for Women. That hospital has a place in the historical record because it was founded shortly after the end of the Civil War to serve women who were arriving into the city in search of missing soldiers.

"I always loved the name Debbie," Billie Jean said. "That's probably because of (1950s film star) Debbie Reynolds. I know Bob wanted a boy, but we had boys later." Bob says that "Debbie has always been special. I didn't care if it was a boy or a girl. I just wanted a healthy child."

Bob was so taken with his first child that he made it a point to write Debbie and Billie Jean's names into the mortar work on top of every chimney he finished and also in the moisture-proof sealant around windows. There are still many homes in Arlington today with Debbie and Billie Jean's names permanently etched into them.

With the Virginia side of the family growing and beginning to prosper in the Washington, D.C., area, Bob's parents, Claude and Mary, decided to move to Virginia with the younger children, Margene, Claude Jr., and fraternal twins Carl and Jane. Claude had come from a broken home, so he was motivated to unite the family.

Lee had a job waiting for Claude, who at 57 immediately went to work with his older boys Charles, Lee, Jim and Bob. After four decades as a carpenter, Claude found bricklaying to be a challenge. You need good eyesight to be a bricklayer and his eyes weren't as sharp as they used to be. But the fact that his family was together once again filled him with joy.

Although he was nearing 60, Claude—whose own father dazzled crowds with his circus high-wire act as the family story goes—still had some daredevil in him. In the tall structures that his sons were creating, Claude had the skills to dance across the top edge of six-story buildings or dangle his long legs over ledges while taking in the view like an agile hawk.

"Daddy would scare me to death," Bob recalls. "Daddy was fearless of heights and I didn't like heights at all. Still don't." Bob's mother couldn't stand to watch her husband's escapades and would dash inside once he started his acrobatic moves. The boys would try to talk their father down, but their protests only encouraged him. "He always said if you were afraid, you would fall," Lee said. "But if you weren't afraid, you wouldn't fall."

That pretty much summed up the attitude of the Warhurst family as they marched into the second half of the 20th century.

Bob's skill at bricklaying kept him occupied during the daytime, but he felt the need to bring in even more money for his growing family.

Billie Jean's grandmother's brother, Joe Robertson, owned a detective business—the Interstate Detective Agency—on Washington Boulevard in Arlington. Bob asked him for a job as a "gumshoe," as detectives were known in those days.

The federal government, military and lobbyist companies were expanding in the post-Korean War years, and Washington was awash with newcomers spilling into the area to grab up lucrative jobs in the fast-growing nation's capital. With all that societal upheaval, extra-marital affairs were on the rise due to the sudden mixing of ambitious men and women in the bustling and exciting city. Because many of these illicit affairs were consummated at night, Bob had to spend his nighttime hours tracking the couples.

"Mostly it was divorce cases where you followed someone to see where they went and what they did," Bob explains. "I would park up the street from the target husband or wife. I could see them, but they couldn't see me. I was too slick to be caught. I was trying to find out what the husband or wife was doing and report back. I'd write in my notebook what I saw and call it in to the boss."

Just in case the police questioned him, Bob carried an "official" Interstate Detective Agency badge in a well-worn leather case as part of his credentials. But Bob's bricklaying workload would often wear him out, making it difficult to stay awake during the wee hours. So Bob enlisted new bride Billie Jean and younger brother Claude to join his late-night forays. A neighborhood girl started calling Claude "Tracy," short for Dick Tracy—the comic book detective. The name stuck and Claude became widely known as Tracy for the rest of his life.

"I'd be so tired from working all day," Bob says. "If they came with me, I could get a little sleep and not worry about the suspect getting away without me knowing."

In the three years he worked for the agency, Bob handled about 35 cases. Sometimes Bob's natural flamboyance got in the way of his need for stealth. Tracy talked Bob into buying a fancy new white Pontiac Grand Prix automobile that was quite conspicuous.

"I bought that car out of stupidity," he says. "I couldn't afford it."

IN THE FALL OF 1961, BOB, BILLIE JEAN and three-year-old Debbie were living in the tiny apartment in Fillmore Gardens. But with the October 28 birth of their first son, Robert Jr., and the acquisition of three horses, they knew that their expanding family needed to find a new place to live.

Without a barn of his own, Bob kept Comanche, his paint horse, and Peg and Big John, Claude's large Belgian work horses, in an abandoned barn in McLean, Virginia, near Lee's house. "Daddy loved nothing better than being in a wagon with horses," Bob says.

Bob was still looking for just the right place one year later when brick salesman Bill Phillips, who knew Bob owned horses, told him about a house with acres of land available to rent in Vienna, a new suburban enclave about 15 miles west of Washington, D.C., that still had some wide open spaces. That same night Bob visited the house on Ninovan Road. "I lit up like a Christmas tree," he says. "It wasn't perfect, but almost."

For $300 a month (about $2,300 in today's dollars), Bob could rent a three-bedroom home with about four acres of land, including a barn and fields for their small stable of horses. Bob was unable to purchase a home because he had not yet acquired the sizable down payment that was required at the time. "We couldn't even afford to buy a setting hen," Bob says.

The Vienna house was home to Bob, Billie Jean, Debbie and baby Rob, as well as Bob's parents and younger siblings Margene, Tracy, Carl and Jane. Ten people squeezed into a three-bedroom house was a tight fit, but the family loved being together under one roof. The home had just one bathroom, but "it was better than having a bathroom outside like when we were growing up," Bob says.

Bob's mother would fix dinner for everyone, who gathered around a picnic table and wooden benches placed in the dining room. Pork, pinto beans, green beans and turnip greens were staples of their diet. After dinner, the family would gather around the huge stone fireplace in the living room. Bob splurged and bought their first color television set. Like many Americans, the TV was their window into the historical events of their generation. From there, they and the rest of the nervous nation followed the tense game of nuclear poker between the United States and the Soviet Union during the 1962 Cuban Missile Crisis.

"I was scared to death," Bob recalls. "The Soviet Union was such a huge power and their ships were coming to Cuba with nuclear missiles. If they fired their missiles at Washington, D.C., we would all be blown up. I thought seriously about taking (Billie Jean) and the kids away from D.C. Then (Soviet Premier Nikita) Khrushchev backed down when we put up the blockade, and they turned around. It was very scary, and it all happened very fast."

The early 1960s were a tumultuous time for Washington D.C., and the nation. But in the shady suburb of Vienna, two families would become a united force that would define the rest of Bob Warhurt's life. The Warhurst and Williams families would eventually create and build Merrifield Garden Center, but first they had to be introduced.

Of course, Bob was the catalyst.

The Warhursts had recently moved to their Ninovan Road home. That area is now a popular suburb just outside the river of auto traffic known as the Capital Beltway, but at that time it was country and the "next-door neighbors" lived about a quarter of a mile away.

Once they were settled into their new dwelling, Bob rode his Pinto horse bare-back down the tree-lined, one-lane dirt road to introduce himself to the Williamses.

"Bob doesn't know any strangers," Billie Jean said.

Bob knocked on the back door of the Williamses' house and out came Hampton Williams III—better known as Buddy—and his beautiful wife Doris with daughter Wanda wrapped around one leg and son Hal around the other leg.

"Hi guys, I'm Bob."

When he returned home, Bob told Billie Jean, "You've got to meet the Williamses. Buddy is a good guy. You'll like his wife, Doris, and they have two young kids." The Williamses took a liking to their friendly new neighbor, too. "We found we had a common interest in horses," Buddy said.

Buddy's early family history was much different than Bob's. Doris said Lord Fairfax granted Buddy's great, great grandfather, the first Hampton Williams, 434 acres of land in Fairfax County. That land became known as Woodford. Hampton Williams moved to Washington, D.C., to work in the U.S. Treasury Department.

Later in his career, he became private secretary to President James Polk. Hampton Williams' second son, Franklin Williams, also had a notable career. He fought with Confederate Army war hero John Mosby in the U.S. Civil War. Mosby's Rangers were guerrilla fighters, making daring night raids across U.S. Army lines to destroy supply lines and thwart communication before vanishing into the darkness.

Woodford became a popular summer destination, said Wanda (Williams) Flanagan, Buddy and Doris's oldest child. "It was on a hill, and there was a constant breeze," she said. "It was calm and nice and pretty." In its heyday, vacationers from Washington D.C., took the train to the mansion. Woodford was passed down through the generations. When the family needed money, they sold parcels of land. "They gave property away for potatoes," Doris said. "By the time Buddy's dad got it, it was probably down to 30 acres or so."

Buddy was born and raised on the famous Woodford property, where there were always horses, for income and recreation. Buddy's father operated an equine boarding facility on the site. There was a big pine tree at the top of the hill that was a stiff challenge to climb. "When you climbed to the top, you could see the Washington Monument," Wanda said. "My dad did it, his dad did it." When Buddy's father was 17, he took a dare and walked across the railroad trestle near their property. He slipped and fell on the tracks, getting electrocuted. He had difficulties talking from then on, although Bob could always seem to understand him.

Buddy and Doris, whose maiden name is Irvin, had known one another since childhood. Sparks began to fly when Buddy, who was two years older than Doris, drove the school bus that took Doris to Falls Church High School. "He was a big shot," Doris recalled. In those days, older students drove the school buses instead of professional bus drivers. As a teen, Buddy was a volunteer firefighter, just like his father. There were dances every Friday night at the firehouse, and Doris talked her parents into letting her go to them with a girlfriend. Doris and Buddy often danced, although Doris had many suitors.

After they married in 1958, Buddy and Doris settled into a cottage on the Woodford property. Two years later, they moved into a small, but new house that Buddy's sister and brother-in-law had built on one acre of the property. The house was not quite finished when the brother-in-law got transferred out of the area, so Buddy bought the house, which was no more than 1,000 square feet with three bedrooms, a bathroom, a kitchen, a living room and a screened-in porch. They had three horses. "We didn't have money," Wanda said. "The horses ate before we did. The Warhursts were even worse off than we were. It was hard, but it was fun. We were happy."

The land where Bob and Billie Jean were renting an old house was once owned by Herbert Williams, one of Franklin Williams' sons who was interested in horticulture. Wanda said Herbert hybridized an apple tree with five or six varieties in his orchards. "The state gave him an award," she said. "They were really into horticulture. It's in our blood."

In the 1990s, developers purchased the remainder of the Woodford property. Now what's left is a small section of upscale houses known as Williams Hill, including a small family graveyard, where the remains of Franklin Williams rest.

ON A HOT, HUMID FRIDAY AFTERNOON in July 1963, Claude was working with his boys on building a new split-level home for a customer in the woodsy Virginia suburb of Mantua. As the day wore on, he began to feel unusually weary, and he slowly climbed down from the high scaffolding to take a rest in the shade.

"I could sit here 'til morning," said Claude, mopping beads of sweat from his face.

Claude, 62, like so many men of his age, wouldn't hear of going to the doctor. He was determined to wait and see how he felt after the weekend.

"We knew it wasn't good, but we just aren't people to go to the doctor," Bob says. "He laid around on Saturday. I saw him eat a little ham. That wasn't good, but that's what he was used to eating."

On Sunday morning, Claude remained in bed, skipping a backyard picnic with his wife's sister and brother-in-law, Lela and Howard Willis, who were visiting from Russellville. Monday came and Claude wasn't feeling any better. Bob's brother Jim brought their father to see Dr. John Judson, who took one look at him and immediately sent him to a heart specialist in the same building. While in the cardiologist's office, Claude suffered a heart attack and was rushed to Arlington Hospital. Claude rallied over the next few days and his stabilized condition helped the family keep high hopes for his recovery.

On that Wednesday night, Bob, Billie Jean, Lee and Bob's mother Mary visited Claude in the hospital after work. Claude was propped up in bed with wires and tubes taped to his arms and chest. He had his eyes focused on the tiny hospital TV set because his favorite show, "Wagon Train," was about to start. He was a big fan of the main character, Major Seth Adams, played by actor Ward Bond. Major Adams was a character Claude could empathize with: a Southerner who led his family and others across the country after the Civil War to settle down in a place where they could get a fresh start.

"Y'all go on now," Bob remembers his father saying. "Bob's got to work tomorrow and I'll ride with Major Adams."

At 3 a.m., the darkest hour of the night, Bob got a frantic call that Claude had taken a turn for the worse. Bob, Lee and their mother sped to the hospital, where they received the sad news that Claude had died. Later that day, Bob knocked on the back door of Buddy and Doris's house. Doris opened the door and Bob burst into tears. "Daddy died last night," he said.

"My heart just broke in two," Doris recalled. "Here's this big, tall, strong, macho man standing in front of me with tears rolling down his face. It really made an impression on me. He loved his father so much and he was just heartbroken. It showed another side of him."

Claude's funeral was held at Pearson Funeral Home in Falls Church. Although he only lived five years in Virginia, Claude's funeral was packed with people who loved and respected him. As a Mason and a Shriner, Claude was given a Masonic funeral service, which Bob says "he would have loved." A large procession of mourners drove behind his hearse to the National Memorial Park in Falls Church, where Claude was laid to rest.

It wasn't long after Claude's funeral that Bob's mother longed to return to Alabama. Jim was chosen to drive her and their younger siblings Margene, Tracy, Carl and Jane back to familiar Russellville. Jim returned to Virginia with his mother's old, wood-burning cooking stove in the back of his truck. "Mother said she would never use it again," Bob said.

Claude's death and the return of his mother and the younger children to Alabama caused Bob to think hard about his life in Virginia. After mulling it over, he decided that he didn't want to be a bricklayer for the rest of his life. Despite his obvious skills, Bob realized that aside from the tough physical challenges of the job, bricklaying couldn't provide a steady paycheck.

"You couldn't work if it was raining, snowing or too cold," he remembers. "I just didn't feel like it was the smart thing to do anymore. It came to me pretty plain. It was time to find another job."

At that time, Bob and the rest of Lee's crew were busy building homes in Mantua's Ridgely Estates neighborhood. Always observant, Bob noticed that the young couples who had purchased the homes would often drive by the job site after work to check on the progress of their new homes.

Something clicked in Bob's mind, much like one of those light bulbs above a character's head in a comic strip. Not one to shy away from a good idea, he decided then and there what was going to be his Next Big Thing: collecting trash.

He had seen a trash man in his neighborhood eating steak for lunch. "If that guy can make a lot of money picking up trash, I can certainly pick up trash," he thought.

The next afternoon, a homeowner stopped by and Bob threw down his trowel, jumped off the wall he was building and announced with authority, "I'm your trash man!"

Younger brother Carl said Bob was "always looking for something else. He wasn't satisfied laying brick. His wheels were always turning. They still are."

Ridgely Estates had about 60 new homes under construction. Bob moved in fast to sign up the newcomers before they moved into their new homes, always introducing himself as "I'm Bob Warhurst and I'm your trash man," not once asking if they wanted or needed such a service. Calling on his strong personality and sense of showmanship, Bob rode his beautiful horse Goldfinger—a Palomino with a golden coat and platinum mane and tail—through the neighborhood. As everyone marveled at the sight, Bob signed them up for trash disposal. Within a year, all 60 homes were under contracts.

Bob was now exactly where he wanted to be, doing the thing he wanted to do while supporting his wife and growing family. He had fast horses and even faster cars. Life was good. Looking around at what he created in such a short time, Bob wondered, "Why didn't I leave Alabama and come here sooner?"

CHAPTER FOUR

ANYTHING TO MAKE MONEY

Once he saw the fast-growing opportunity, Bob did not hesitate to start the Warhurst Trash Company in 1963. He started off with a few customers he would service in the morning before he went to his main job working for Lee as a bricklayer. At 25, Bob was at the peak of his strength, 6-feet-tall and a wiry 185 pounds. He would need every ounce of that power to muscle the thousands of cans of household trash into his truck every week. He added more customers as the area boomed, and that meant his hours of masonry work declined. After about a year, he left bricklaying altogether.

"I hated to lose him," Lee admitted. "But you can't stand in the way of progress."

In the early 1960s, there weren't many homes yet with kitchen garbage disposals. The first household disposal was the In-Sink-Erator, created in 1927 by architect John W. Hammes in Racine, Wisconsin. But the device would not be used in 50 percent of U.S. homes until 2009, according to the 2009 American Housing Survey conducted by the U.S. Census Bureau. Most homes separated their household waste into dry trash (paper, cardboard, leaves, etc.) and wet garbage (food scraps and liquids)—almost all destined for landfills. According to the U.S. Environmental Protection Agency, only 5.6 percent of U.S. municipal trash and solid waste was recycled in the early 1960s. By 2010, the rate increased to 34.1 percent—a trend that would later prove critical in Bob's business progression.

Always a showman, Bob rode Goldfinger through new neighborhoods to drum up business. Eventually he was forced to give his top horse more rest and Skate, a sorrel mare, would be saddled up to market the growing business. At the pinnacle of his trash business, Bob serviced as many as 2,000 homes, first at Ridgely Estates in Mantua, then Stonewall Manor in Vienna and Greenbriar in Chantilly. "We didn't hesitate to sign up with him," recalled Stella Matalas, who lived in Stonewall Manor. "He was instantly lovable. Very nice, polite, down to Earth." Billie Jean mailed handwritten bills to customers every quarter. Homeowners paid $5.50 every three months for twice-a-week curbside pickups and $7.50 for behind-the-house service. Eventually Bob discovered that behind-the-house service was difficult because of locked garages and angry dogs. He dropped that service for new customers but honored his deal with his existing 80 customers and elderly folks.

"Back then, we didn't have the ability to hook up a can to a truck," Bob recalls of the days of hard, physical work that he and his crew endured. The back-breaking routine involved driving the trash truck to a customer's house, lifting the heavy, smelly cans and carrying them to the truck, where they would dump the trash. Then they would hop back in the truck and drive to the house of their next customer. "We had to pick up the cans—no matter how big the can was," Bob says. "If we had a really heavy can, we doubled up on it. You would do thousands in a day. A lot of people had three or four cans. I was in and out of the trash truck for years."

Bob's hardscrabble childhood prepared him well for the physical work. He says that although he would get tired from the lifting, he wouldn't get sore. His hands were calloused by years of manual labor and seldom protected by gloves. His first trash truck, a green 1949 Chevrolet half-ton pick-up that he bought for $200, was small by today's standards and often temperamental. "It was wore out when I bought it," Bob says. "It jumped out of second gear. You had to hold it to keep it in gear."

When the truck was full, Bob climbed in the back and stomped the trash down. He saw that new homeowners used a lot of cardboard when moving into their homes, so he used the cardboard sheets to build up the sides of the truck bed. When he reached the dump, he would rake the heavy, compacted trash from the truck. The landfill charged $13 a cubic yard. "It was on the honor system," Bob recalls. "There were no scales back then. Now they weigh it." The landfill was about eight miles from his routes and he drove the trash truck there three or four times a day for nine years. To save money, Bob burned the cardboard in an outdoor fire pit at his home.

"It was hard work," Bob says. "No question. We did it in rain, sleet and snow. I thought of it just like the U.S. mail. The trash had to go. No matter how hard it rained, we kept going. Some days I'd come home with icicles hanging from my hair and clothes."

As soon as he could, Bob bought a red 1959 Ford F600 truck from Lee. That truck had a 14-foot-long bed. "We could haul 10 times as much as the other truck," Bob says. "The bed lifted up, dumping the trash with no more raking." The more efficient operation allowed Bob to hire a couple of men to help pick up the trash and to widen his service area. One of those men was Donnie Nelson, now an electrician in Charleston, South Carolina. "Those were some great times," he said. "It was hard work, but we had fun doing it."

A third truck—a 1955 Garwood Load Packer—was a revolutionary, single-axel design with a 13-cubic-yard capacity. Bob painted the used truck blue. The final truck in the Warhurst Trash Company corral was a big, 18-cubic-yard Chevy packer. Bob put in a new motor and used it until he sold the trash business in 1972.

Despite his aggressive business instincts, Bob kept to his country ways even as the Washington, D.C., area began to grow into a crowded and impersonal metropolitan area. Whenever he heard that a customer had lost a job or had health problems, Bob would tell them that they didn't owe him anything for trash services until things got better. And they wouldn't have to reimburse him for the payments they missed, just for the renewed services.

Tim Guy, who grew up on Drexel Street in Stonewall Manor, still remembers his excitement as a young boy when Bob let him hop on the back of the trash truck. "It was big time fun!" Tim said. "I thought it was so cool that I could ride on the back of a trash truck. Who could do that?"

Tim is now Merrifield Garden Center's foremost plant expert. But there is an even better story: Bob picked up trash for Tony and Bev Ostroski in Stonewall Manor. They became his in-laws two decades later when their daughter, Lynn, married Bob's oldest son Rob. "I bet they never thought their daughter would end up marrying the garbage man's son!" Bob said.

When the day's trash service ended, the sun was still high in the sky. Bob strongly believed there was no reason to let daylight hours go to waste when there was money to be made. So Bob and his crew would often spend the rest of their day tackling odd jobs that he had lined up.

"Bob would do anything he could to make money," Donnie Nelson said. "We'd mow lawns, rake leaves. You never knew what you would be doing until you got there. I guess that's why he is where he is now. He's a go-getter."

Bob was developing a stellar reputation as an honest, can-do man who would accept any job. You name it—bury dead horses, plow snow, take down a tree, repair brickwork—Bob did it. And he did it with skill and speed. And he didn't charge much.

BOB THINKS A LOT ABOUT BUSINESS, but he also thinks a lot about fun. And he has the most fun when he has a lot of friends with him.

Bob's father once asked him if he would like to join the Masons, a prestigious global fraternal organization with a majestic granite temple in Alexandria and a membership roll that included U.S. presidents. "Before he died," Bob recalls, "Daddy said, 'No one will ever ask you this again. Would you like to be a Mason?'"

The Masons were well established and had a strong organizational structure. Bob preferred to form his own clubs with good friends, pursuing his passion for driving fast cars and riding horses.

"Daddy, thanks for asking," Bob said. "I really don't have time to do it."

Bob was indeed busy with his growing family and his business ideas. But there was something about horses that touched his soul. He even took his old dog with him on horse rides, draping Duke across the saddle when the 35-pound yellow-mix hound could not keep up.

In 1963, Bob and Buddy Williams began their first joint venture when they started the Rockin' F Riding Club. The "F" stood for Fairfax. Billie Jean and Doris Williams rode a bit with the club, too. "It's fun when you're associated with people you like," Bob says. "It's like being a kid and getting people to play baseball."

One of the Rockin' F Riding Club's objectives was to promote the Western style of riding, which was often ridiculed when compared to the more popular and genteel English discipline. The Western style evolved from American cowboys, who favored a deep saddle with a horn and tended cattle on sprawling ranches with one hand on the reins.

"Western riding in Northern Virginia was almost a joke," recalled Wanda (Williams) Flanagan, Buddy and Doris's oldest child. "(Bob and Buddy) wanted to change the perception. That it wasn't people who didn't know how to ride. They really were trying to come across as horsemen, not just rednecks. They looked for members who had experience and money to share their knowledge, people who could take us to the next level."

Bob hired local instructors to give group and individual lessons to club members. "The more we worked at it, the better we got, and then we were able to teach those skills to other people," Bob says.

The Rockin' F Riding Club rode in parades in Vienna, Virginia, and even took part in the large, annual National Cherry Blossom Festival Parade in Washington, D.C., along with military bands, dozens of ornate floats and politicians waving to the crowds from fancy convertibles. Decked out in white pants and a red shirt embroidered with the club name, Bob rode his beloved Goldfinger in the big parade. The club members also rode their horses to visit friends in their neighborhoods, which were still wooded and veined with dirt trails. They even rode their horses on errands. At the local 7-Eleven convenience store at the corner of Gallows Road and Electric Avenue in Dunn Loring, Virginia, a horse was killed when it was frightened and reared up, then came down on a metal stake hitching post. When he heard the horrible news, Bob sprang into action. The Rockin' F Riding Club donated and installed a traditional horizontal hitching post—just like the ones in cowboy movies—where horses could be tied safely.

While this was going on, Bob's mother brought back 13-year-old twins Carl and Jane in 1964 from the family's Russellville homestead, where they sought refuge after Claude's death. They moved in with Bob and Billie Jean for the summer. Brother Tracy had already migrated back to his older brothers in Northern Virginia in 1963 and sister Margene had gotten married.

As summer drew to a close, Bob's mother began making preparations to move the twins back to Alabama. But Carl said, "We told her we wouldn't go back. We were bored to death there. We were used to being here." She relented and brother Lee found them a small house to rent in Tyson's Corner, not too far from Bob and Billie Jean's house.

For the rapidly growing Rockin' F Riding Club, Bob wanted to expand the fun with a show ring. Borrowing a friend's bulldozer, Bob created a respectable ring in the side of the hill near Buddy's house. The club members could not afford a grader, so they painstakingly raked the ring. The kids pitched in as well, picking up rocks by hand to save the horses from injury.

Every Saturday throughout the summer and fall, club members competed in traditional rural equestrian sports, including barrel racing, pole bending, jousting, goat tying and pleasure class. Barrel racing was a timed contest where riders guided their horses in a clover-leaf pattern around three barrels. In pole bending, riders navigated their horses around six poles arranged in a line—similar to slalom skiing—to see who was fastest. Jousting, also called Spear the Ring, was where riders used a wooden pole to snag shower curtain hook-sized wooden rings hanging from a horizontal post. For goat tying, riders jumped off their horses, tied a goat's legs and jumped back on their horses. And pleasure class was a chance to show the horse's obedience through figure-eight riding.

Donnie Nelson, Bob's trash helper who lived in Dunn Loring near the Warhurst's house, had a small paint horse named Tonka that he kept in Bob's stable. To practice for the goat tying event, Donnie had Debbie and her friends run around the show ring while he tried to throw a rope around them.

Bob competed in a handful of pleasure and barrel racing events, but he recalls, "I was busy running the show." Bob was an expert with the bullwhip, which could recoil in the air at the speed of sound. The "crack" of the whip is the tip literally breaking the sound barrier, according to Scientific American magazine. His prowess was so great that Bob could even knock a lit cigarette out of brother Tracy's mouth with his 14-foot-long, leather whip.

Bob built a two-level judge's stand, and would climb to the top with a microphone and make announcements with aplomb, while Doris worked below taking money and registering entrants. It cost a couple of dollars to enter an event. The club members went so far as to hire an official judge. Prizes were awarded to the first four places. Carl still keeps a cardboard box filled with his ribbons. He also has his Rockin' F Riding Club silver belt buckle and membership card.

Carl acquired his steed, a brown quarter horse with a white face named Cindy, for $150, which he faithfully paid off in $10 monthly installments. "It was a long time before I could buy a saddle," Carl said. "And I always wanted saddlebags, but I never could afford them. We didn't have any money for anything. Bob didn't have any money back then, either. He had a growing family and the trash business. We had a lot of fun and we didn't have a lot of money."

During events, a concession stand was set up with hot dogs, sodas and candy. "For us kids, it was downright fun," Wanda said. "We had backyard horses. We loved them. We didn't know they were bad. It was all we could afford."

Ten-year-old Debbie had a horse named Misty, who was a mix of thoroughbred and Arabian bloodlines often referred to as Anglo-Arab. "She was a jumping horse," Debbie recalled. "But she hurt her foot so they sold her to us." Debbie competed in pleasure class and barrel racing.

The highlight of the season was the end-of-year banquet, where a small forest of shiny trophies was presented to the year-end award winners. It was a dress-up occasion for the members. Bob and Buddy looked sharp in their dark suits with button-down shirts and skinny ties, so did Billie Jean and Doris in their sweetheart dresses with their hair put up in buns.

For about six years, Bob served as president of the Rockin' F Riding Club. He says he also served as president of the Northern Virginia Western Horse Association and the Virginia Cutting Horse Association. Cutting horses were originally used by cattle drivers to separate individual calves or steers from the rest of the herd for branding or other purposes through an intricate, dance-like motion.

In addition to calming strong-willed horses, Bob showed the Williamses his healing powers. "One of our cousins lived with us growing up," Wanda said. "She had warts on her feet. She always wore socks because she didn't like the way her feet looked. Well, one day Bob held her foot, rubbed her warts and said something under his breath. The warts went away. I'm not kidding. He's a good witch!"

Later Bob even treated an FBI agent who was shopping at Merrifield Garden Center. "He had awful looking warts on his hand," Bob says. "I said, 'Would you like me to get rid of those warts?' We were in the azalea patch. I took his hand and did my thing. Weeks later, I saw him. He said, 'It has something to do with the soil, doesn't it?' I told him that I couldn't tell him. It's a gift."

Bob says he started removing warts when he was about 19. "I just felt like I could do it," he says. "Something told me I could. I surprised myself, though, the first time I did it. It was so natural."

Whenever he sees anyone with warts, Bob offers to take them off. He estimates that he has removed warts on more than 50 people over the years. Word spread that he could get rid of warts and mothers used to bring their children to the garden center for his treatment.

"I've often wondered myself how I do it," he says. "Maybe it's the chemistry in my body. I've asked some learned people. I've never gotten a good explanation."

Even today, Bob meets people who received his wart cure 30 or more years ago. They say, "Remember when you removed my warts?"

BOB'S DRIVE TO BE THE BEST AT EVERYTHING is a constant theme in his life and that desire didn't stop with his trash collecting business.

"In school, I wanted to win all the races," he said. "Laying brick? I wanted to be the best. I wanted to do it better and faster than anyone else. Even when I was in the trash business, I wanted to be the best."

Bob claims he was so punctual that "people could set their clocks by me." And attention to detail was a high priority. "I would set the cans back properly with their lids on top and I made sure there was no trash left on the ground," he says.

In his nine years of collecting trash, Bob never missed a day on any route, until his son Larry Ray Warhurst came into the world. Although Virginia is considered a Southern state, winter weather in the mid-Atlantic can be as raw and cold as New England and February 19, 1965 was no exception. "It was extremely cold with a bitter wind," Bob remembers. "It was one of the coldest days I've ever seen."

Bob was out on his trash run when he saw a car behind him flashing its lights and honking the horn. It was his neighbor, Virginia Sanderson. Bob climbed down from the truck and met her on the wind-blown street. As the icy winds whipped around them, she told him that Billie Jean had gone into labor and he needed to get home to take her to the hospital. There were no cell phones in those days, of course, and Mrs. Sanderson nervously drove Bob's route, hoping to find him before the baby arrived at the Warhurst home on Ninovan Road. Bob rushed Billie Jean to the Columbia Hospital for Women—where all the Warhurst children would be born—then waited nervously in the hallway until a nurse told him he could go to the viewing area.

"You've got to see this!" the nurse said.

In the nursery, Bob saw his second-born son Larry, a 10-pound, 11-ounce baby who entered the world with strong muscles and intense curiosity. In fact, not long after he was born, Larry was able to move his head side-to-side using his fists to push his large head back and forth to take in this bright, beautiful new world and the faces of his amazed parents.

For the first and only time, Bob didn't complete his trash service run. But the next morning, he fired up the truck and finished his appointed rounds.

IF YOU SPEND ENOUGH TIME OUTDOORS, sooner or later Mother Nature lets you know who is the boss. Mother Nature usually gets the last word. Bob discovered that in 1965.

As he drove down Ninovan Road in Vienna on his way home from work, Bob noticed that the sky had turned dark as a large thunderstorm was moving in his direction. Heavy rain began falling and thunder was booming as he pulled into his driveway.

He flung open the truck door to make a quick dash into the house about 80 feet away. As his feet hit the ground, there was a huge flash of bright light and the loudest noise he had ever heard. In that brilliant moment, his arms flew straight out to both sides and he was frozen in time. Bob had been struck by lightning. Then he suddenly collapsed in a heap on the ground.

"It's not a good feeling to be struck by lightning," Bob says. "You can actually feel the lightning go right through you. It's like the crack of a whip. I'll never forget the feeling. I can feel it now."

Just as quickly as it began, it was over. Bob began to slowly wiggle his fingers and toes, making sure his appendages still worked. Once he learned he was unharmed, Bob jumped up and rushed safely into the house, thankful to have survived his brush with death. Coincidentally, as Ninovan Road crosses the nearby Washington and Old Dominion Railroad Trail, its name changes to Electric Avenue.

ON MAY 19, 1966, BILLIE JEAN DELIVERED another son named Donald Wayne. One night shortly after they brought Donny home from the hospital, Bob and Billie Jean were talking in the kitchen when they saw 15-month-old Larry walking in holding the newborn under his arm like a football.

"We about dropped our jaws!" Billie Jean said. "Larry was so strong he climbed up the side where the railing was lowered and scooped him up. He could have dropped him! From then on, we kept the railing up."

The following year on July 13, 1967, Bob and Billie Jean had their fifth and final child, another boy named Richard Kevin.

"We had five kids and five horses!" Bob exclaimed.

For the first week or two, Bob and Billie Jean called their new son Ricky, then they decided he looked more like a Kevin than a Ricky. From then on, he was known as Kevin.

To take care of his growing family, Bob needed to find bigger and better ways to make money. Bob's natural penchant for business has always served him well, but when he hatched an idea for a new financial product in 1967, he ignored the nagging little voice in his head.

Credit cards were becoming popular with consumers, but Bob was smart enough to see that the laws of physics also applied to money. For every action, there is an equal and opposite reaction. The credit card companies were charging early-adopting merchants a big fee to access their services because of the novelty of charge cards. Bob, as usual, had a counter-intuitive idea. He based his Cash Plan card on businesses giving customers a discount, as much as 15 to 30 percent, for paying cash. For $15 a year for the Cash Plan card, customers would receive a plastic card with their name on it, much like a regular credit card. But instead of having to pay a card fee plus an interest fee on their outstanding balances, they paid less at the cash register.

Bob's idea was that businesses would benefit in the long run because the discounts would drive customers their way. He designed Cash Plan signs for store windows that looked like dollar bills. His pitch: "Use Cash and Save Here."

"I signed up as many stores in Fairfax as I could, maybe 40 or 50," he says. "I had furniture stores, gas stations, hardware stores and restaurants."

But Bob didn't get a cut of the customer cash from the retailers, just the one-time $15 fee. He soon realized that he should have listened to his own doubts. He spent $10,000 and a lot of effort trying to make the Cash Plan work, but he couldn't turn a profit.

"I never had a great feeling about it," Bob says now. "I did it for about a year and a half and then I just decided that I wasn't going to do it anymore. I didn't have a lot of money. We didn't even own our house. I've made some mistakes. But you can't let it get you down."

As his record shows, by sheer hard work and persistence, Bob would find a path to his true calling, his destiny. But at this point, the road ahead would be literally full of dirty work, twists and turns, heavy lifting and the kindness of strangers.

CHAPTER FIVE

TURNING TRASH INTO CASH

Bob Warhurst's boyhood in economically depressed Alabama gave him an education in thrift and the need to make the most of every opportunity. The time he killed and slaughtered the hog at age 12, everything but the squeal was put to use. That trait would continue into his adult years as a trash collector. Not everything his clients placed on the curb was garbage or useless. The Washington, D.C., area economy was booming and in the Northern Virginia suburbs the emerging disposable society was not adverse to bringing in the new and tossing out the old.

The first item Bob ever plucked from the trash was a stainless steel pitcher with a crack in the handle. Billie Jean boiled it and sterilized it.

"We're still using it after all these years," she said.

Today, that old pitcher sits prominently in the Warhurst's big, shiny kitchen. It's a reminder of how far the family has come.

Before the term "recycling" was used, the Warhurst Trash Company was turning household discards into usable items that could be resold, transformed or traded.

"We would always take an extra truck and park it at the entrance of the subdivision," Bob recalls. "If we saw a bicycle or a chair or something worth keeping, we'd go back."

While Bob drove the trash truck to the landfill, a helper would go back on the route and pick up the discarded treasures. The booty varied from the truly useful to the semi-salacious. Playboy magazines were a hot item and the crew would glean 40 to 50 magazines every day. Bob found two .45-caliber pistols in the original plastic wrap, a set of golf clubs and fencing equipment in one home's trash. Thinking the expensive items were tossed out by mistake, he knocked on the door.

A woman answered and promptly informed him that, "We're divorcing. You're welcome to it." Fifty years later, Bob still has one of the pistols. He traded the other gun years ago for 100 wooden 2x4s and a .38 pistol.

"If someone threw away a lawn mower, I'd take it," he says. "I'd collect all the lawn mowers, broken chairs and take the parts and make them whole. Someone would throw away a mower with a broken wheel and another person would throw one away with a faulty engine. If a couch had a broken leg, I fixed it. All of a sudden, I had a whole lot of everything."

Bob's thriftiness became legend and his trash customers began setting aside items, such as chairs, tables, ironing boards and scooters, for him. "Bob's a likable guy and people were good to him," Billie Jean said. "People saved books and clothes for us. People would even wash and iron the clothes and set them aside for us in a separate box. We got so much stuff. He would find a good sofa, better than the one we had, so we'd switch. Everything we got came from the trash."

Bob stored everything in the garage of their Ninovan Road home, where he also kept a workbench and tools to make repairs. They also recycled clothing. "We never bought any clothes for the kids when they were growing up," Bob says. "We had our choice." Oldest son Rob remembered it differently. When asked if he got his toys and clothes—which included out-of-style bell-bottomed plaid pants and checkered shirts—from the trash, Rob replied with a smile, "Unfortunately."

Having a dad who was a trash collector was sometimes problematic for the Warhurst kids. Billie Jean remembered that when Debbie was in the fifth grade, all the kids were asked to stand up and tell what their dads did for a living. She refused to do it. "She told me she didn't want to tell," Billie Jean said. "The kids always wanted to say he did something else." Bob would tell them, "It feeds you and clothes you. Don't ever be ashamed."

Looking back, Bob says, "I was always proud of being a trash collector. It was a good, honest way to make a living." And, as destiny would soon prove, trash collecting would create opportunities the Warhurst family could never have imagined.

In 1968, the Washington, D.C., area was in turmoil. Opposition to the bloody war in Vietnam had spawned an angry counterculture that was protesting in the streets around the U.S. Capitol and the White House. Then the worst came. On April 4, 1968, Martin Luther King, Jr., was assassinated in Memphis, Tennessee, where he was leading a protest by janitors for better wages. Just 63 days after King's death, U.S. Senator Robert F. Kennedy, who was against the war in Vietnam and had just won the California Democratic Primary for U.S. president, was shot in a Los Angeles hotel kitchen moments after delivering his victory speech. He died early the next morning on June 6, 1968. Following the death of Robert F. Kennedy, Republican Richard M. Nixon defeated Democrat Hubert H. Humphrey to become president in 1968. In the coming years, America would learn of another Washington tragedy: Watergate.

But in the suburbs, life in America was rolling along, and affluence was turning what had been sleepy country roads into busy thoroughfares that tied Virginia to the nation's capital. The expansion of the federal government brought another wave of civilian office workers for the FBI, the Pentagon and other federal agencies.

As Bob was amassing a large amount of clean and usable items from his trash runs, he decided to organize the process he had been running out of his truck into a viable business. He found an ideal site at the corner of Jermantown Road and Lee Highway in the Kamp Washington section of Fairfax, Virginia that he rented for $300 a month. The 1,600-square foot main building came with an adjoining metal warehouse and an outdoor picnic table. Bob called it "The Tradin' Post," and its mission was selling the goods he found in the trash for cash. His move from casual neighborhood sales to a bricks-and-mortar retail building was a big step for what would eventually be one of the nation's most successful independent garden centers. The lessons he learned as a child worker from Miss Hendrix and her little country store back in Alabama would become valuable.

His first order of business was building a big, 20' x 4' plywood sign with 2' high letters that spelled out The Tradin' Post and affixing it to the front of the store to attract the attention of thousands of people driving by every day. There was no budget for radio, television or newspaper advertising. Even so, his customer base steadily grew by word of mouth and people driving by. One day Bob realized that the store's entrance was inconvenient to the drivers who might wish to come to the store immediately after seeing the sign. The driveway that led into The Tradin' Post was about 300 to 400 feet off the less traveled Jermantown Road, instead of the much busier Lee Highway. So Bob borrowed a backhoe, carved out a new entrance and driveway off Lee Highway and put down asphalt with the help of a neighbor.

At the start, Bob's whole family was involved. The building was subdivided into a room for clothing with his mother in charge, another as a showroom for expensive antiques and other pricier items and a third room for fabrics and other household items, such as couches, chairs, lamps, bookshelves and mirrors. "I gave the clothing room to my mother," Bob says. "She got to run it and keep the money."

Bob started out only selling items he found in the trash. Donnie Nelson, who helped with the Warhurst Trash Company, remembers Bob regularly reminding him and the other workers, "If you see anything good, save it for The Tradin' Post." Donnie said, "Bob would find stuff in the trash and try to sell it. I'd say, 'No way that will sell.' The next day, it'd be gone."

Bob soon supplemented his trash treasures with products he purchased from peddlers who frequented the store, as well as long-distance suppliers. He would drive 650 miles round trip to High Point, North Carolina, to buy couches, chairs and tables. He would also make the 500-mile round trip to Scranton, Pennsylvania, for bolts of fabric, needles and thread to feed the growing numbers of home seamstresses inspired by the postwar boom in electric home sewing machines and mass-produced clothing patterns.

"I wanted to get as much stuff as I could," Bob says. "Once you have customers coming, you want to load up."

The biggest seller at The Tradin' Post was Playboy magazine, which was plentiful in the suburban trashcans and could be resold for 25 cents. "Women would buy them for their husbands," Bob says. "We'd sell 15 or 20 a day. We always had a nice selection of them." Bob sold items other merchandisers wouldn't touch, such as used mattresses. "I built me an 8' x 8' x 8' wooden chamber where I sterilized and fumigated them," he says.

Estate sales were not yet as common as they are today, but The Tradin' Post became just the place for families to make a little cash by selling some sad family memories. "One time a man called me and said his wife died and he just wanted to get the stuff out of the house and move on with his life," Bob says. "I think I paid him $1,200 and I sold about $25,000 or $30,000 out of it. I didn't know what it was worth. But I called a couple of ladies who knew antiques and they helped me price the items."

Bob's son Larry Warhurst recalled that they once had a white spacesuit with an interlocking helmet for sale. "They kept it in the bathroom, probably to keep someone from stealing it," he said.

In no time, The Tradin' Post was a popular place that hummed with noise and excitement as family members, shoppers and peddlers mingled in the building. The Tradin' Post brought out the showman in Bob and that led to some real monkey business. To drum up sales, Bob brought in two hard-nosed partners with jungle instincts and the agility to climb the corporate ladder. Their names were Mike and Cheetah—and they were real monkeys. They lived in cages in the warehouse next to The Tradin' Post, and their antics soon made them stars throughout the store. They were especially fond of Bob and went into a frenzy every time they heard his truck pull up.

"One of them would hold my hand," Bob fondly recalls, "but you couldn't trust them. You never know what they might do. They were fast. They could grab your glasses out of your shirt pocket." In one memorable stunt, one of the monkeys grabbed a lit cigar out of Bob's mouth and popped it into his own mouth—lit-end first!

One family in particular fell in love with Mike and Cheetah. They visited the monkeys every weekend and brought them cookies and bananas. As winter neared, Bob realized the store was not the best place for the monkeys. Bob wanted to find a good home for them, so he gave the monkeys at no charge to the couple who adored them. Bob personally delivered the monkeys to their new home and he says, "when I closed the front door to leave, I could see the monkeys were already on top of their curtains!"

Meantime, the Warhurst family was settling down in their cozy home on Ninovan Road in Vienna, just about three miles as the crow flies from the place where Bob would one day open his first garden center. The area was not as cosmopolitan as it is now, with the huge Tyson's Corner mega-mall, multiple highways and Metro rail lines crisscrossing every which way.

Back then, the area was still a little bit country. The closest thing to a mall was Maple Avenue, the main road that runs through Vienna. That's where the family bought their clothes, ending the embarrassing era when the Warhurst kids had to wear items scoured from Bob's trash business. Maple Avenue was a big step up, with Curly's, Kinney Shoes, Samson Sporting Goods, a Safeway grocery store and a Bob's Big Boy for an occasional treat of burgers and frosty milk shakes.

Maple Avenue was also the place where pediatrician Dr. Ronald

Barsanti looked after the Warhurst kids, including the biggest kid of all, Bob.

After taking their five children to Dr. Barsanti for years, Bob and Billie Jean got to know him. Bob rarely left work to visit a doctor himself, but when he did, he felt comfortable with Dr. Barsanti. The receptionist would roll her eyes when Bob would come in, asking to see the good doctor. She would hem and haw about how Dr. Barsanti was a pediatrician and did not treat adults, but Bob would insist that she tell the doctor that he was there and wasn't feeling well.

Bob had to sit in the waiting room, squeezed into the biggest chair he could find in a room full of kid-sized furniture. And, after a while, the nurse would come out and announce, "Mr. Warhurst, the doctor will see you now."

There is no record of Bob receiving a lollipop.

Bob's very independent childhood in the 1940s was typical of that era and especially of rural Alabama in the final years of the Great Depression. He didn't have a lot of parental limits on what he could and couldn't do. Once he became a father, he passed that ethos on to his kids. They could do anything they wanted, within reason. "We had no rules," Bob's son Donny said. "But if you ever crossed that line, you knew you were gonna get a beating.'"

With 25 acres of woods and pasture to roam and rumble on horseback or the seat of a motorcycle, the Warhurst kids had a happy childhood filled with memorable adventures and boisterous fun. There were a lot of animals in the mix: horses, dogs, cats, two goats and a pregnant pig. "I remember being outside a lot," Debbie said. "There were lots of woods and open spaces. The neighbors lived across the field, not across the street."

In the winter, the rolling terrain was perfect for slipping and sliding. "The Sandersons had the best sledding hill in the area," she said. "We had a great time sledding on the snow." Store-bought sleds were out of the question, so the kids used metal soda pop signs that they found in their rented home. In the warmer months, horses became the entertainment. "I loved horses and the idea of cowboys," Kevin said. "I can still remember Rob mucking the stalls one day and me sitting on a fence post watching him while "Tie A Yellow Ribbon Round The Old Oak Tree" played on the radio."

The Warhursts and their good friends and neighbors, the Williamses, will never forget the Labor Day weekend they took their kids and horses about 35 miles to the country village of Waterford in Loudoun County, a beautiful place of rolling hills, abundant creeks with cold, fresh water and a history steeped in the bond of horse and man in both sport and battle, especially during the Civil War. Escaping from the growing urbanization of the Washington, D.C., area became a priority for the Warhurst and Williams families, whose roots in the countryside were deep.

"We went all out," recalled Doris Williams. "We rode horses and chopped wood. We cooked meals over the campfire."

All around them was some of the most gorgeous land in the United States. Centuries-old farms were outlined with miles of hand-laid stone fences, intricately set by local masons who refused to use cement, preferring to cut each piece of fieldstone to fit snugly against the next. This was the place steeped in the early history of the nation, some gallant, some cruel. The Potomac River was just beyond several forested ridges of the Catoctin Mountains, fed by creeks—locally called runs or branches.

Both the Revolutionary War and the U.S. Civil War were fought in these hills, but the only battles going on at that time were between historic preservationists trying to hold tight to the history and developers seeking to bring the Washington suburbs farther out into Virginia. Tiny Waterford fought off suburbanization and to this day clings precariously to its heritage. Many historic fox hunts are still held in the area, with the hoots and hollers of the field masters and whippers-in holding tight to that equestrian discipline and social order.

The Warhursts and Williamses preferred a simpler way, with family close. Their horses chased only fun, not animals, and the trails they rode always brought them back to campfires and homemade meals under the stars. Doris and Buddy rented a camping trailer for the weekend. One night it rained, and they shared their cozy space with the Warhursts, who were sleeping in the back of their horse truck.

Dawn turned the eastern sky purple and gold. "I remember fixing eggs, bacon and coffee for breakfast, and my, how good it smelled," Doris said. "The special thing was we didn't have a lot to worry about. We were young and we had fun. Most people don't have fun anymore."

When he was growing up, Bob didn't have any store-bought toys, so when his boys got to the point where they could handle fast motorized fun, he made sure they had all the horsepower they needed to turn the throttle hard on the rolling dirt trails near their home on Ninovan Road.

The Warhurst and Williams families had friendly sports rivalries. When Bob bought a beautiful, new Honda CL70 for his nine-year-old son Rob for Christmas, Buddy wanted to get a motorcycle for his son Hal, too. But Buddy bought a QA50, a mini bike without the power to satisfy a 10-year-old boy. So Bob bought the mini bike from Buddy and put it under the Christmas tree for Larry, who was five. Buddy went back to the Honda dealer and bought the same motorcycle for Hal that Bob had gotten for Rob.

"We were freaking out," Larry said. "It was so cool to have motorcycles."

Bob taught his boys the basics of riding, but he believed that experience was the best teacher, a theme in his life. As Rob and Larry gained experience riding motorcycles, they also took their younger brothers for rides on their bikes. Bob's son Donny caught the motorcycle bug, too. When he was in middle school, Donny and his friends lusted after a Honda CB360T motorcycle, a fast twin-cylinder, four-stroke machine that was parked outside the firehouse that they passed every day on the way to and from school. He excitedly told his parents about it at dinner, but he didn't expect to get the Honda because it wasn't cheap and it had a lot of horsepower for someone his age. One day, the motorcycle was no longer at the firehouse. Donny and his friends were disappointed, knowing that someone had bought it.

Later that day, Donny came home from school and there was the motorcycle parked in the driveway.

"Whose is that?" Donny asked. "I got it for you," Bob said.

"It was incredible," Donny recalled. "My friends couldn't believe it. I couldn't believe it, either."

The Warhurst's three-bedroom house on Ninovan Road was divvied up with Bob and Billie Jean in the master bedroom and the four boys camped out military style in a small room next to their parents with two sets of bunk beds. "Before we went to bed, Mom always checked us for ticks," Larry recalled. Rob would tell ghost stories to frighten his younger brothers, tales of severed heads searching for lost bodies, bloody ghouls hiding under the bed, waiting for little kids to fall asleep.

Debbie was by herself in a big bedroom far from the other two rooms. She wished that she could have swapped her much larger room with her brothers, but Billie Jean wanted the four rambunctious boys close to her room so she could keep a close eye on them. She kept the roughhousing boys at bay by threatening, "Don't make me tell your dad!"

But Debbie wasn't beyond her own missteps. Debbie remembers getting in hot water with her parents after botching the important after-school job of removing trash-collection checks from their mailbox. She wasn't careful about taking them home one day and dropped many of them on her quarter-mile walk home from the school bus stop. For days, Debbie and her parents scoured the dirt road and grass spots for wayward checks. "I was in big trouble,"

Debbie recalled. "But once the boys came along, anything I did was nothing compared to what they did."

When a harsh word wasn't enough to keep the boys in line, Billie Jean maintained law and order with a whack from a long-handled wooden spoon. "She was famous for her wooden spoons," Rob said. When they were young, Billie Jean would spank the boys with her bare hand. But one day, mischievous Larry slipped a hard-cover book in the back of his trousers so when his mother spanked him, her hand took the force of the blow instead of his behind. After that, she always used a wooden spoon to dole out punishment. "When Dad got home, he'd take a belt to us—hard," Rob said. "We'd beg her not to tell on us. If she told him, we'd be in for it. Then we were scared out of our minds."

With Bob busy working most of the time, Billie Jean held the family together with her motherly tenderness. She made sure meals were prepared, homework was done, school activities attended and Band-Aids applied to skinned knees and broken hearts. She would not take the title for herself, but Billie Jean is regarded by many as a "saint." She is always there for Bob and their children, tending to their every need with a warm smile and a kind word. When he gave her guns, motorcycles and a fancy sports car for gifts, Billie Jean would just smile, even though she had no use for such things. She saw her mission in life as supporting Bob, and although she was comfortable offering advice to him in private, she never questioned him. She was the strong foundation that allowed Bob to reach as high as he could imagine.

Although they loved their parents equally, Kevin said "we were always a little bit fearful of Dad, especially when we were younger. He was very big and strong, a man's man. He worked hard and didn't make a lot of small talk. If he spoke to us, it was because he had something to say. Dad was always a little bit mysterious to me. I know he loved us, but it was a tough love. He talked about hard work, doing the right thing, minding your manners, listening to your mother, et cetera." There was always much more love than anger at the house on Ninovan Road. Bob created the Pizza Night family ritual, which still exists today. Money was tight in those days, so Bob waited to buy groceries until Friday night after customers had paid their bills.

Bob realized that "we're buying stuff we couldn't afford because we're hungry." So Bob and Billie Jean made a habit of eating pizza before doing their grocery shopping.

Their favorite Pizza Night spot was Pizza Fair on Maple Avenue in Vienna, about a mile from home. Sometimes Bob and his brother Carl picked up the pizzas by horseback. Other times, Bob put all four boys on his motorcycle for the trip. "Two boys on the gas tank, one behind me and one on the handlebars," he says proudly. They took the Washington & Old Dominion trail next to the railroad lines, which were no longer in use. That trail is now the W&OD pedestrian and bicycle trail that funnels thousands of runners, walkers and cyclists into and out of Washington D.C., every day. But back then, it was the Pizza Night Express.

Then as now, the Warhurst house was the place to be every Friday night. Family and friends all wanted to join the fun. "You never knew who was going to show up," Larry said. "There could be 30 people there. People would stop by for 10 minutes or four hours."

WHEN BOB WAS GROWING UP, children were expected to help out around the farm with whatever needed to be done. So when the Warhurst Trash Company was short of workers, Bob naturally turned to his oldest son Rob.

"Sometimes I held him out of school when someone didn't show up for work," Bob says. "Rob drove the trash truck when he was nine years old."

When Bob first told his son that he wasn't going to school, Rob's initial reaction was, "Man, this is awesome!"

Then reality sunk in. Even though he was big and strong for his age, Rob had no experience driving a huge, four-speed truck filled with garbage through the hilly tangle of suburban growth in Northern Virginia.

"I remember being nervous," Rob said. "There were lots of hills in Stonewall Manor, which was hard because the truck was a stick-shift."

The large steering wheel felt like the wheel of an ocean liner to Rob, who had to sit on two phone books to see over the dashboard. He had to use his whole body to engage the clutch pedal with his outstretched foot while shifting the gears with his right hand and steering with his left.

But Rob knew his father was expecting him to come through for the family.

"He wasn't someone you could tell, 'I don't want to do the hills,'" Rob said. "You just had to figure it out."

Rob drove the trash truck half a dozen times and remembers the Fairfax County Landfill as "a playground with sea gulls flying around it."

He's still amazed at his feats.

"It's kind of hard to believe when I think about it," Rob said.

Although the Warhurst family no longer lived in the countryside of Bob's Alabama youth, the old ways of the Deep South were never forgotten. In the winter of 1969, Bob decided it was time to take his family to see Russellville.

"I wanted to show them where I lived," Bob says. "We drove to Florida with a camper on the back of a pick-up truck, which was fancy for people like us. On the way back home, we stopped in Alabama and went to Miss Hendrix's country store."

At the store—the site of Bob's first job at the age of seven—several elderly men were smoking and sharing town gossip to while away the day. In the middle of the store, there was an old-fashioned potbelly stove, stoked red hot to stave off the chill in the air.

Kevin, who was not quite two, dropped some candy near the blazing hot stove. No one noticed as he bent down and picked up the candy with his right hand, while using his left hand to balance himself on the stove. He began howling in pain and pulled his seared hand off the stove as fast as he could.

"He burned his hand really, really bad," Bob says. "He was just a toddler and didn't know anything about a hot stove."

In the chaos of Kevin's screams, Bob's country instincts took over and he immediately asked for "someone who takes out fire," a healer with the powers to return a serious burn to unblemished, healthy skin.

Someone shouted "a lady up the street" was such a healer. Bob grabbed young Kevin in his arms and the entire family rushed to the camper to seek out the healer. In a tiny, tree-shaded, low-slung house just a few feet off the road, Bob found her.

"My son Kevin just burned his hand," said Bob in a calm voice because he never shouts or raises his voice, not even in an emergency.

The healer, a poor, elderly country woman in a long dress, flung open her door and ushered the strangers inside. "She began doing her magic stuff," Bob says. "She took his hand in hers and began saying things under her breath. I didn't say anything to her. I was so overwhelmed with what was happening."

Back out in the camper, Billie Jean recalled, "We could hear Kevin screaming. He wasn't in there five minutes when the screaming all of a sudden stopped. Debbie and I looked at each other and started crying. We didn't know what happened. You always think the worst." What Billie Jean and Debbie couldn't see was that Kevin had been healed and had fallen into a deep, peaceful sleep. "There were no blisters, not even a sign of a burn," Bob says.

Bob believed in healing powers, based partly on his own power to cure warts.

"I thought it was an art that should be passed on," he says. "Every time I went back to Russellville, I chased around trying to find the healer. I even went to a nursing home, but I could never find her. It was real, though. I saw it with my own eyes. I was so impressed. I'm still looking for her actually. Or someone like her."

The story of Kevin's encounter with the "fire healer" is often repeated in the family. For Kevin, the miracle was an important moment of his life. "I was so young I don't remember it," he said. "Sometimes I feel like I remember parts of it, but I'm sure that's because I've heard the story for so many years."

By the time he was in high school, Kevin began thinking about the event in a different way. "I thought it was really cool and mysterious," he said. "I feel like I was part of something kind of special, even if it's somewhat confusing and unexplainable. As I've grown into adulthood and become a father, I've thought about it a lot more, especially when my kids were young and would get really sick in the middle of the night and have to go to the emergency room. Parenting is such a joy, but there's this awesome responsibility and worry that comes with being a parent. It makes me think back to what my parents must have felt having a small child get a really bad burn and the panic of what to do when something like that happens."

IN THE WARHURST FAMILY IN RUSSELLVILLE, Alabama, work was everything. It had to be that way for the family to survive the Great Depression, World War II and the droughts that decimated farming in the South.

When Bob followed his older brother Lee to Virginia for work in the booming post-World War II years, they spent their days in back-breaking labor so they could afford to bring family members to a new place with more opportunities and better pay.

Getting an education was not a priority. But in 1970, Bob's youngest brother Carl became the first member of the family to graduate from high school. Carl credits his girlfriend, Sheila Crunkleton, now his wife, with encouraging him to finish his schooling at George C. Marshall High School in Falls Church, Virginia.

At Carl's graduation, only Carl's mother, Billie Jean and young Debbie attended the ceremony from the family. They watched Carl proudly accept the first-ever Warhurst high school diploma. The other men in the family were working.

Bob's wheels were always turning. He was always looking for bigger and better things. For all the long hours and hard work at the Warhurst Trash Company and The Tradin' Post, he was not turning much of a profit.

"My saying is if you deal in nickels, you're going to make nickels," Bob says. "McDonald's is the exception to the rule. It works for them because of the volume. I needed to deal in something more valuable."

Although the inside of The Tradin' Post was filled with cast-off treasures, Bob had ample room outside the store and warehouse. He was thinking of something to sell to expand his business.

Near The Tradin' Post on Lee Highway was Garden World of Virginia.

Bob couldn't help but notice their bustling parking lot, which overflowed with traffic on weekends. Cars left with their trunks and back seats filled with beautiful plants, while bigger trees poked out of the beds of pickup trucks headed to the many new suburban homes popping up in the area.

Bob decided to start selling beautiful shrubs and trees at The Tradin' Post, beginning with some of Washington, D.C.'s most cherished plants, azaleas and cherries. He did not have connections with any growers, but he used his winning personality to work out deals with area nurseries to acquire plants at discounted prices. Not only were the beautiful plants more profitable than most of the other items at The Tradin' Post, Bob came from an agricultural background and liked growing plants and knew how to take care of them.

This would be a great way to make a living, he thought. A great way.

One night, after another exhausting day of slinging trash and peddling second-hand goods at The Tradin' Post, Bob came home and told Billie Jean that he was going to open a nursery.

"A nursery?" Billie Jean said. "You don't even babysit our own kids very much."

"Not that kind of nursery," Bob replied. "Plants and trees and flowers."

"But you don't know much about it," Billie Jean said.

"I can learn."

CHAPTER SIX

BOB AND BUDDY'S GARDEN CENTER

In 1971, Bob Warhurst was 32 years old, married with five kids. Some people might have settled down to the rhythms of running the Warhurst Trash Company and The Tradin' Post, but that's not Bob's way.

"I was always anxious to try something new and different," he says.

His "new and different" turned out to be a garden center.

Not long after hatching the idea based on how well his plants were selling at The Tradin' Post, Bob approached his friend and neighbor Buddy Williams to see if he wanted to join him in the venture. "Buddy, I'm going to open a nursery," Bob said. "Do you want to go in with me?"

Immediately, Buddy said yes.

"I had so many other things going—the trash business, The Tradin' Post," Bob says. "I had my hands full. I needed help and I liked Buddy and his family."

The first step was to find a great location. Bob and Buddy explored different options and eventually found a plot of land in Manassas, Virginia, that they rented on a month-to-month lease. But after a few visits to clear the land, Bob thought that area wasn't yet ripe for the type of garden center he wanted to build. But its time would come. Not the kind of people to let things get them down, Bob and Buddy soon hopped in Bob's pick-up truck to look for a new place to set their roots. Pulling out of their Ninovan Road neighborhood into Vienna, Bob drove south down Gallows Road and turned left at Lee Highway in the small industrial area known as Merrifield, Virginia.

Like Columbus coming ashore in the Americas, Bob declared, "This is it!"

Merrifield was just outside the busy Washington Beltway that moved tens of thousands of vehicles around the nation's capital. All of Bob's entrepreneurial instincts were buzzing. One of Bob's greatest strengths is to see beyond the present moment and visualize what might be possible. He looked around a weedy, junk-strewn lot filled with scraggly brush and abandoned, rusty cars occupied by weeds. But Bob saw huge potential: The lot was next to an Exxon gas station at a very busy intersection at the corner of Gallows Road and Lee Highway. His mind began racing as he scanned the scene, visualizing the potential of the property.

Bob always trusted his gut feelings, especially when it came to making money. He was so excited that he pulled over at the gas station and immediately called a friend who was a real estate agent to find out who owned the land. Bob learned the site was about eight acres and owned by Mary Fuchs, a wealthy Washington socialite. Wasting no time, Bob and Buddy rented less than an acre from her for $325 a month, which is about $1,900 in today's dollars.

"It was just a little piece of land," Billie Jean said. "But I remember Bob saying, 'It's going to be great! It's a good location right by the intersection.' It was a lot of money. We had to watch every dime. Everyone worked hard. It was scary, but wonderful. It's almost like Bob had a gift of knowing just what to do."

Once the land was secured, Bob and Buddy worked hard to clean up the property and open the nursery as soon as possible. After their shift ended with the Warhurst Trash Company, Donnie Nelson, Bane Dudley and Solomon Hicks came over to the garden center. Although he was just renting, Bob didn't need Mrs. Fuch's approval to make sweeping changes to her property. With axes and chainsaws, they removed the stubborn weeds, roots and stumps. The first accomplishments were the creation of the parking lot, walkways and roads—all gravel—inside the boundaries of the site.

Garden beds were built with railroad ties.

Bob was deep in his element. At night, he could hardly sleep, thinking of how he would make their little corner of the world a successful business.

The building where customers would pay for their purchases was a small red barn. Today, the relic is still standing at the company's largest and newest store in Gainesville, Virginia, near Manassas, the town where Bob and Buddy had first thought they would start their garden center. Those 8' wide x 10' x 8' barns were originally built and sold at The Tradin' Post.

Before the garden center could open, it needed a name and a sign. Bob and Buddy put up a 4' x 8' plywood sign that they had painted white. They hired a painter to add the words. "We were going to call it 'Bob and Buddy's Garden Center,'" Bob remembers. "The painter was up on a ladder with his brush. He had already started painting the letters BOB."

Then Bob had a vision and yelled, "Hold up! This little area is called Merrifield. We'll call it Merrifield Garden Center."

"That's okay with me," Buddy said.

Less than a month after signing the lease, Bob and Buddy opened Merrifield Garden Center on April 9, 1971.

"That's Bob," Billie Jean said. "When he wants something done, he wants it done right away."

Not everything was ready to go. Bob wasn't a plant expert—not yet, anyway—but he knew sales and he knew people. From Day One, his objective was to offer top quality plants, a superior selection and expert advice. Forty-three years later, those objectives haven't changed. "We wanted to be the best nursery we could be," Bob says. "You just do the best you could do. It took hard work."

Merrifield Garden Center opened on Good Friday. Not expecting much business, Bob and Buddy's wife, Doris, were the only workers that first day. They sold tulips and a few other potted flowers out of the trunks of their cars with a small selection of shrubs and trees.

Bob had picked up the plants in his old, open-bed trash truck from growers in New Jersey and Delaware.

Their first sale was a $64 shrub. "I was so excited I called everybody," Doris said. "I sold a bush! I didn't even know what kind it was. In those days, $64 was a fortune. That was my weekly paycheck. I couldn't wait to put it in the bank at the end of the day."

Merrifield Garden Center sold $1,500 worth of plants the first day and $45,000 total the first year.

"As soon as it opened, people came," Bob says.

Billie Jean wasn't surprised. "I knew it would be a hit," she said. "I had been with him long enough to know that whatever he touches turns to gold. He has good ideas and good feelings. I think you're born with it. He's not afraid of anything, especially work."

Bob's knack for marketing was already in top gear. He recruited family and friends to park their cars next to Lee Highway, where he would fill their trunks with beautiful plants. He purposely left the trunks open to attract the attention of people driving past the garden center. "A crowd brings in a crowd," Doris said.

When Merrifield Garden Center opened, there was no water on the property. Bob made friends with Dan Keay, who owned the corner gas station, and received permission for his employees to use the restroom at the gas station. Mr. Keay also let Bob and Buddy connect hoses to his water spigot so they could water their plants. After working all day, Bob would water the plants in the nursery one at a time with a garden hose. "I couldn't leave until every plant was watered," Bob says. "Sometimes I would be there until 10 p.m., 11 p.m., even midnight."

Later that year, Bob built his own irrigation system. He did most of the work himself. While working in the ditches, Bob's strong, six-year-old son Larry helped out by handing him tools, fittings and pipes. "A kid can do a lot at six or seven years old if they want to," Bob says. Bob's two oldest children—Debbie and Rob—were busy with school activities and his youngest children—Donny and

Kevin—were too small to offer much assistance.

Not long after going into business together, Bob and Buddy decided to form a corporation. They agreed that Bob would serve as the president and chairman of the board and that Buddy would be secretary-treasurer. "Buddy and I had been friends for several years and we got along great," Bob says. "But now that we were in business together, we agreed it was important to spell everything out. It was a great partnership, but we both knew that someone had to have the final say on all business decisions and we decided that person would be me."

Bob's foray into the landscaping and gardening business came on the heels of one of the most famous efforts to beautify the nation's capital. That plan was most closely associated with Claudia Alta Taylor Johnson, better known as "Lady Bird" Johnson. She became the First Lady of the United States when her husband, U.S. Vice President Lyndon Baines Johnson, was elevated to president after John F. Kennedy was assassinated in November 1963. President Johnson won the election in 1964, and soon Lady Bird created the Committee for a More Beautiful Capital, bringing together philanthropists, civic leaders and the government in an effort to promote and protect the beauty of the natural landscape. Some two million daffodil and tulip bulbs, 137,000 annuals, 83,000 flowering plants, 50,000 shrubs and 25,000 trees were planted as the result of Lady Bird's 1965 "Beautification" plan, according to the Lady Bird Johnson Biography at the National First Ladies' Library. Many landscapers learned their trade under the federal Jobs Corps program, which carried out the work.

In the summer of 1971, Bob and his team constructed a 12' x 20' building near the little red barn to house the cash register and basic gardening supplies, such as grass seed, fertilizer, watering cans and garden hoses. They painted the new building white to match the cross beams on the barn.

"It was hectic," recalled Wanda (Williams) Flanagan, Buddy and

Doris's first child. "I remember Bob going back and forth to The Tradin' Post." Buddy worked at the garden center between shifts as a Fairfax County firefighter.

Later that year, Bob gave The Tradin' Post to his younger brother Tracy, and Billie Jean left the popular second-hand store to start working full time at Merrifield Garden Center. "When you are married to someone who is such a hard worker, you've got to be a hard worker yourself," Billie Jean said. "You can't sit home and eat bonbons."

The Warhursts and Williamses did whatever work needed to be done. "God bless Mom and Billie Jean," said Kim (Williams) Myers, the youngest of Buddy and Doris's three children. "They ran the registers, stocked the shelves, helped customers and fixed us breakfast, lunch and dinner!"

Bob and Buddy tried many strategies as they worked to establish a foothold in the community, which at that time lacked the large supermarket and drug store chains that now seem to have a building on every block. "We would take on any job we could just to keep the wolf away from the door," Buddy said. Selling Fourth of July fireworks was one idea. Selling fresh produce was another, but the reality was that selling a perishable commodity takes a lot of time and coordination. Bob and Buddy had to drive to Washington, D.C., before sunrise to buy their fruits and vegetables from the supplier. Their round-the-clock efforts started to take a toll. "We were zombies," Buddy said. To make matters worse, they were not bringing in much of a profit. So Bob went back to his original theory: If you deal in nickels, you're going to make nickels. "I made the decision that we should concentrate all our efforts on the nursery part," he recalls.

For the first two years, Bob and Buddy didn't take a salary. All profits went back into the garden center. As the garden center began to take off and develop a customer base, Bob soon realized he needed more help. He didn't have to look farther than Garden

World of Virginia, which was near The Tradin' Post on Lee Highway. Bob was good friends with Pete Lonardelli, owner of Garden World. Pete let Sam Aylestock, one of his young employees, work part time at Bob's new venture. Sam was 16, had a driver's license and knew about plants—important credentials in Bob's world. Sam also came with landscaping experience. He had started working in the fifth grade for a landscaping company.

For a while, Sam worked part-time at both Merrifield Garden Center and Garden World. Bob thought the world of Sam and got Pete's permission to hire Sam full time.

"He offered me 25 cents more an hour than I was making at Garden World," Sam said. "That was big money, like going from $1 to $1.25 or maybe $1.25 to $1.50 an hour. I went with Bob."

It was a decision that would change both of their lives.

Sam started as a loader at Merrifield, hefting customers' purchases into their trucks and cars, everything from straw bales and flats of petunias to bags of mulch and pea gravel. In keeping with Bob's unspoken rule that employees should do a little of everything and a lot of hard work, Sam even went on trash runs with the Warhurst Trash Company when Bob was shorthanded, riding on the back of Bob's famous trash truck on the hills of Mantua.

Bob learned from Sam about the need to protect their plants from harm in the sometimes bitter Northern Virginia winters. They dug long ditches, made beds of landscape timber, placed the plants (both container grown and balled-and-burlapped) and insulated them with sawdust, a process called heeling in. Bob's frugality had no bounds. He made regular trips to a sawmill in Lorton, Virginia, about 15 miles from Merrifield, to pick up free sawdust that he also sold to customers for horse bedding.

Sam was a walking encyclopedia and often came to Bob's aid when customers had questions, initiating a practice of sharing plant knowledge from experts to customers that soon evolved into a hallmark of the Merrifield brand. Sam remembered the time he was helping heel in the trees and shrubs for the winter when a customer asked Bob if he had any variegated holly. Bob ran down the aisle saying, "Sam, Sam, do we have variegated holly?"

"Yes," Sam said. "Right over there."

"Sam, what's variegated mean?"

"That just means the leaf is two shades."

Today, Sam chuckled and said, "Bob didn't know much about plants, but it didn't take him long. He's a person who has a sixth sense as to what will work. Many times I heard him say, 'I think I'm going to try this.' You might as well mark it down. It will be gold."

Bob's strong business sense and Sam's seemingly endless energy kept the business going even in the cold months when most nursery owners shuttered their doors and vacationed in warmer climates. "Winter was coming and Bob wanted to keep me on," Sam recalled. "He said, 'Let's sell firewood!'"

Sometimes things didn't go the way Bob or Sam intended at Merrifield Garden Center, but it was in both of their natures to turn a problem into a life lesson. When Sam was 16 and still a neophyte in the ways of big trucks and the world of business, Bob asked him to deliver a dump-truck load of gravel to a home in the Fairfax County neighborhood of Greenbriar.

"Bob gave me a 10-minute lesson and let me go," Sam said. In that lesson, Bob told him to shovel the gravel out of the truck and not to dump it. An older employee was waiting at the home to help Sam in scorching 102-degree heat and vicious Virginia humidity.

When Sam drove up, the older employee told Sam where to dump it.

"I said, 'No,'" Sam recalled. "Bob said, 'Don't dump it, shovel it.' I'm 16 years old. The other employee was 24 and just out of the Army. He tells me, 'We're not shoveling the gravel. Dump it.' He intimidated me."

Sam disobeyed Bob and tried to dump the gravel, but the size of the load exceeded the dump truck's capabilities. The truck broke and hydraulic fluid spread everywhere. They shoveled the gravel, then Sam nervously drove the broken truck back to Bob.

"Bob and I had been together about a year," Sam recalled. "I thought he would fire me, but he didn't get mad. With a stern look on his face, he said, 'When I give you a job to do, do it like I said. There is a reason.' Then he was fine and we were fine. He gave me a second chance. It was an important lesson I needed to learn about obedience and trust."

Bob didn't yell at Sam because that's not something he does. "I think you're out of control when you yell," Bob says. "It's not my nature."

Sam worked at Merrifield Garden Center throughout high school. "Bob asked me if I would consider going to college to study horticulture," Sam recalled. Bob told Sam that he would pay his way through college. "That was really tempting," Sam said. "The only reason I didn't was because I was focused on entering the ministry. As a born-again Christian, I felt that was a higher calling, although I appreciated Bob's offer."

Bob says Sam was like a son to him. "Sam was great," Bob says. "We loved Sam. Still do. He's a very, very special person. He's the epitome of goodness, as far as I'm concerned." Sam Aylestock is now an associate pastor at Valley Forge Baptist Church in Collegeville, Pennsylvania. His ministry has taken him around the world and he has spoken to thousands of people. "I tell stories of Bob wherever I go," he says. "It was homespun wisdom and character. We need a lot more people like him in this country. He treated people like family. He wasn't just concerned about the business but about the relationships."

In 1972, Bob approached Mrs. Fuchs about expanding Merrifield Garden Center's footprint. Bob and Buddy rented another three acres from her, providing the garden center with much more room to display and sell its wares with nearly four acres of land. With this new land, they built a 36' x 36' main building that remains the centerpiece of the Merrifield store.

It was around this time that Bob sold the Warhurst Trash Company to his older brother Jim. Bob had owned the business for nine years, but the garden center was flourishing and he was too busy to keep an eye on the trash business.

Bob still felt loyalty to his customers and always believed that his trash service was like the U.S. Postal Service: it had to go on despite rain, snow or the gloom of night. "All through these years, I was paranoid about not picking up the trash on time," Bob says. "After I sold it, I actually had nightmares about not picking up the trash on time. Seriously, I had nightmares for six or eight months. I'd see the wind blowing all the trash down the street. Then I would wake up and be so happy that it was just a nightmare."

Jim operated the business for 17 more years before moving to Montana because of his arthritis. Since he was a Warhurst, Jim refused to retire and opened a country store and gas station. Jim lived in Montana for the rest of his life and died in 2004 due to complications from a fall.

MERRIFIELD GARDEN CENTER HAD BEEN OPEN for a little more than a year when it received a very famous customer: Washington Redskins Coach George Allen. He had taken over the Redskins in 1971 and instantly returned the team to prominence after two decades of losing. They won the National Football Conference Championship and a place in the 1972 Super Bowl, where the Redskins lost 14 to 7 to the American Football Conference's Miami Dolphins.

"He wanted to buy some plants and we became friends," Bob recalls of their first meeting. I probably got invited four times a year to his suite at RFK Stadium. It was one of those invitations you don't want to turn down."

Allen's chauffeur would drive the coach's black limousine to Merrifield Garden Center, where he would drop off three or four tickets for Bob to watch the games from his impressive suite. Bob usually brought along Billie Jean or a couple of their children.

"I think Coach Allen thought I brought luck to the team," says Bob, who is superstitious. "That's the only reason I could figure he kept inviting me."

But Bob's son Larry was not surprised that the celebrated coach was interested in Bob and his honest, hard-working sensibilities. George Allen, who led the Redskins to the playoffs in five of his seven years as head coach, was a serious man who favored old-fashioned values over flash and self-promotion. He was known for leading the charge, "Hip, Hip, Hooray!" in the locker room after victories. "It doesn't matter where you come from or your background," Larry said. "When you find someone who is genuine, you are drawn to them. People are drawn to Dad. They like him and they like being around him."

Merrifield Garden Center did landscape work at Allen's spacious home in the upscale area of Great Falls, Virginia. Larry remembered going to the Allen property several times. It was there that he met the coach's children, including George, Jr., who would go on to become governor of Virginia and a U.S. Senator, and Bruce Allen, now the president and general manager of the Washington Redskins.

"He had a big house," Larry recalled. "I'd go over there and just hang out with him. He was like a big kid. We'd lift weights. We played basketball, but we could only play half court because George Jr., had a steer's head—a skull and horns—stuck up in the hoop at the other end of the court. (George Sr.) was very generous. He gave me tennis shoes, a bunch of footballs, hats and whistles. He even gave me (Redskins running back) Larry Brown's practice jersey. (Coach Allen) was a neat guy and his wife (Henrietta, more commonly known as "Etty") was really nice, too."

Bob would give Merrifield Garden Center landscaping services to Redskins star receiver Roy Jefferson in exchange for Redskins game tickets. Bob in turn passed out some of those tickets to Merrifield customers, a clever marketing move that encouraged buyer loyalty. Forty-three years later, giving customers tickets to sporting events and concerts is still a treasured Merrifield tradition.

In 1973, as Merrifield Garden Center was becoming more established in Northern Virginia and the Washington, D.C., area, Bob asked Coach Allen about buying hard-to-get season tickets for Redskins games. The very next day, the Redskins' ticket manager called Bob and asked when he could stop by the stadium. "I'm on my way!" Bob said. An assistant ticket manager walked Bob around the stadium, checking out available seats. Bob bought seven season tickets, one for each member of his family. He held those tickets at RFK from 1973 until 1997 when the Redskins' new Jack Kent Cooke Stadium—named for the team's owner—opened in Landover, Maryland. After Cooke passed away and the team was sold to businessman Daniel Snyder, the stadium was renamed FedExField in November 1999.

Bob and Billie Jean attended their first Super Bowl in 1983 in Pasadena, California. They saw an exciting game in which the Redskins defeated the Miami Dolphins 27 to 14 at the legendary Rose Bowl in flower-crazy Pasadena, a fitting venue for the owner of a garden center. The next year Bob and Billie Jean returned to the Super Bowl, this time in Tampa Stadium where the Redskins lost to the Oakland Raiders 38 to 9.

After attending back-to-back Super Bowls, Bob became a member of a group of 10 Redskins season ticket holders who went to the Super Bowl every year, regardless of the contending teams. While a member of that group of enthusiastic fans, Bob got to know many of the Redskins players and coaches, including legendary coach Joe Gibbs, a man who Bob held in great respect and admiration.

"I had a chance to meet Bob when I first got to Washington," Coach Gibbs said. "I've always appreciated his support and passion for the Redskins."

The Super Bowl trips were one of the few times that Bob and Billie Jean took trips together and just relaxed. Bob loved the football and Billie Jean enjoyed all the pomp and circumstance associated with the biggest game of the year. Just spending time alone with Bob was a victory for her. The Super Bowl group disbanded in 1992, the year Redskins Coach Joe Gibbs retired to concentrate on his NASCAR team.

IN NOVEMBER OF 1973, AFTER 12 YEARS OF RENTING their house on Ninovan Road, Bob and Billie Jean were finally able to buy their own home on Byrd Road in Vienna, Virginia, about three miles from the growing Merrifield Garden Center.

"I loved living at the old house on Ninovan Road, but I remember the excitement about moving to a new house," Bob's son Kevin said. "There was a sense of pride associated with it. This is OUR house."

The three-bedroom, one-bath home cost $39,000, which Bob financed with a mortgage. The home was a tight fit for their family of five children, but Bob bought it because of its close proximity to the garden center. The ever-resourceful Warhursts made the most of the small house. Bob and Billie Jean had an upstairs bedroom, Debbie had a room and Donny and Kevin shared a room. Personal space was so tight that Rob and Larry had to share a waterbed in the basement for awhile. "We made do with that until the next year," Bob says. "Then we built an addition."

At this time, the family's wonderful times riding horses and motorcycles was beginning to wind down. Bob was putting in so many hours at the garden center there was not much time left to ride anything and his kids were moving on to sports and school activities.

The family was down to just one horse and one dog.

Although he worked seven days a week to build his business, Bob was a proud father who always made time to see Debbie's choral concerts and watch his sons play football, basketball and baseball. In her senior year, Debbie made the elite madrigal singing group. The boys were all outstanding athletes. "You had to play sports or go to work so we played every sport," Larry said. "We still had to work Sundays, though." To this day, Bob hears stories about Larry's prodigious grand slam home run for Marshall High School. "I recently saw a guy who after all these years still remembered Larry hitting that huge home run over the left-field fence," Bob says. "Larry hit the ball out of the park, over the roadway and cul-de-sac and it was still sailing high in the air when it went into the woods near the treetops."

In the early 1970s, the popular hairstyle for young men was long hair touching the shoulders and often "feathered" as in the styles worn by young pop stars. But Bob was never a fan of men having long hair, so when his oldest son Rob grew his hair out, Bob couldn't take it.

"C'mon here, boy," Bob said. "I'm going to cut your hair. It's too long."

"No, no, no!" said Rob, as his father grabbed a pair of scissors and began cutting big swaths of Rob's hair. Frugal Bob never sent his boys to the barber shop when they were younger.

While he could lay bricks as precise as a laser beam, Bob lacked the ability to make Rob's hair look like anything an image-conscious 13-year-old boy would want.

Then things went from bad to worse. "He couldn't get it level," Rob said. "He kept working on it. When he was done, there wasn't much hair left. I freaked out. How could I go to school? I was old enough to know this wasn't good. I wore a hat for about a month I was so embarrassed."

When they were out hunting, Bob would often cut Rob's hair

with whatever device was handy, such as tin snips, a hand tool used to cut sheet metal.

MERRIFIELD GARDEN CENTER HAD BEEN OPEN only two years when the U.S. economy started to slide as a result of a series of global events. An "energy crisis" developed in 1973 after the Organization of Arab Petroleum Exporting Countries (OAPEC) declared an oil embargo after a series of world events. That resulted in a decrease in gasoline available to U.S. drivers. With gasoline in short supply, long lines formed at gas stations as irate drivers steamed. Fist fights often broke out when angry motorists vied for the last gallons of precious fuel. To avoid violence, various rationing plans were devised by states to peacefully share the limited supplies. One of the most common being the "odd-even" method, where drivers whose license plate numbers ended in an odd number could purchase gas only on odd-numbered days. The same plan covered even numbered days. Some states tried a "green-yellow-red" plan in which "green days" were unrationed, "yellow days" were restricted and "red days" no gas could be sold. To reduce gas consumption, the federal government instituted a 55 miles-per-hour speed limit, down from the previous limit of 70 mph.

"I anticipated what was going on and knew we needed access to gas for our trucks and equipment," Bob says. "We put in a 5,000-gallon tank in the ground, filled it with gasoline and saved it."

As it turned out, Bob didn't need to tap his reserves. The owner of a gas station next to the garden center let Merrifield Garden Center vehicles fill up at his station after he closed to the public every evening.

After a couple of years, the U.S. government dropped rationing and gas prices rose, leading to consumer frugality, energy-efficient lighting and fuel-saving cars and trucks.

Meantime, Bob and Buddy were continuing to build their team

at Merrifield Garden Center. Sam Aylestock had been the first non-family employee at Merrifield, but Howard Saunders was the first professional hire. In 1973, Bob met Howard, a Fairfax County Extension Agent who was making one of his regular visits to the garden center.

With his long hair and sideburns, a steady supply of Swisher Sweets cigars in his shirt pocket and an impressive degree from the vaunted Virginia Tech horticulture program, Howard made a big impression on Bob.

"I walked in and Bob was digging a huge tree," Howard recalled. "I asked him, 'How will you get it out of the hole without breaking up the root ball?'"

Bob's instincts told him that Howard was the man who should be their general manager. Bob offered him the job on the spot, saying, "I want you to work for me."

Bob was not one to swoon at fancy degrees and years digging in the library instead of the dirt. But he realized that a horticulture degree was a valuable asset for his budding business. Howard had practical experience, too. While growing up in Hampton, Virginia, he worked at McDonald Garden Center.

"I had a nice government job," Howard recalled. "This was a start up. But I saw that it had a lot of potential."

Howard told Bob he would be happy to work part time to see how it went.

"I could tell right away Bob was a sincere person," Howard said. "He would live up to whatever he promised. He said if Merrifield made money, I would make money. I thought it was worth giving a chance. I thought if we got to 100 employees it would be fat city."

Howard began full time on March 1, 1974. He became the company's 11th employee, including family members. Bob convinced Howard to start at the same salary he was making as a Fairfax County Extension Agent and work six days a week instead of five.

"We thought we were the cat's meow when we got Howard,"

Doris said. "I thought he was the smartest man who ever walked on two feet."

Like all Merrifield employees then and now, Howard did a little bit of everything. But one of his primary duties was plant acquisition, building relationships with growers and bringing customers a burgeoning variety of beautiful plants. Once again, Bob's country instincts proved accurate. In Howard Saunders, Bob found a smart, hard-working man who understood the nursery industry and plants, a side of the business that was growing rapidly as the Washington, D.C., area was expanding into the suburbs. Merrifield Garden Center was on its way.

"Howard helped make Merrifield Garden Center what it is today," Bob says. "He brought horticultural expertise, experience and a knack for knowing exactly what our customers are looking for."

Two years later, Bob's knack for spotting talented workers brought Peg Bier into the Merrifield family. Peg is a petite, slender woman who radiates energy and creativity. She lived less than five minutes from the Warhurst home in Vienna and their children often played together, but she said she had never met Bob because "he was always at work."

Married with four children ages 9 to 17, Peg was a stay-at-home mom, as was the culture of that time. But she was not shy about getting her hands dirty. Raised on a prominent 1,000-acre peanut, corn, cotton and cattle farm outside the Georgia town of Boston, Peg's life had been rooted in the Earth.

When she and her family moved to Vienna, Peg continued her love affair with plants in the Five Hills Garden Club. The club had entered the prestigious Old National Guard Armory Flower Show—as famous as the Philadelphia Flower Show is today—and had borrowed an array of beautiful plants from Merrifield Garden Center for their display. After she returned the plants, Peg sought out Bob to thank him personally. She showed him photographs of the colorful arrangements and eye-pleasing designs.

"Did y'all win?" Bob asked.

"Yes, we got first place," she proudly stated.

Bob's instincts started buzzing. Immediately he could see that Peg could bring the design element to Merrifield. He wrapped a big arm around her tiny shoulders and asked, "Why don't you come and work with us some? We need help with silk flowers, designing and the garden shop. We want to do more with it, but there are only a handful of us. Would you give us just one day a week and help us get started?"

Peg recalled that, "He's a big guy with great ideas. It sounded like fun." But she had to think hard because in those days most women stayed at home with their children. The working world was a man's place. My greater ambition was to be the best wife and mother I could be," Peg said. "It was not work. But I was drawn to the challenge."

Peg told Bob she needed to talk it over with her husband Dick, an architect, before accepting.

"I thought once she got to know us, she might want to work more," Bob says.

Bob didn't need a human resources department to tell him who to hire. Once again, his instincts led him to a relationship that has lasted nearly 40 years. Peg would become a major force in Merrifield's early drive to success. In addition to the silk and dried flower business, she was one of the protagonists in the expansion of Merrifield's perennials department, taking a modest selection in the 1970s to more than 6,000 varieties and prime-time display today.

Peg was an early supporter of the four season and container gardening trends, expanding the stores' reach outside of spring and fall. She started the company's popular free seminars and workshops, bringing the beauty of flowers to thousands of homes in the area. She also was a driving force for Merrifield's Christmas shops, now a Washington, D.C., must-see during the holidays with an astounding array of artistically decorated trees, custom bows and collectible ornaments.

"Peggy was a wonderful addition to our company," Bob says. "She's very innovative and always seems to be on the cutting edge. She's very talented with growing plants and design."

Merrifield Garden Center was Bob's "baby," as he likes to call it. But Bob also found time to follow other dreams.

When he was a young boy in Russellville, Bob liked to lie on his back at night in the thick, cool grass and gaze up at the stars. In those days, there was very little outdoor lighting, so the sky was a deep black punctuated with the brilliant, pure silver-white light from stars millions of miles away from Alabama—stars so perfect that they seemed to hover just above his country home.

"It was like you could reach out and touch them," Bob says. "It was so beautiful."

But now, a grown-up Bob decided to take a big chance and attempt to get closer to those stars. In the deep cold of the winter of 1977, with fewer work distractions, Bob channeled his energies into something new: learning to fly airplanes.

CHAPTER SEVEN

FLYING HIGH

Bob Warhurst is not a man with many fears. He takes life by the horns and wrestles it to the ground. But there was one thing he was deathly afraid of: heights. He certainly did not inherit that from his grandfather, a high-wire circus performer, or his father, who had a penchant for walking along the narrow ledges of tall buildings like an acrobat without a net.

Bob's fears extended to airplanes, although in the Great Depression, not many planes flew over the family farm. Seeing those planes, Bob remembers thinking that "there ain't nobody in there. It just seems too far-fetched." Bob's acrophobia was deepened when he was 13 years old by a horrible and tragic accident. In 1951, Dr. William H. Spruell, a prominent Russellville, Alabama, surgeon known for his gentle bedside manner, was giving Boy Scouts rides in his airplane one day. While on a flight with a Boy Scout in the seat next to him, Dr. Spruell suddenly lost control of his small plane and crashed into a field about a half mile from the Russellville airport. The crash and deaths shocked the community. Not only was a beloved doctor dead but also a young man on the cusp of adulthood.

Young Bob was horrified by the double tragedy and could not shake the memories of that fiery crash, his nightmares filled with images of the young man, someone just like him, trapped in the plane as it screamed toward the ground. Decades later and an adult on his way up in the world of business, Bob was invited by Pete Lonardelli, owner of Garden World of Virginia, to fly with him on his personal plane to visit nurseries in Florida. After a month of avoiding Pete's invitations, Bob decided it was time to conquer his fear. "I was always afraid to fly," Bob says. "I thought the plane would fall out of the sky. But then I thought, they can't really all be crashing."

When he has big decisions to make, Bob tries to acquire as much first-hand information as possible. So he drove over to the nearby Manassas Airport to acquaint himself with small aircraft up close. For several days, he observed planes take off and land, and he went inside the airport to talk to some of the pilots. "I realized that the planes weren't crashing all over the place," he says. "Planes were taking off and landing, and everyone was safe and happy. I added it all up in my mind, and I got to thinking it would be nice to see my friends back in Alabama. I told Pete I would fly with him if we stopped in my hometown on the way back home. Once I made up my mind, I was okay."

In January 1970, Bob flew in an airplane for the first time in his life with his friend Pete behind the controls. "It was kind of scary, but I overcame it right quick," Bob recalls. After spending a day in Florida visiting nurseries, Bob and Pete took off the next morning to Russellville, Alabama. Not long after takeoff, Pete asked Bob if he wanted to fly the plane. "I held the controls and I was hooked!" Bob says. "It was exhilarating! Kind of like going on a carnival ride you really like."

When it came time to fly back to Virginia, snow flurries disrupted the last leg of their journey and they were forced to cut their flight short and spend the night of January 16 in a motel in Knoxville, Tennessee. To make matters worse, Bob missed his wedding anniversary. It was the first and only time that he was not with Billie Jean for their annual Chinese dinner, a tradition dating back to their wedding day. They flew home the next day when the weather cleared. Bob said Pete let him steer the plane again. "It was a great feeling to actually fly the airplane," Bob says. "I came back and scheduled me a lesson."

But Bob was so busy working that he had to drop the lessons after his first session. He did not return to flight school until 1977, when a brutally cold winter kept customers away from the nursery. Bob started flying lessons again on January 5, 1977, at Piedmont Aviation in Manassas, Virginia. He brought books home and studied hard. On his first solo flight, "I flew like 25 minutes," Bob recalls. "I went on a nice flight to Warrenton and Culpeper. When I got back, the instructor said, 'I forgot to tell you. You're not supposed to leave the pattern for your first solo flight.' The pattern is the airspace around the airport. I was very confident and certainly at ease." After the flight, the instructor cut a big swath in the back of Bob's shirt, which is a long-standing tradition after a new pilot's first solo flight.

Always one to put his all into every endeavor, Bob earned his license for single-engine planes in only three months and seven days on April 12, 1977. On the night he earned his license, Bob was up past midnight, giving family and friends rides over the Shenandoah Mountain range cities of Warrenton, Culpeper, Front Royal and Strasburg. Bob stayed so late, the folks at the airport gave him the keys to lock up. "I'm surprised people flew with me," Bob says. "Night flying is more dangerous. You can't see the ground. It's a lot more challenging if you can't see the ground."

Whenever he wanted to fly, Bob would rent an airplane. He typically rented a Piper Archer, a single-engine, four-seater. An all-metal, piston-powered light aircraft, the plane could reach speeds of 160 mph. Sometimes Bob chose a Piper Arrow, an even faster model. For those who have never flown in a small plane, the experience is like flying in a car, only the plane is narrower than a car. You're cruising at about 140 mph or more and you could go almost anywhere, as there was very little restricted air space. That freedom was eliminated after the September 11, 2001, attacks. Instead of looking at highway signs, the pilot looks down and follows rivers and roads. The practice is called visual flight rules (VFR). The more advanced method is known as instrument rated, in which the pilot uses navigation tools and speed/altitude gauges to determine his position in three dimensions. Bob isn't instrument rated, which involves a significant amount of flight school time. Time is something Bob is always short of, but he did learn to fly with the basic instruments for emergency situations.

Larry Warhurst, who accompanied his father on many flights, is proud of how Bob overcame his initial fears to become a competent pilot. "For someone who only went to eighth grade learning how to fly, that's amazing!" Larry said. "You have to map out your routes and learn the instruments."

With his newfound joy of flying, Bob wanted to share the amazing experience with all his friends. Buddy's wife, Doris, had never flown before. Just the thought of it petrified her. One day Bob and Buddy convinced her to try a quick spin in the sky to overcome her fears. "They said flying was like sitting in a living room chair," she recalled. "They lied."

As they were getting ready to take off, Bob told Buddy to be sure to latch the cockpit door. But somehow the door swung open during the flight, much to Doris's terror. Bob calmly landed the plane and secured the door, and they took off again. Since then, Doris has only flown one more time—a commercial flight to Florida to take a Caribbean cruise. "On the boat, I spent my whole time worrying about flying home," she remembered. "It was the most horrible thing."

Bob flew Buddy, general manager Howard Saunders and other employees to nurseries in nearby states to look for beautiful plants to sell at Merrifield Garden Center. With the plane, they could visit three or four places in a single day, while car travel would have them on the road for days. Bob's passengers were comfortable with him at the controls. Even so, "Just to show how safe Bob was," Howard recalled, "he paid for me to take lessons so I could land the plane."

Looking to expand the number of nurseries they could visit, Bob joined a flying club to have more readily available access to planes. The small group of investors jointly owned three aircraft: two, four-seat Mooneys and a six-seat Cherokee that were housed at Washington Dulles International Airport. Bob stayed in the club a few years before buying a Cherokee 6 airplane with friend Bob Lederer, who was the executive director of the American Association of Nurserymen.

Bob once flew Buddy and Howard over the Hudson River to the Teterboro Airport in New Jersey. They visited nurseries in Connecticut to learn about the wholesale plant business. That trip convinced them to move forward with their own wholesale plans, in which they sold plants and gardening supplies to landscape contractors, builders, golf course owners and municipalities. "Flying to New York was a big challenge for me, a country bumpkin," Bob says. "I never saw so many planes in the air at once. I flew straight over the Statue of Liberty. We were 300 feet above it. I had never seen it before."

Bob was so close he could see Lady Liberty winking at him.

The idea of even seeing the Statue of Liberty would have been amazing to Bob's parents, who never drove a car, let alone flew in a plane. His mother's goal was to live until the age of 70 and flying in a small plane didn't look like a good route to that number.

"She said she would fly with me when she turned 70," Bob says. "And the day she turned 70, she told me she wanted to go flying. I flew her all around Washington, D.C. She loved it! She brought peanuts to pass out to the other passengers. I told her she was the stewardess. Daddy would have loved it, too."

Going fast in airplanes wasn't all that fascinated Bob. From the time he was a teenager growing up in Alabama, Bob always had an eye for sharp cars. It was that love of cars that led him to start the car club back in the mid-1950s shortly after moving to Virginia.

Bob and Buddy began their tradition of buying matching cars, starting with Lincolns and moving on to Cadillacs, Jaguars and eventually Mercedes-Benzes. Bob and Buddy started their relationship riding horses, but now they were wealthy enough to buy the best on four wheels. Bob's 1974 Lincoln Continental Mark IV was painted gold and Buddy's was silver. The Mark IV was a long car with two doors, big comfortable seats and a powerful engine, certainly a luxury vehicle. After a long day at work, Bob often drove his flashy cars straight to the ballpark to watch his boys play sports. He would still be wearing his work shirt with "Bob" and "Merrifield Garden Center" patches sewn on the front, well-worn overalls and dirty work boots.

"My dad was kind of a big deal to my friends," Larry remembered. "He always had a wad of money in his pocket. Back then, anyone who had a Lincoln Continental had money. They thought, 'That guy is set.'"

Bob kept that roll of bills to give cash to people who needed a helping hand, a practice he still keeps. If someone can't make a mortgage payment, needs a new set of tires to get to work or holds back a smile because of a crooked tooth that requires straightening, Bob is known to dig deep in his pockets. "It gives you goose bumps when you hear how he has touched people," Bob's son Donny said. Bob can never forget how he felt as a child growing up in rural Alabama during the Great Depression, and his family had to struggle just to put a plate of vegetables on the dinner table. He never wants anyone to feel like he did back then.

"The man has touched so many people's lives, and not just minimally," Merrifield Plant and Design Specialist Peg Bier said. "I remember many times seeing him reach in his pocket to give someone money because they needed it. Billie Jean is very sharing, too. She just doesn't wield the pocketbook like he does."

Bob and Buddy's growing wealth gave them the ability to turn spur-of-the-moment ideas into reality. Bob called Buddy one night and said, "Let's go to Florida tomorrow!"

Packed in their shiny new cars, Doris recalled, "We took off for Florida. We thought we were big and bad. We followed Bob. Of course, he was speeding. And of course, we were the ones who got caught. I paid extra insurance for five years for that!"

Even so, they treated their children to a fabulous vacation at Walt Disney World in sun-soaked Orlando. With their business growing and the Washington, D.C., area booming, the Warhurst and Williams families had seen their biggest and most fabulous dreams come true. Their kids went on ride after ride and ate whatever they liked. Tanned and relaxed in the Florida sun, their future was so bright, they really had to wear sunglasses.

A BIG FACTOR IN BOB'S SUCCESS AS A BUSINESSMAN is his ability to quickly size up potential employees. Because of his own unique rise to the top, he knew the best person for the job wasn't always the smooth-talking, well-educated applicant with a sterling resume, but a gritty, hands-on survivor who showed his work history with the calluses on his hands and no fear of hard work and long hours.

If Bob had a profile for the type of employees he was looking for, it was an honest person who was always hustling and had no tolerance for those who were not. If they loved plants, that was a big plus, because they could be taught to become experts.

In essence, Bob was looking for someone a lot like himself.

In 1975, Tim Guy was just 16 and a freshman at George C. Marshall High School in Falls Church, Virginia, when he rode his skateboard to Merrifield Garden Center to apply for a job. He was motivated because his best friend had recently been hired at a fast-food restaurant. "I wanted to get a job, too," Tim recalled.

Tim didn't know much about plants, but he liked being outside. He thought Merrifield Garden Center would be a better fit than a greasy, fast-food restaurant. Merrifield had only about 15 employees at that time and Bob wasn't ready to hire one more. "Sorry, I really don't have anything right now." Tim wouldn't take "no" for an answer, and for the next month he skateboarded to the store once a week to ask for a job. After his fifth trip, Bob hired the tenacious teen.

Like many of the company's current managers, Tim started at the loading dock, shouldering bags of mulch and potting soil into the back of station wagons and filling truck beds with trees and bushes with bulging, burlap-covered root balls. Tim spent hours filling topsoil bags, unloading trucks, helping customers and watering plants to Bob's exacting standards before searching for another task to complete. It was hard, dirty work but Tim quickly built a reputation for hustle and a love of plants.

"We learned plants pretty quickly, because Howard would quiz us about the azaleas and hollies as we unloaded them," Tim recalled.

Within a year, Tim became one of the store's top salespeople. "He already knew more about plants than most people," Bob says. Tim soon realized that this was how he wanted to spend the rest of his life, surrounded by the beauty of plants in the outdoors. After graduating from high school, Tim enrolled in Virginia Tech's prestigious horticulture program and earned his degree.

Tim was an avid gymnast who was on the varsity team at Marshall High School and the club team at Virginia Tech. While working at Merrifield Garden Center, he coached at Karon's Gymnastics Center in Fairfax. When he was 37, Tim snapped both his Achilles' tendons while attempting a back-flip followed by a front-flip. He had to use a wheelchair to move around for three months but insisted on working six days a week helping customers at the store. What's more, he built waterfalls and landscapes while crawling on his knees. "That speaks volumes about the kind of work ethic that Tim has," Bob says. "We're very fortunate to have him as part of the Merrifield family. He'll do any job that needs to be done with a smile."

Over the years, Tim has become one of the foremost horticulture experts in the Mid-Atlantic states. Every day he puts his encyclopedic knowledge of the plant world to work for Merrifield's customers.

Another employee in the same mold was David Watkins. In 1976, David was a senior at Vienna's Madison High School and worked a part-time job washing trash dumpsters, a job he didn't much like.

"A friend told me that Bennett's (Bennett's Nursery in Vienna) was hiring for landscaping for $3.50 an hour," David said. "I weighed about 110 pounds back then and Tom Bennett looked at me and said they didn't have any work."

His next stop in the job search was Merrifield Garden Center.

Bob spit tobacco and one eye twitched with a nervous tic that suddenly started when he first opened the garden center. He looked at David's long hair and scrawny build and asked, "You any good?"

"Yeah, I'm good," the teenager replied.

As David remembered it, Bob offered him $2 an hour, 35 cents below minimum wage back then. David was hired on a Wednesday and started the very next day. On Saturday, Bob gave him a raise to $2.25. On Sunday, David was up to $2.50. David thought, "Man, this is the place to work."

Bob looked beyond the long hair and slim build to see that David had the potential to be something special. He was a smart, ambitious and hard-working kid who was eager to learn. David worked every day of the week, just like Bob. He finished school at 11:30 a.m., then worked noon to 5 pm at the garden center before heading over to Tyson's Corner, where he worked a second job cleaning restrooms in a high-rise office building. On Saturdays and Sundays, he worked all day at the garden center.

"I felt that David was like me," Bob says. "He'd do anything he needed to do to make money. I don't think any work is bad. I was never embarrassed about being a trash man. David washed dumpsters and scrubbed toilets. I related well to that."

On his first Saturday, David met Tim Guy, who made a lasting impression by doing back flips off the back of a truck, and the two kids went to lunch across the street at Roy Rogers. It was the beginning of a lifelong friendship.

David remembered starting at the loading dock, where Bob's then 14-year-old son Rob gave him his first lessons in customer service: 'Be friendly to customers and say 'Yes, sir' and 'Yes, ma'am.'"

After a few months, Bob asked me if I could drive a stick-shift," David recalled. "I said no. He asked me a few more times and I changed my answer to yes. So I started doing deliveries."

Like Tim, David went to Virginia Tech and worked at the garden center on his breaks. When David and Tim were short on cash, Bob would lend them money to help them get through the semester. David studied economics, finance, management and insurance. When he was through with college, David was planning to drive to Texas with some friends to make their way in life. They had no money and no prospects. When he caught wind of David's plans, Bob invited him over to his house and told him that he had a promising future with the company.

"David's a once-in-a-lifetime employee," Bob says. "I recognized that right away. His mind is quick and he knows how to get things done."

David knew how the garden center worked and his schooling helped solidify his already impressive business acumen. Bob showed him his beautiful home and swimming pool, and told him that if he stayed, he, too, could live like this one day.

"You're probably not going to know these friends in five years," Bob told him. "It's better to take care of your family. You're going to have a wife and kids someday. Going to Texas with these guys isn't looking out for your future. Stay and work with us."

David told Bob on the spot that he would stay. "The hardest part was calling my friends and telling them," he said. Bob offered David a salary of $15,000 a year. David thought $16,000 was more in line with what he should make with his schooling, and Bob considered that fair.

At the age of 22, David took over Merrifield's landscaping division. He's still overseeing that operation and has helped it grow much larger. Landscaping isn't David's only job. He's also one of the company's top managers.

"David and Tim live their lives to please people," Doris said. "When you do that, you can't help but be successful."

Under Bob and Buddy's direction, Merrifield Garden Center was rapidly growing and building a loyal customer base. They were selling mainly trees and shrubs with a few annuals and perennials. The small store was stocked with just enough seeds, bulbs and gardening supplies to meet the anticipated needs. But soon the demand exploded.

"Word spread about our customer service, quality and selection," Howard said. "It's something Bob still insists on."

Gail Crocker, a customer since the early 1970s, said she feels at home at Merrifield. "Why go anywhere else?" she said. "They have the best of everything."

The fast growth was almost overwhelming. The parking lot was covered with gravel and employees took bags of lime to mark out parking spots. When customer demand for topsoil exceeded their supply, workers would frantically go to a large dirt pile at a neighboring construction company, pull out the weeds and fill empty mulch bags with dirt. When truckloads of mulch arrived, workers had to unload the 40-pound bags by hand—900 bags in a truckload—and carry them to the sales floor or storage area. There was no forklift.

Bob and his team worked constantly to expand the selection of plants offered as more and more customers visited the store. They quickly upgraded the parking lot from gravel to paved asphalt and added on to the store. The expansion projects seemed endless:

brickwork, roofing, plumbing, carpentry, electrical and irrigation installation.

"I love work because it's a challenge every day," Bob says. "You have to use your best wits. You have to think all the time and anticipate what might happen next."

Carl, Bob's youngest brother, a self-trained carpenter, plumber and electrician, was instrumental. He started out working nights and weekends for Bob while he was employed for a company that handled carpentry work for steak houses. As the garden center expanded, Bob brought Carl on full time.

"When I came to Merrifield, it was a busy time," Carl recalled. "We were working a lot to keep up with everything."

The workload was hard, but a sense of mission was forming, a belief that something special was happening, and everyone wanted to be a part of it. They worked as if there was no tomorrow, but tomorrow always arrived with even more demands.

"Bob wasn't afraid of hard work," Peg said. "That's what was required at the time. He was right in the middle of everything. He didn't just tell you what to do, he was right there in the middle of it helping you do it. And we were all having fun. It was very special. We knew we were growing. We set the pace. We were leaders, not followers. You just knew it was going somewhere."

OF THE FIVE CHILDREN IN BOB AND BILLIE JEAN'S family, Debbie is the oldest and the only girl. Like all of the kids, she worked at the garden center while growing up, becoming a cashier while in high school.

"College was never talked about in my house," Debbie said. "All my friends didn't have a choice. They were going to college. I had to decide if I wanted to go. I got good grades in school and I took the SATs. My first goal was to be a secretary. I always thought of the nursery as part time."

To reach her objective, Debbie took shorthand, typing and business classes at George C. Marshall High School, earning the "Business Student of the Year" award.

But when her senior year was almost over and she had to decide on a profession, Debbie considered her love of music and decided to become a radio personality, a disc jockey. She applied to and was accepted at James Madison University in Harrisonburg, Virginia, which had a good broadcasting program. As her high school graduation drew closer and the prospect of leaving her close-knit family and many friends loomed, Debbie got cold feet.

Billie Jean could see that her daughter was troubled, so the two drove from the garden center to nearby Dunn Loring Park for a mother-and-daughter, heart-to-heart talk. As they sat on the child-sized seats of the swing set, moving back and forth in the shadow of the park's many trees, Debbie confessed to her mother that she was having second thoughts about leaving for college.

"If it's about the $100 deposit," Billie Jean told Debbie, "that doesn't matter."

Billie Jean recently said, "Debbie was such a homebody that to go off someplace, well, she just wasn't ready. I told her to follow her heart."

Debbie decided to stay home and not go to college. But about two months later when her friends started leaving their homes for the excitement of college, Debbie recalled, "I had a horrible feeling. I'm not going to school and I don't have a full-time job."

Once again, mother and daughter drove to Dunn Loring Park. Billie Jean repeated her advice to "follow your heart." Debbie called James Madison to see if she could get her place back in school. There was an open spot in the broadcasting program, but the dormitories were full. One of her friends was going to Northern Virginia Community College—known as NOVA—in Annandale, Virginia. Debbie checked into NOVA's degree offerings and discovered that the school had a broadcast engineering program. She eagerly signed up for classes, such as "The Introduction to Tubes and Transistors" and "The Fundamentals of Direct Current."

Looking back, Debbie recalled, "The classes included me, another girl and 27 guys. I barely made it through the classes, but I had a lot of dates."

As she started the second quarter of her freshman year, Debbie wondered what in the world she was doing in broadcast engineering. That wasn't what she wanted to do. Her future had been in front of her all along: Merrifield Garden Center. For the first time, she started thinking about working in the family business as a career.

"We're so glad she made that decision," Billie Jean said.

Debbie joined NOVA's Phi Beta Lambda Business Club and enrolled in its two-year associate degree program in retail merchandising. She then transferred to Radford University after her father, now a full-fledged pilot, flew her downstate to look at the campus. Debbie went on to graduate from Radford with a degree in marketing. She became the first in her family to earn a college diploma.

"College isn't for everyone," Bob says. "But she was college material."

After graduation, Debbie came back to Merrifield, taking over the company's advertising efforts. Debbie is still Merrifield's advertising director and host of "Merrifield's Gardening Advisor," the company's long-running TV show, which proves that there truly is no place like home.

Debbie said family members are held to different standards. "You have to work harder, put in more hours and be ready to go in whenever you are needed," she said. "But the rewards are incredible. You feel like you are part of something really important and something that really means something to you. From a young age, I always felt like my opinions and suggestions really mattered."

In 1977, Bob and Buddy were still renting the land for Merrifield Garden Center from Mary Fuchs. One day, Mrs. Fuchs asked Bob if he wanted to buy the four acres.

"I'd love to, but I don't think I can afford it," Bob told her. "How much do you want for it?"

Mrs. Fuchs told him that she'd sell it for $425,000 and that if he gave her a down payment of $50,000, she'd finance the remaining $375,000 at a rate of 8 percent over 15 years. Bob agreed.

A few days later, Mrs. Fuchs called him back. "Mr. Warhurst, if you can give me a $75,000 down payment, I'll reduce the price by $25,000 to $400,000," she said.

"I'll try my best!" Bob replied.

Bob remembers that he "borrowed and begged" to get the $75,000 down payment. They paid off the $325,000 in the allotted 15 years. The 8 percent interest rate seems high today, but inflation drove rates up significantly in the late 1970s. That $325,000 price—adjusted for inflation—would be about $1,275,000 in today's dollars.

Bob and Mrs. Fuchs developed a close friendship over the years. She owned an apartment building in Arlington, Virginia. Because of their relationship, he helped her with maintenance of the building at a lower price than other companies would have charged.

During the holidays, Billie Jean would bake Mrs. Fuchs a pound cake. Bob delivered the delicious cake and a beautiful wreath to Mrs. Fuchs every Christmas Eve. Over cups of hot coffee, Bob and Mrs. Fuchs shared holiday memories and enjoyed the fresh-baked cake.

WHILE HE IS INDEED A VERY HARD-WORKING MAN who demands the best from himself and those around him, Bob also has a spontaneous side that made it exciting to be around him.

In 1977, on the day after Christmas, Bob gave the family its first trip to the ski slopes. They drove to Bryce Mountain in Basye, Virginia, where the whole entourage rented boots and skis. "I must have fallen 50 times that day," Bob says. "I don't know how I didn't break something."

Bob, Billie Jean and their children grew to love the sport and visited some of the best and most popular ski areas in the Appalachians, such as Snowshoe and Liberty. Out of the blue, Bob might say, "I'm thinking of going snow skiing tomorrow." Many times the adventure would actually begin that day and everyone—Bob's family and Merrifield employees alike—would take off with no idea of when they would be coming back.

"It was an incredible treat to go off on a ski trip back then," Peg recalled. "None of us had enough money to do that. Bob paid for everything. When it was slow, like in January or February, he loved treating people to a good time."

Bob and his employees piled into Bob's 32-foot camper and drove to Liberty, where they would rent ski equipment for an exciting day on the slopes. For many employees, it was their first time on skis so Bob gave them lessons. "He had a unique method that was quite an experience," Peg said. "I remember getting behind him, and holding on. By the time we got to the bottom of the hill, I knew how to ski! He loves showing people how to do things—skiing, planting a tree or whatever it might be."

Winter ski trips became a tradition for the Warhurst family and the Merrifield Garden Center staff. Long before team-building became a popular management tool, Bob recognized that employees perform better at work if they share fun adventures together. For example, the Warhurst family and 10 to 12 Merrifield employees took trips for many years to Elk Mountain in Pennsylvania. They stayed in a charming, old farmhouse that was owned by one of the growers from whom Bob and Buddy bought plants. The group would start the day with a hearty breakfast in the large dining room before hitting the slopes. "Rob would ski backwards down the slopes and videotape us," Tim recalled. "It was insane. Video cameras had just come out and they were heavy. I could barely ski forwards. Then at night after dinner, we'd watch the videos. It was a blast."

Besides fast planes, fast cars and fast skiing, Bob wanted to hand down to his sons the great experiences he had as a young man hunting in Alabama. He took his boys hunting at a friend's house on 630 acres of woods and open fields that were planted with corn and soybeans in Gainesville, Virginia. For longer trips, Bob took them to the George Washington National Forest in the family camper. Bob parked the camper on his friend Jack Burns's property next to a scenic river in Harrisonburg, Virginia. After a long day of hunting, the Warhursts would join Jack and his hunting buddies for a big meal in his cabin and listen to hunting stories. The boys would wake up early to the heavenly aroma of scrambled eggs and biscuits that Bob was making.

Hunting trips were quite an adventure for the Warhurst family. Not only did they provide a great bonding experience between Bob and his four sons, these adventures produced many funny stories that continue to be talked about to this day.

Bob's son Larry remembered being called to the office of his junior high school one morning. He heard over the school's loudspeakers: "Larry Warhurst, come to the office please." Larry was nervous, wondering what was wrong. When he got to the office, he found his dad sitting there in his coveralls.

"Let's go hunting!" Bob exclaimed.

Bob taught all his boys how to hunt once they turned 10.

"I wanted them to experience it, and if they liked it they could stick with it," Bob says. "Larry's a great hunter now."

Bob's youngest son Kevin remembers anxiously waiting for his 10th birthday so he could join his older brothers on the hunting trips. "When your time came and you were finally able to go, it was almost like a rite of passage that took you from being a boy to becoming a man," Kevin recalled.

Kevin will never forget his first hunting trip. He was so excited to finally get a chance to walk through the woods and hunt with his oldest brother Rob. They stopped next to the side of a mountain, where Kevin plopped down in front of Rob to patiently wait for a deer sighting. Rob instructed his little brother to keep still and not make any noise or they would scare away the deer. With such a peaceful setting, Kevin fell asleep in no time. Rob later woke him up and asked if he wanted a Pepsi. "I was real thirsty and wanted that Pepsi so bad," Kevin recalled. "I reached behind me for the bottle, and I could feel that it was warm. So I turned and looked at it and saw that it was yellow. I discovered that Rob had drank the Pepsi and peed in the bottle before giving it to me as a joke. We still laugh about it."

Bob was later part of a group that bought 904 acres of land in southern Fauquier County, Virginia. The "904" is just an hour's drive south from the Washington, D.C., metropolitan area, but insulated from urban life by the Quantico U.S. Marine Corps Base to the east and the Phelps Wildlife Management Area to the west. The land was a hunter's paradise, thick with quail, turkey, deer, rabbit and squirrels. The group later converted the land into 18 lots and named it Seneca Lake Estates after the 64-acre lake at its center.

Bob created a new family ritual in which the Sunday after Thanksgiving would be set aside for family "shooting" day. He takes sons Rob, Larry, Donny and Kevin and son-in-law Rob Capp and his 11 grandchildren to "904" to shoot guns at targets that Bob designed and had custom-built for these outings. The day is special for the kids, because they can see Bob in another light: outdoors in the woods, smoking a cigar, relaxed and enjoying himself without dealing with business. By teaching the kids how to safely handle and shoot firearms, he's sharing an important part of his rural heritage with them, giving them a skill to pass on to future generations of Warhursts.

Merrifield Garden Center was continuing to grow. Now that he had bought the property in Merrifield from Mrs. Fuchs and was successfully making the payments, Bob was ready to expand.

In 1979, after many years of searching in Fairfax County, Bob and Buddy bought land for their second store, now known as the

Fair Oaks location, on Lee Highway, about eight miles west of their original store. The 33 acres cost $211,000.

"My thought was that to have the kind of nursery we wanted to build, we needed to have a lot of land," Bob says. "This location was big enough to allow us to carry a larger inventory of plants and have plenty of room to grow. I thought it was cool to have both stores on Lee Highway."

The Fair Oaks site turned out to be ideal. The 1996 connection of the nearby Fairfax County Parkway to busy Interstate 66 brought much more traffic to Lee Highway and the Fair Oaks store.

It was around this time that Bob began to realize that he was making a lot of money.

"I remember in the late 1970s," Bob says. "My tax man told me how much money I had made. I said, 'Hey, I'm a real millionaire!' It was a nice feeling, but I didn't have time to gloat. I had to build on it. I didn't want to lose it."

Bob's boyhood home in Russellville, Alabama, had no electricity or running water.

Claude Rea (Warhurst) holds his young son Bobby, who was dressed as a girl.

Bobby (bottom row, far left) and brothers Jim (directly above him) and Lee (top row, third from left) are shown with a few of their cousins in Alabama.

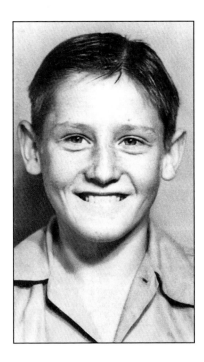

Bobby got his first job at the age of 7 to help put food on the table.

When he was barely a teenager, Bobby bought a used 1936 Ford and found a license plate for it in the junkyard.

Bobby's family: (top row) Lee, Charles, Jim and Bobby and (bottom row) Margene, Jane, Mother, Daddy, Tracy and Carl.

Bobby left school for good in the eighth grade and moved to Virginia to make his way in life.

If he worked hard, Bob believed he could accomplish anything.

Bob's love of cars reached a new high with his 1956 Chevrolet Bel Air convertible.

With Bob and Billie Jean, it was love at first sight.

At their wedding, Bob's brother Lee was the best man and Billie Jean's sister Joann was the maid of honor.

Bob loved to ride Nifty Five, a quarter horse owned by his good friends and neighbors, Buddy and Doris Williams.

Bob spray painted one of his trash trucks blue.

Bob led the Rockin' F Riding Club in the annual National Cherry Blossom Festival Parade in Washington, D.C.

The original Merrifield Garden Center opened in April 1971 at the corner of Lee Highway and Gallows Road. This photo was taken a few years later.

The Warhurst family in 1972: (front row) Donny, Bob, Kevin, Billie Jean and Larry and (back row) Debbie and Rob.

Bob (far left) and Sam Aylestock (red shirt), the first non-family Merrifield employee, had fun at Sam's going-away party before he headed off to college in 1973.

Under the direction of Bob and his partner Buddy, Merrifield Garden Center grew at a fast pace. This photo was taken in the early 1980s.

Buddy Williams, Howard Saunders and Bob Warhurst are shown preparing to fly to a plant grower.

The Warhursts played in the waters of Lake Anna.

Bob coached the Merrifield Express basketball team, which won all of their regular season games for more than four years.

The "Real" Santa at Merrifield Garden Center attracted kids of all ages, even Bob.

Bob visited the White House and met First Lady Barbara Bush.

The cast and crew of "Merrifield's Gardening Advisor" cable television show: (standing) Bob, Diane Hawthorne and Peg Bier. (Front) Debbie Warhurst Capp and David Yost.

Bob built his dream house at historic Hope Parke in Fairfax, Virginia.

Bob shared his family and his happy life with Tommy McVean, who lived with the Warhursts for five years.

Bob presented an award to Tommy's brother, Andy, for 25 years of service at Merrifield Garden Center.

Merrifield's founding families: Bob and Billie Jean Warhurst and Buddy and Doris Williams.

Bob's brother Lee (left) was the greeter at Merrifield's Fair Oaks store and his brother Carl (right) has been Merrifield's facilities manager for nearly four decades.

Bob and U.S. Supreme Court Justice Clarence Thomas pose for a photo at one of Bob's Fourth of July parties at Hope Parke.

Bob (far right) is shown at a board meeting of Virginia Heritage Bank, which he co-founded in 2005.

For Bob, family is everything. This photo was taken in October 2014. (Seated from left) Harley, Whitney, Billie Jean, Bob, Debbie and Sarah. (Standing from left) Kevin, Grace, Karen, Chris, Donny, Madison, Leslie, Larry, Jake, Chance, Rob C., Danny, Lynn, Rob W., Ashley, Bobby, Lyndsey and Kyle.

Bob and Billie Jean have been happily married for 57 years.

The original Merrifield Garden Center opened in April 1971.

Bob and Buddy opened their second store, the Fair Oaks location, in Fairfax in December 1988. Five years later, their new building, shown here, opened directly across the street.

Gainesville, the third Merrifield Garden Center store, opened in December 2008.

CHAPTER EIGHT

FUN IN THE SUN

Bob played almost as hard as he worked while climbing up the business ladder. In 1977, Bob bought a beautiful new Sea Ray water ski boat that he took to Pohick Bay, just south of Alexandria, Virginia. That spot was a mecca for fun-seekers due to its close proximity to the growing Washington, D.C., metropolis.

The Sea Ray would be filled to the brim with Bob, Billie Jean, their five children, assorted girlfriends, a boyfriend and a cooler. King, their beloved German shepherd, would sit at the bow of the boat, his nose sniffing the fresh air as the Warhurst family soaked up the sun.

"We stayed on the boat the whole day," said Rob, Bob's oldest son. "It was like a home. That was part of the fun." The only time they stepped off the boat was to eat the lunches they brought to one of the picnic tables that dotted the shores of the big park on the Virginia shore.

Bob soon got bored with Pohick Bay, so he started asking around about nearby places to water ski that had clear and deep water. The name that kept coming up was Lake Anna, a scenic spot in Spotsylvania County, a little more than an hour's drive south from his family's home in Fairfax County.

Virginia Electric and Power, now Dominion Virginia Power, had just created Lake Anna to cool their nuclear reactors, which provide the heat to run the big steam generators that make the electricity to power the nation's capital. The lake had a "cold side" with fresh water to cool the generators and a "hot side" with water discharged from the power plant.

A few years later, Bob and Buddy bought two "cold side" waterfront lots with a total of five acres. It was a great place for the two families to enjoy boating, jet skiing, water skiing, playing volleyball or horseshoes, riding motorcycles or just relaxing in a hammock.

"We worked hard for everything we've got—both families," Buddy said.

For many years, Merrifield Garden Center held company picnics at Lake Anna, featuring huge cookouts with barbecue chicken, hamburgers and hot dogs. Hundreds of employees and their families would make the trip. Bob taught many of them how to water ski. Bob taught Matt Bier, Peg's son, how to barefoot waterski.

"As long as his business is well taken care of and then some, when it's time to have a good time he has a good time," Matt said. "Work hard and play hard. It's consistent with my own spirit. Some people will never know how to have a good time. Bob's not one of them."

As for Bob, he loved to drive the boat. He soon became fascinated with using the boat for more than just water skiing. Bob bought a kite that could be attached to people with a harness that would allow them to rise as high as 70 feet above the water. He later bought a parasail that could take them as high as 150 feet.

As the oldest son, Rob was always the first to take on a challenge, which often led to some close calls. When Bob asked if he was ready to fly, Rob said "I haven't read the instructions yet."

"Don't worry about the instructions!" Bob replied.

Peg was caught up in the action and was one of the first to join in the parasailing escapade. "When Bob first bought the parasail, it was such a thrill!" she said. "You ran down a hill, jumped and it took off."

Unlike parasailing at the bay or the ocean today, where you take off and land without worry from a platform attached to the back of the boat, the Warhursts took a more adventurous approach. The person who was going for the ride was strapped into a harness and stood on a hill. The parasail was connected to the speedboat with a 250-foot rope. A group of people held up the parasail while Bob would slowly pull the boat forward and let the parasail fill up with air. Then Bob would hit the gas and the person started to go up, often dodging the dock, the light pole or the sea wall depending on which way the wind was blowing.

"This was the country folk's version of enjoying these new toys," Bob's son Kevin recalled. "It was a bit scary at times but a lot of fun."

One time Bob came up with a fun challenge: try to create a pyramid on water skis, like the formations they saw on television programs.

"We did it just to see if we could do it," Larry said. "Dad was convinced we could."

Building the pyramid required six people: three skiers on the water, two standing on the shoulders of those skiers and one standing on the inside shoulders of the two people below. Kevin was the youngest and smallest skier, tipping the scales at 95 pounds. So Bob chose him to climb up the wall of bodies to the top of the pyramid. All six held tow ropes and Bob steered the boat.

After many tries, they accomplished the remarkable feat of strength and balance.

"Dad always wanted to make it fun and interesting to keep you wanting to come," recalled Rob, who was one of the three broad-shouldered skiers at the bottom of the pyramid.

The boys also had the thrill of riding wetbikes, an early type of jet ski. Wetbikes became famous in the hit movie "The Spy Who Loved Me" when James Bond hopped on the speedy machine to chase a villain. "It was powerful and fun," Bob's son Donny recalled. "Unbelievable! Everyone wanted to go."

As word spread among their friends, the Warhurst kids realized they were fortunate that their family was now able to afford big toys and fun times at the Lake Anna property.

"It was neat to tell people about it," Kevin said. "Not to brag or anything—that's not how we were raised—but because I was proud of where my parents had come from. I think people understood that because they knew the kind of people we were. We're not fancy or anything like that. They would hear that my dad bought a nice car or that we bought a beach house. But then they'd see him at one of our baseball games and see he was wearing overalls and driving a dump truck filled with topsoil. They knew how hard he worked. I was always proud but humble."

BOB HAS A BIG HEART. Like many men of his generation, Bob showed his love with his actions, not his words. One example of this was how he was willing to share his family and their fabulous life with a kid who needed a little family support at the time. That kid was Tommy McVean, Jr.

Kevin and Tommy became friends on the first day of sixth grade in 1978 when Tommy's family moved to suburban Vienna from the rolling hills of Warrenton, a historic town in Virginia's horse country. On the first day of school at Freedom Hill Elementary School in Vienna, newcomer Tommy was asked to stand up and introduce himself to his new classmates. He made quite an impression with his loud, plaid suit and flashy Nike sneakers.

Tommy told everyone that his dad, Tommy McVean, Sr., worked as the equipment manager for the Washington Redskins and its coach, George Allen. After class, Kevin told Tommy that he and his father attended a lot of Redskins games and also knew Coach Allen. From that point on, Kevin and Tommy became best friends and started hanging out at Kevin's house after school, a place where Tommy immediately felt at home.

"When I first met Bob, I was a little intimidated," Tommy recalled. "He's bigger than life. But it's amazing how he's able to make you feel like a friend when you first meet him."

For Tommy, spending time with the Warhurst family was very special for several reasons. Not only was it a fun place to hang out, the Warhursts always had a lot of food in the house and Tommy was a big kid who loved to eat. "Tommy could hide three cookies in his mouth and still carry on a conversation and you would never notice it," Bob says.

There was a reason for Tommy's hunger. "I came from a broken home," Tommy said. "Their family unit was so strong. There were home-cooked meals seven days a week. I wasn't used to it."

Tommy soon became part of the Warhurst family, spending many nights with them watching ball games, riding motorcycles, jumping on the trampoline, swimming at Freedom Park pool and going out for dinner.

Bob was always looking for fun things that his family could do together. On July 4, 1980, Bob strolled into the backyard of his Vienna home with his son Rob. Sweeping his outstretched arms across the yard, Bob turned to Rob and asked, "Would you guys like a swimming pool?"

Rob answered with an emphatic "Yes!"

So Bob designed a kidney-shaped pool and Jacuzzi, but he didn't intend to build them himself because he had never done it before. He reached out to some local pool contractors and found a guy who would do the job for $25,000, but his work schedule was so crowded he couldn't build the Warhurst pool until the following year.

Bob called another contractor and received the same bad news: "Not this year." Bob doesn't take "no" for an answer. So he found a couple of pools under construction, carefully observed what the workers were doing and decided that he could build his own pool.

Bob is not one for lengthy contemplation. He's a man of action. After being out of town for several days, Bob's daughter, Debbie, was surprised to come home and find several big trucks at the house.

"I thought, 'What's going on? We had our landscaping done the year before,'" Debbie said. "I walked in the backyard and there was a hose put together in the shape of a kidney. I should have realized that if Dad couldn't get the swimming pool done, he'd do it himself."

It only took Bob and his makeshift team a month to build the beautiful pool. Bob worked with his brother Carl and a few others, including Rob, Larry, Donny, Kevin and Tommy, who helped with digging and fetching tools. At one point, Bob was working in the deep end of the pool, and Tommy was waiting to hand him a heavy piece of steel rebar. Bored with the wait, Tommy began talking to Kevin and accidentally dropped the 40-pound, 16-foot piece of rebar right on Bob's head.

The worksite went silent. A chill went down Tommy's spine.

"I thought I was kicked out of the house," Tommy recalled.

But Bob didn't say a word. He just gave Tommy a look that said, "Boy, be more careful. Pay attention to what you're doing."

The new Warhurst swimming pool was 10.5 feet in the deep end, where the diving board was attached. It held 45,000 gallons of water. Where could they get that much water? "I borrowed some hoses from the nursery and asked five of our neighbors if they'd let me hook up to their spigots," Bob says. "They were kind enough to say yes. It took 24 hours to fill up the pool with the five hoses. We enjoyed the pool so much."

Bob added to his family's recreational properties in 1981 when he and Buddy bought a two-bedroom, ocean-front condominium in Ocean City, Maryland. A year later, they bought a second condo. When the Warhursts traveled to the beach, the family of seven squeezed into the family station wagon, with Bob, Billie Jean and Debbie in the front seat, Rob, Larry and Donny in the back seat and Kevin sharing space with the luggage and gear in the fold-down third row. "Going to the beach is one of my fondest childhood memories," Kevin said. "I remember crossing the bridge that takes you to Ocean City and seeing the water, the sailboats and the seagulls. I would take in the smell of the ocean air as it wafted through the car windows."

Life was wonderful for the family, with the kids playing in the water all day, building sand castles and body surfing. At night, they went to the boardwalk, played Putt-Putt golf and ate pizza, Thrasher's French Fries and funnel cakes. But Kevin said, "I don't think the beach was Dad's thing." Bob liked to work on the condominium or visit friends while the kids played in the water and enjoyed the sunshine.

"He used to go to the beach with us," Debbie said. "After a while, he'd start searching for projects to do, like looking for new appliances. He used to take us to Frontier Town. He said it reminded him of Alabama." Frontier Town is a tourist attraction with Wild West-type shows. Bob's children and grandchildren still use the Ocean City condos for a couple of weeks every summer, as do Bob's brother Carl and the Merrifield Garden Center managers.

"I enjoyed it all as much as my family did," Bob says. "When you're young, you have the energy. You get to where you can't do that anymore. I lost interest in the beach. I couldn't run or walk on it anymore. I don't like the sun. The sand is hot. I'd rather be at work."

Work has always been a family affair for the Warhursts, from laying bricks in Arlington and picking up trash in Mantua to peddling second-hand items at The Tradin' Post and selling plants and garden supplies at Merrifield Garden Center. While growing up, all the Warhurst kids worked part time at Merrifield Garden Center when they weren't playing sports or participating in other activities.

So did Buddy and Doris's kids. "I grew up at the garden center," said Kim (Williams) Myers, who was born the year before Merrifield opened. To take care of her, Buddy and Doris put a camper on the back of their truck and parked it next to the little red barn. "I was like the Merrifield rug rat. It was fun. And it still is." Kim was deadheading—removing faded flowers—when she was a toddler in diapers.

Work is not a four-letter word to Bob. It ranks up there with "love" and "life." "Work" was the first order of business every day and the last thought at night. First-born son Rob was Bob's shadow every day. "I was around him all the time, even as a little kid," Rob said. "I watched and learned and tried to do as he does. He used to do every little project to make money. I remember riding on the tractor to plow snow. He had me shovel sidewalks, even if we didn't get paid for that, so the customers didn't have to park their car and walk through the snow to their house. He was like a machine: push, push, push."

When Merrifield Garden Center opened, Rob was nine. His first job was loading plants and products into customers' vehicles. "I was tall for my age, and big," Rob said. "So being a loader wasn't a problem." At 16, he started making deliveries as well as many other jobs that needed a strong back. He acquired carpentry skills while working with his uncle Carl. All the while, Rob was learning about plants and helping retail and wholesale customers.

Rob's then-girlfriend and now wife, Lynn Ostroski, remembered how he would tell her, "Dad just called. I have to go to work. I have to do deliveries." Lynn said Bob would frequently call Rob out of school. "Rob was always working," she said. "While we were playing outside in the snow, Rob was snowplowing at all hours of the night. They had to work when most kids were playing."

College wasn't in the forefront of Rob's thoughts. Education was rarely discussed in the family. Work was his life, just as it was for Bob. Rob inherited his father's knack for pleasing customers and an eagerness to learn all he could about running a garden center. He dedicated his life to helping make his father's dream come true.

In high school, Rob enjoyed playing sports and spending time with Lynn, who went to Marshall High School with him and worked as a cashier at Merrifield. A lanky receiver, Rob played four years of varsity football for the Marshall Statesmen. After missing most of his junior season with a broken leg, Rob came back strong his senior year and caught an 85-yard touchdown pass in a win against arch rival Madison.

One of Rob's favorite things about his senior year was playing with his younger brother Larry, who made varsity as a freshman. Strong as an ox and chiseled from head to toe, Larry was a unique talent. A powerful fullback and a punishing linebacker, Larry was well known throughout Northern Virginia for his size, strength and athleticism. As a sophomore, Larry injured his back during a drill in training camp. "I couldn't straighten up," he recalled. "I went through two-a-days with my back messed up and I couldn't do it anymore. I thought, 'I'm tearing myself up.'" So after the first game of his sophomore season, Larry gave up sports for good. As gifted as he was as an athlete, he seemed to find more peace and happiness in hunting, fishing and just doing his own thing, not confined to a rigid practice schedule.

Larry began working full time at Merrifield after he graduated from high school.

"It was a plan on my end," Bob said. "I wanted all my kids to work here. I know they each have their own interests and talents, but I thought it would be neat if we all worked together in a true family business. Larry and his wife wanted to move away and work with horses. I encouraged him to work at Merrifield. I've encouraged all the kids and made sure they knew what the garden center had to offer. I've always tried to keep this a family business. It's wonderful we've been able to do it. People ask, 'Isn't it difficult to run a family business?' I tell them, 'Not when I'm the boss.' Somebody has to be the boss."

Bob's son Donny said most family businesses don't last. "It's hard to work with your family all the time," he said. "But we all get along and do different things. I'm good at one thing, Larry's good at another. Same with Rob, Kevin and Debbie."

Larry put aside his dreams and joined the family business.

"In the early 1980s, I wanted to do agriculture real bad," he said. "I love agriculture. Cattle. Dad said we're going to buy a farm. We never bought a farm, but maybe some day I can do it. I think I'd be good at it. I always envy people with a family farm, one that's been there for five generations."

In 1984, Donny graduated from Marshall High School. A standout linebacker, punter and field-goal kicker, he went to New Mexico Highlands University to play football. But after just two weeks, Donny realized that New Mexico wasn't for him, and he returned home. He went back to work at Merrifield Garden Center and took classes at Northern Virginia Community College, earning his associates degree in horticulture. He continued his studies at the University of Maryland before settling in at Merrifield, where he does whatever is needed. He's a very talented carpenter and can build whatever he sets his mind to.

"I love working at the nursery," Donny said. "There are so many different things to do. If we don't know how to build something, we figure it out. The only pressure is to live up to the name. No one in their right mind can expect you to. My dad is so far beyond anyone I've ever met. If you come close to what he wants you to become, you've done a good job."

The route between higher education and working at Merrifield was difficult for Donny to navigate because of Bob's aversion to formal education. "I would say, 'I want to go to college and study,'" Donny recalled. "And he would say, 'You don't need to go to college.' Or I would say, 'I want to study business,' and he would say, 'You don't need to study business. You hire managers to run the business.'" Donny knew as early as eighth grade that he wanted to work at the garden center. "So wanting to go to school wasn't about moving on," he said. "It was about trying to better myself within the nursery. But Dad never wanted me to go to college. But when I did, he paid for it all."

In the 1980s, Debbie, Rob and Larry all got married and started families of their own. Larry and Leslie Garrison were married in Upperville, Virginia, in 1984 and Leslie gave birth to Bob and Billie Jean's first grandchild, Chance Ray Warhurst, on May 7, 1985.

Also in 1985, Kevin became the last of Bob and Billie Jean's five children to graduate from Marshall High School. Like his older brothers, Kevin starred in football. As a senior, he rushed for nearly 1,200 yards and was the fourth-leading running back in the Northern Region, which was comprised of 28 high schools in Northern Virginia. Kevin considered playing football at Boston University, where he was offered a scholarship, but decided to enroll at Virginia Tech instead.

THE SUMMER AFTER THEY GRADUATED from high school, Kevin's best friend Tommy was working full-time at Merrifield Garden Center and staying at the Warhurst house most of the time. Bob and Billie Jean considered him a son, and Tommy even called them "Dad" and "Mom."

That summer, as the Warhursts were preparing for their annual July stay in Ocean City, Maryland, Bob pulled Tommy aside. "We're getting ready to go out of town," Bob told him. "You need to stay here and watch the house and feed the dogs. When we get back, if you're going to stay here—and you're welcome to—you need to start paying rent."

Tommy was thrilled. That meant the move was permanent. He paid $300 a month in rent, which included utilities and food. He kept a neat and tidy bedroom, which had a bed, large dresser and a couch. He bought a large stereo system to play his favorite music, mostly 1980s rock stars Bruce Springsteen and Elvis Costello. The Warhurst home became his home for the next five years.

Debbie married Rob Capp in March 1985 in Vienna, Virginia. When they met, Rob was working as a medical technologist. He continued this line of work for a few years before changing careers and joining the family business.

In June 1986, Rob Warhurst and Lynn Ostroski were married in Vienna. Lynn earned a degree in decision sciences and information systems from George Mason University in Fairfax, Virginia, and was prepared to accept a full-time position with Control Data Corporation. But Bob realized what an asset she could be to the family business and offered her a full-time job. She has worked at Merrifield ever since, most recently serving as the company controller. "If I was going to be part of the family, I wanted to be part of the business," Lynn said. "People think having your own company is so much fun. Yes, but it's a lot of work. They look at it as you can come and go when you want, but you have to be here to make sure it's working smoothly. You give up your life to be here and help make it work."

With Bob leading the way, Merrifield Garden Center was growing at an even faster rate than his family.

"Bob's philosophy has always been that if you think you've reached the top, you start going downhill," said Howard Saunders, the company's first general manager. "He was always looking for new things we could do to make the company grow."

Bob and his brothers, Lee and Carl, built a beautiful addition to the main store building to open up more room to sell silk and dried flowers, and other home decor items. "You think about bosses who are dressed up," said Merrifield Manager Tim Guy. "Bob helped with whatever we were doing. If there was a ditch to be dug, he was right there next to you. He was always working." Bob and his team decided to call the new room the "Oak Room" because the walls were lined with oak. It still has that name today. "We wanted to make the room look different from the rest of the store," Doris Williams said. Bob and his brothers also put down the brick for the floor. Bob recruited design experts Peg Bier and Joyce Eisenman to help with the brickwork, showing them how to take a spoon to tamp down the mortar between the bricks. Although Peg and Joyce had no experience in masonry, Peg said "Bob wanted everyone to be able to do everything."

To promote Merrifield's new silk and dried flower business, Peg suggested offering free seminars and workshops to customers. She had attended many seminars herself and realized their value, saying "You make a wonderful room of friends. I felt we could build our silk and dried flower business if we could teach customers how to arrange them."

Bob loved the idea. He may only have an eighth-grade education, but he is a big fan of learning. He thought it was important to empower customers to be successful decorators and gardeners. The free seminars were enthusiastically received by old and new customers alike. It was not uncommon for more than 100 customers to cram into the Merrifield meeting room.

Educational seminars have been a staple of Merrifield Garden center ever since. Twice a year, eager gardeners rush to their mailboxes to see if the new seminar schedules have arrived. In January, it's the Winter/Spring edition. In September, they receive the Fall/Holiday schedule. Competition is fierce for a space on a folding chair for many seminars—especially those presented by Bob, Peg and Merrifield plant specialists David Yost, Larry Shapira and Karen Rexrode. Their talks are typically standing room only with even more gardeners listening in the hallways. Merrifield also brings in guest speakers, such as garden luminaries Andre Viette and David Culp.

Merrifield is now known for its wide array of free seminars—more than 70 are offered in a year—for gardeners of all abilities, covering a wide range of gardening, landscaping and decorating topics.

Bob and Peg's intuition about the free seminars also helped grow the company's bottom line. "The more we talked, the more we sold," Peg said.

In the early years, Christmas at Merrifield Garden Center quickly became a local holiday destination. It sold handmade ornaments, such as angels made of pipe cleaners and ribbon, and potpourri, as well as fresh-cut Christmas trees. Making the angels was painstaking work, but Peg said "it was fun and they flew out the door."

Bob and his managers decided to up the ante and completely transform the garden center from a place with garden supplies, fertilizers and pesticides into a winter wonderland. To bolster the store's collection of holiday decorations, Bob, Billie Jean and Doris took a train to New York City to order the latest and greatest holiday decorations at a popular trade show. They had never done anything like that before. Most vendors had come to them. With a shoestring budget, the three of them shared a hotel room, with Billie Jean and Doris sleeping on the bed and Bob on the couch.

"It was quite an experience," Doris recalled. "We were a bunch of country folks. We walked the streets, not knowing where we were going or what we were doing. We didn't know what to buy."

They didn't bring heavy coats and were unprepared for the frigid temperatures, so they could only walk a few blocks before darting inside a store to warm up. Once they reached the trade show, they selected products mostly from Kurt Adler, a prominent importer of holiday decorations. Then months later while Doris, Billie Jean and the Merrifield team were setting up their trees and displays in the store, a Kurt Adler representative came to visit and showed them how to string lights around a Christmas tree in a dramatic way no one had ever seen before. "We had the most beautiful trees around," Doris recalled. "There were 15 to 20 strands of lights on each tree."

That started the Merrifield tradition of fabulous holiday displays, each with its own distinctive theme, decorations and tree. The displays were and are simply spectacular, with a phenomenal quality and selection of decorations. Merrifield's designers won't buy themed packages, so a holiday display could have products from 15 or 20, even 30 vendors. The result is a Christmas Shop that can be found nowhere else.

Another tradition caught on, too: the Merrifield bow. "I taught everyone how to make the Merrifield Bow," Peg recalled. "Billie Jean and I would make 100 in a night." It was just a traditional bow with a beautiful loop in the center to hide the wire, but Peg had a strong sense of branding and dubbed it the "Merrifield Bow," which it's still called today.

"I often tell people we're the bow capital of the world," Bob says. "People come from all over for the bows. Some people buy 40 or 50 bows. I don't know what they do with all of them."

To take the holidays a step further, Bob bought a flocking machine to make the entire store—even the ceiling—look like the North Pole with simulated snow. Employees built a 15-foot tunnel out of 2x4s, burlap and wire and flocked it so customers felt like they were walking through a snow tunnel.

Sometimes the creativity was a bit too much. Peg was asked to make a holiday wreath out of dog biscuits, which Merrifield was selling. "The wreath was cute," Peg said. "A customer was interested in it, picked it up and started screaming. I ran over and saw that two little mice were sitting on the bottom of the wreath, eating away. With all that burlap, we had made a beautiful home for mice."

Merrifield Garden Center became an even bigger holiday destination when John Buckreis, who often visited the original store as a garden supply salesman for Arett Sales, became Santa Claus.

A natural showman and pitchman, John serviced territories in Pennsylvania, Delaware, Maryland and Virginia, and was looking to get off the road.

John grew up in St. John's Orphanage for Boys on the outskirts of Buffalo, New York. He started playing Santa in 1944 when he was 14 years old. He went door-to-door in wealthy neighborhoods asking people for toys to give to kids at the orphanage.

With no money for a Santa costume that first year, John made one out of an old bed sheet that he dyed red with Tintex. He used white cotton for the fur trim, a rope for a black belt and his black galoshes for boots. He made a wig out of spun glass and glued a fake beard to his face. He looked so odd in his homemade Santa outfit that he decided to greet the children from outside the windows of the orphanage. By the time he put down his roots at Merrifield Garden Center, John had perfected his routine. He brings flair to the role, and when in his costume and ringing his bells, children could swear he really is Santa.

John's goal is to give kids the true meaning of Christmas through the spirit of Saint Nicholas. A visit with this Santa is an experience, with sing-alongs next to a creche, a sprinkling of star dust and a chance to sit with Santa in an antique sleigh built in the 1800s.

Santa's appearances became so popular that John insisted that his "Santa Wonderland" be created in one of the warehouses on the property instead of the store so as not to inhibit sales.

"He's a great Santa," Bob says. "We call him 'The Real Santa.'"

Now John needed a job for the other 11 months of the year.

"You can work in the store," Bob told him. "Let Doris do the buying and Peggy the arranging."

"I don't want anyone's job," John said. "I want to be your troubleshooter. I want to be up front by the registers when someone comes in with a sick or a dead plant."

Bob said, "We send those people to Howard in the other building. We don't want anyone coming in the store with a dead plant."

John, who has a degree in horticulture from New York State College, convinced Bob to try his idea. John set up a table near the cashiers and hung up a sign that read "Plant Clinic." He even wrote out "prescriptions."

When customers called with plant problems, Bob would say, "We've got a plant doctor, Dr. John. He'll take care of all your plant needs." The name stuck, for both Dr. John and for the Plant Clinic.

This remarkable free service was a big hit with customers, who now had a place to go to find out what was wrong with their plants and how to fix the problem. The Plant Clinic resonated with Bob, who likes to think of plants as people, as living organisms instead of decorating accessories in outdoor living spaces. He can't stand to see a plant die because of improper care. When a plant dies, he says "it's like losing a friend that was depending on you to keep it healthy."

The Plant Clinic and plant doctors became a mainstay at Merrifield Garden Center. When it comes to saving the life of a treasured friend, Bob believes that no plant should be left behind.

IN 1977, BOB SERVED AS PRESIDENT of the Northern Virginia Nurseryman's Association, now called the Northern Virginia Nursery and Landscape Association (NVNLA). Peg Bier went with him to the monthly meetings and took notes. At one NVNLA seminar, they met Andre Viette, a noted perennial grower who owns a farm and nursery near Fishersville, Virginia. Andre began giving them perennials on a consignment basis to get them started.

"They sold like hotcakes," Peg remembered.

The Merrifield Garden Center staff was unfamiliar with perennials, and their lack of knowledge led to some humorous situations. Peg recalled one time they received a yellow variety of hosta. "We didn't grow hostas on the farm where I was raised," she said. "The hostas came in and they were yellow. We fertilized the heck out of them, trying to turn them green. Then we realized they were supposed to be yellow!"

Another time, Bob acquired 8,000 to 10,000 chrysanthemums from rooted cuttings and his team planted them in 8-inch, plastic mum pots. They were purchased in late May, grew all summer and were sold in August and September. The mums needed to be "pinched" to encourage more blooms. Bob always finds a way to make chores fun, especially when a large group of employees are involved. He organized pinching parties, saying "It's pinching time!" And he gathered up everyone who was around him and told them, "This is how you do it, guys."

The mum-pinching parties went deep into the night. "Mom and Dad and Carl would have the headlights on their trucks turned on so we could see," Kim recalled. "I thought it was fun. Now it sounds insane. Your thumb and pointer finger would be green for weeks."

They pinched mums for the next four or five years, but eventually stopped because the need for twice-a-season pinching made them too labor intensive and more suppliers began offering mums to garden centers.

Now the perennial section is viewed as an integral part of the nursery, earning even more square footage as colorful annuals. Perennials have a shorter bloom time than annuals, but they don't perish after the first frost. They come back year after year to bring color and interest to the garden.

Bob's love for the biggest and best toys extended to the garden center. "Bob loves toys," said Byron Wates, Jr., owner of Area Landscaping and the historian of the NVNLA. "Anything that has a motor on it, he loves it. If he reads about something, it probably won't be long before he has it. You can truly say if the guy who dies with the most toys wins, he wins."

Bob is willing to take a chance and buy an expensive piece of equipment, figuring it will eventually pay for itself. In 1977, Bob became enthralled with a $50,000 tree spade. "It's the ultimate toy for a landscaper," Byron said. "It's one of the most marvelous inventions of our industry." A tree spade consists of a number of large steel blades that encircle the tree, digging into the ground and then lifting the entire tree, including its roots and soil, out of the ground. Tree spades can transplant any tree but are typically used to move specimen trees of high value or large shade trees where clients demand immediate gratification, such as a shade tree that is 15' to 20' tall, a 30-year-old Japanese maple or a 15' Southern magnolia.

While it did cost a lot, the tree spade quickly did the work of a large crew working with shovels and a backhoe. For a large company such as Merrifield Garden Center, the cost savings could be significant.

Bob first tried out the new tree spade at the home of Stella Matalas, a Merrifield customer who did a favor for Bob. In return, he asked if she needed any work in her garden. As it turned out, Stella wanted to have an overgrown arborvitae removed. The debut of the new machine was a success. "It was brand new and he was very excited about it," she recalled. "It pulled the huge plant right out of the ground."

Byron was building his own company at the time and didn't want to invest that much money in a single piece of equipment. So he hired Bob to help him remove trees many times.

"I love Bob Warhurst," Byron said. "He's a guy you can love. He's such a generous man. You don't call another company and borrow their equipment. This is not something that happens every day." Bob appreciated that Byron always treated the tree spade like it was his own, so Bob eventually let him rent and use it without his supervision.

In addition to the tree spade, Bob was one of the first garden center owners in the area to purchase a crane to lift large boulders and trees into difficult to reach areas without damaging lawns and gardens, a Wood-Mizer to turn logs into lumber and a ready-mix concrete truck for top quality concrete, which is made to order on site to eliminate waste.

Byron recalled the time he was using the Wood-Mizer at Merrifield's Fair Oaks store and a Merrifield employee told him that the company now owned a kiln to make kiln-dried firewood. "Nothing surprises me," Byron said. Merrifield's computerized kiln, which holds 24 cords of wood at one time, features six temperature sensors that monitor heating of the wood to a core temperature of 150 degrees over three days. This process results in insect-free firewood that is easier to light, burns better, produces more heat and can be used immediately. Merrifield even offers septic tank cleaning, and Byron scheduled an appointment. "(Bob) even came himself!" Byron said.

It was over this period of time that Bob refined his management style. He hates meetings, reports and confrontation. He doesn't like to sit in an office. He runs the company by common sense and instinct, traits which have always served him well.

"Bob would give me advice along the way," said David Watkins, a Merrifield manager who studied business at Virginia Tech. "It was always a common sense approach. In school, it would have been more analytical. But I could see in the first few months of working with Bob that he knew people and he knew common sense. What Bob says has always made more sense to me than what I learned in school.

"To my knowledge, Bob spends very little time looking at reports. If you have customers standing in line, you don't have enough employees. If you've got employees standing around talking, you've got too many employees. If your customers are asking for products, you don't have enough products. The reports just confirm what you're already looking at."

Seven years after Merrifield Garden Center opened, Bob was looking for a way to give back to his regular customers. "One morning Bob woke up and said, 'I think I'll have a festival,'" Billie Jean said. "Bob is always trying to make people happy. I don't know how he comes up with all this stuff. I think he stays up all night thinking."

The annual Fall Festival was like a country hoedown, with Merrifield's founding families dressed in their best western outfits. The men wore cowboy boots and hats, jeans and plaid shirts with pearl buttons. The women wore big skirts, white blouses trimmed in lace, white aprons and straw hats with wide brims.

It became a huge event, with thousands of people who came for delicious food, country music provided by live bands, square dancing, horse-drawn carriage rides, pony rides, an auction, an antique car show and more than a hundred juried crafters and exhibitors handpicked by Bob in his travels to craft shows. To accommodate all the cars and exhibitors, Bob convinced neighboring landowner Charles Dunn to allow access to his open field next to the garden center.

Bob rigged up an elaborate barbecue pit and vendors sold hot dogs, hamburgers and all the goodies children love, such as funnel cakes, snow cones and cotton candy. The air smelled of apple butter simmering in a big pot. There were costume contests and every child who entered received a crisp dollar bill from Bob.

In 1994, after 14 years of caramel apples and do-si-dos, Bob looked around at the huge crowds—he estimated 10,000—and couldn't see a lot of the regular customers who supported his business for many years. In addition, the large crowds made it difficult for customers who wanted to come into the store to shop and buy.

What started as a way to say thanks to his loyal customers evolved into a bigger and bigger headache that cost Merrifield Garden Center about $50,000 every year. With access to the Dunn property in doubt due to the possibility it would soon be converted to townhouses, Bob had no assurance that there would be enough parking for future festivals. The time had come for Bob to end the festival.

Bob Warhurst's instincts told him—and the nursery business showed him—that owning land was critical.

One of Mark Twain's most memorable quotes could have been attributed to Bob: "Buy land, they're not making it anymore."

Although Merrifield Garden Center was turning a good profit, Bob was always looking for new opportunities to make money and decided to try his hand at real estate.

CHAPTER NINE

A SIXTH SENSE

While much of the nation was struggling in the mid-1980s with inflation and the decline of major industries, the Washington, D.C., area was booming thanks to the Reagan Revolution and its pro-business policies.

Although huge deficits left over from the Vietnam War were still dragging down the nation's economy, President Ronald Reagan's sunny optimism and a willingness to restrict a flood of cheap imported goods made his "Morning in America" catchphrase a reason for cheer.

It was the perfect launching pad for Bob's plan for success. In the mid-1980s, Bob saw that Northern Virginia in general and the Merrifield area in particular were becoming popular places for homes and businesses near the ever-expanding Washington Beltway and Metro subway system.

There was land available, but the growing population was beginning to fill in residential and commercial space that had been mostly bucolic just a decade earlier. Growing up in rural Alabama taught Bob that land was a precious commodity that had both financial and emotional value. It is Bob's gift to see clearly that the buying and selling of land was always about more than money. This gift would serve him well in the coming years.

Merrifield Garden Center had become very profitable, but Bob was never one to sit on his wallet if there were opportunities to make money. "When you're like me," he says, "you're always trying to outdo yourself."

A friend told him about a small parcel of land that was available next to the shopping center across from the Merrifield Garden

Center on Lee Highway. Bob bought it for $500,000 and sold it for $1.1 million one year later. A Homewood Suites hotel now stands on that site. But Bob doesn't like to roll the dice. He knows that financial risk is best when spread among partners. Bob and Buddy were already partners in Merrifield Garden Center when in 1985 they created an investment partnership group with a few other local businessmen, including W.R. Owens, Otis Poole, Ray August and Guy Lewis, so they could purchase a 1.5 acre parcel in Merrifield for $500,000. And, as in Bob's first venture, the group sold that property a short time later for $1.1 million.

"That's just the way I'm made," Bob says. "You try something. If it works, you do it again. I thought, 'Investing is a pretty good business to be in. We might be able to do this quite often.'"

Emboldened by their initial success, the group became very active investors. "Bob was never one to tout himself," said Guy Lewis, who was brought into the group by W.R. Owens. "He wasn't one for bragging. We thought he was running a modest garden center, a rental property. It didn't take me long to realize Bob is a smart businessman. He has a great sense of the market. At the time, I think he knew values better than any of us. We kind of stuck to industrial land at the start. That's what he understood the best. We knew industrial land was changing to other uses, making it more valuable."

Bob may look country with his overalls and easy-going manner, but he's no bumpkin. He knows how to use his folksy ways to disarm people in a way that makes it easy to underestimate him. And when they do, that's right where he wants them. He's the opposite of the yelling and screaming stereotype of an arrogant and demanding CEO. He doesn't drink, smoke, raise his voice or lose his temper. Quietly and slowly, he gets what he wants at the price he wants. And the beauty of his approach is that the other person walks away happy, eager to do business again with that simple, country shrub-seller who just happens to be a multi-millionaire.

"If you didn't know the man, you wanted to know him," said John

A Sixth Sense

Buckreis, a Merrifield employee who has known Bob for about four decades. "He has a great smile and handshake. He doesn't mind laughing or chuckling. He's no sourpuss."

Bob has always had a sixth sense about the world, perhaps a talent he acquired from his early life as a country boy in Alabama, where it was common to use healers and mystics tuned in to the rhythms of both nature and people. He seems to be in the right place at the right time, even when others don't see his native logic.

Whatever the source, it served him well in one particular deal that the investment group was wrestling with in Gainesville, a small town west of Fairfax in Prince William County. The group wanted to sell four acres they owned in Gainesville for $2 a square foot. Bob said, "Let's raise the price to $4 a square foot!"

The other partners were dumbfounded.

"That doesn't make any sense," they said. "No one wants it for $2. Now we're going to raise it to $4?"

Despite their misgivings, the group went along with Bob's plan.

"Everyone looked to Bob," Guy Lewis said. "When Bob said something, we respected it." More than six months passed and the property still had not been sold.

"Let's raise it to $6 a square foot," Bob said. "When someone wants it, they'll make an offer. It just takes the right customer."

At their next meeting, Bob shocked everyone when he said he wanted to raise the asking price to $8.

W.R. Owens was so perplexed, he told Bob: "I guarantee you I'll kiss you right in the middle of Lee Highway if we sell it!"

Three months later, WaWa, a national gas station and convenience store chain, came in and paid $8 a square foot for the land.

"I didn't want the kiss!" Bob laughs.

Bob says making money in real estate isn't magic or rocket science. You just have to keep your eyes and ears open for opportunities and stay patient.

"If I see a property that might be worth something in the future,

I'll buy it and hold on to it for five or 10 years or more," he says. "You watch things happen. You see an area start to go up. You understand the times you live in." Bob prefers to acquire income-producing property, but he is willing to buy raw land if the monthly payments on that land are within the project's budget and have the potential for a much greater profit in the future.

The investment group is still together today. They have two pieces of property left: the parcel where the present-day Home Depot in Merrifield is located and a warehouse/office building in Manassas, Virginia.

Outside of the original investment group, Bob accumulated more than 30 additional land holdings in Northern Virginia and Washington, D.C.

IN 1982, BOB JOINED WESTWOOD COUNTRY CLUB, which was about two miles from his Vienna home. Golf was a popular sport and Bob was excited to give it a try, so he bought a set of clubs and asked the pro for a few pointers. Sons Rob, Larry, Donny and Kevin learned to play golf there and it became a lifelong passion for Rob and Kevin. But Bob didn't see it that way. He discovered that playing 18 holes took several hours and he thought that was too time-consuming and kept him from work, his real passion in life.

Bob would play a few times a year with his sons, friends and business associates. When he did play, Bob would hit a long, straight ball. "We were amazed at how he could hit," Rob said. "We would look at each other and say, 'How in the heck did he do that?' We can hardly do it now and we play 30 times a year."

Golf is a sport that takes many hours of practice to place the ball where you want it. Occasional players seldom excel at the game. Bob's secret may be that his lifetime of hard work gave him strong forearms that made his long shots possible. When his kids were young, Bob tore a Yellow Pages directory in half with his hands to impress them. Bob has great hand-to-eye coordination and timing, which made up for his limited flexibility and lack of practice.

In both golf and business, good timing is essential.

At about this time, Rob and his friend Mark Martino were looking for a way to play basketball after their glory days at Marshall High School. They considered playing in the Fairfax Men's Basketball League, but they needed a sponsor. Bob thought it was a good idea and the Merrifield Express was created. No one quite remembers the process, but somehow it was decided that Bob would be the coach. Bob didn't know a lot about basketball, but his people skills couldn't be beat. The team was comprised of Rob, Mark and several of their Marshall teammates, as well as a few Merrifield employees.

One of the first things Bob did was buy uniforms for the team. As the owner of a company in the green industry, he naturally selected green uniforms. It was a good choice because that was the heyday for the most famous green team in sports: the Boston Celtics. Under Bob's direction, the Merrifield Express won all their regular season games for four and a half years. "It was a blast," recalled Mark, who earned a basketball scholarship to then Division II Randolph-Macon College in Ashland, Virginia. "It's as much fun as I've ever had playing basketball with a group of guys." The team had a good center, Warren Denny, who was 6 foot 5 inches tall. Rob and Mark were a few inches shorter and the team as a whole was undersized compared to other teams in the tough league. Bob's plan was to wear the opposition down with an up-tempo style with lots of pressing and fast breaks.

"Bob was so great in the huddle," Mark recalled. "He had a specific strategy for us. He'd say, 'Boys, you better keep shooting. The only way to score is to keep shooting.' As a player, that's what you want to hear and that's pretty much what we did."

The upside of winning is the pride and the glory. The downside is that the pressure grew with each season. "After you win the first year, you try even harder to win again the next year," Bob said. "And then the year after that. It was fun, but it was hard. I was totally into the games. I'd be worn out when the games were over." Rob, who was known for his stellar defense and ability to steal the ball, can't forget the pressure of the winning streak. "We were waiting for someone to knock us off our throne," he said.

Mark, now the director of student activities at Lake Braddock Secondary School in Fairfax County, said he took Bob's advice to heart: "You have to have fun and do what you do best." It influenced how he coached his high school basketball teams at Falls Church High School, Chantilly High School and later at Lake Braddock.

Right about this time, Bob started taking his own advice. He did what he enjoys the most and what he does the best: Focus on making money.

As the garden center flourished and Bob and Buddy's business dealings multiplied, Bob eventually dropped his vacations—skiing the slopes, hunting with his sons, parasailing at Lake Anna and vacationing at Ocean City and its boardwalk filled with laughing kids and warm, sandy beaches. But Bob kept one: the Watermelon Festival back home in Russellville, Alabama. Some successful people find it difficult to look back at their humble beginnings, preferring to see themselves as always wealthy, handsome and powerful.

That's not Bob. Since the Watermelon Festival started in 1980, Bob has attended every year but one when a wedding coincided with the event: the marriage of Kim Williams, the youngest child of Buddy and Doris, to Dustin Myers.

That Bob remains faithful to his roots is remarkable, considering the hard times his family endured in Russellville. But Bob prefers to see his life there as a series of accomplishments that were certainly less significant financially than his success in Virginia, but those hard-won lessons became the foundation of his future. When he visits Russellville, little Bobby Rea still exists, racing in his daddy's big shoes and kissing girls in the dark balcony of the Roxy movie theater.

Russellville is to watermelons what Idaho is to potatoes—a really big deal. In 2013, the Alabama State Legislature proclaimed Franklin County the "Watermelon Capital of Alabama." The festival began as a one-day event and has grown to a two-day celebration of melon thumping, seed-spitting and lots and lots of happy faces smeared with bright red watermelon juice. On the city's main street, known as "the strip," food vendors ply the crowds with the usual summer fare of corn dogs, cotton candy and snow cones. Festival goers are treated to a car show, live entertainment, carnival rides, and arts and crafts vendors.

But the best part of the festival is seeing old friends and making some new ones. One year, Bob had the opportunity to meet State Senator Roger Bedford, a Russellville Democrat. "I like the Watermelon Festival because it's a great chance to see people," Bob says. "Everyone comes out from everywhere for the festival—the good, the bad and the ugly."

If watermelon is the star of the festival, Bob is certainly a very popular co-star. When Bob rolls into town in his luxury Prevost motorhome, it's like a visit from a famous movie star. The motorhome is complete with a bedroom, bathroom, kitchen, dining area, TVs and stereo. The local newspaper has even written about Bob and his fabulous wheels. But what many admire the most about Bob and the Warhurst family is that they have their roots in Alabama red clay and make a point of coming home every summer and taking all their old friends out to dinner in the deluxe motorhome.

"He really has prospered," said Bobby Woodruff, Bob's best friend since grade school. "I'm really proud of him."

Bob still owns the family property in Russellville. Their house burned down a while back, and Bob regularly hires someone to bush-hog the overgrown land. "When we were growing up, the Warhurst family was what you considered poverty stricken," said

Barbara Stanley, the youngest daughter of Miss Annie Mae Hendrix, who gave Bob his first job at the age of seven at her country grocery store. "He never forgot where he came from. That's what I love about him. Most people would never come back to a hick city like this. Some of the U.S. presidents have come from the same background. That shows it's not important where you come from. You would never know about Bobby. You would think he has a PhD. He has a nice voice and a nice vocabulary.

"I believe with all my soul that the hand of the Lord was on Bobby."

No one was prouder of Bob than his mother.

"She was always saying what a good boy he was growing up and how much he looked out for everyone," Bob's son Kevin said. "She took great pride in knowing that he had not only worked hard and built a business, but that he was so well-known and respected in the community."

Bob's mother eventually left Alabama and moved to Virginia for good, settling into a modest home on Prosperity Avenue, less than a half mile from Merrifield Garden Center. With a smile on her face and a piece of spicy Dentyne gum in her mouth, Bob's mother tended to her lovely flowers.

"She was always working with her flowers," Bob's daughter Debbie said. "She would propagate them, water them and fiddle with them for hours. To this day, I have a Swedish ivy plant and a ficus tree that she gave me. She also made beautiful, large macrame plant hangers. I still have a couple of them."

Bob's mother was blessed with a loving family who took care of all her needs. She never learned to drive, but sons Charles, Lee, Carl and other family members regularly brought her to the garden center, where Bob encouraged her to take home any plant that caught her eye. Bob usually stopped at her house at least once a week to see how she was doing. While in Virginia, Bob's mother developed a taste for sausage and egg biscuit sandwiches and coffee from a Hardee's near the garden center. She couldn't drive and she also couldn't walk to Hardee's because of the speeding cars and rumbling large trucks on the roads. But the family made sure she got her coffee and sandwich. They set up a weekly schedule where every day someone was assigned to deliver the sandwich to her. "I think my day was Friday," Debbie recalled. "One of my favorite memories is bringing her a Hardee's biscuit and coffee, and having breakfast with her."

That routine was shattered one spring morning when Bob's brother, Charles, who lived with their mother, called Bob at the garden center to say he could not rouse her. Doris answered the phone and gave it to Bob, who immediately called for an ambulance. But no rescue was possible. Bob's mother had suffered a heart attack and passed away in her sleep on May 6, 1986 at the age of 78, just a few weeks short of her 79th birthday. The day before she died, she had made a trip to the garden center. Her funeral was held at Money and King Funeral Home in Vienna, and she was buried next to her husband at National Memorial Park.

Her death was a powerful blow to Bob that cracked his always-tough veneer. "One of the few times I ever saw my dad cry was at her funeral," Kevin remembered.

Bob had always been a doting son, making sure that his beloved mother never wanted for anything. As a child growing up dirt poor in Alabama, he had taken it upon himself to make sure there was food on the table during his father's long stints away from home working on the railroad. When he became financially successful, Bob showered his mother with money to assure her that those worrisome years of barely scraping by were never a concern for her again. "I made sure she had $3,000 to $5,000 in her purse," he says. "She worried about money her whole life. I didn't want her to worry anymore."

Whenever he asked her, "How's your money holding up?" She'd reply, "I've got plenty!" To make sure her purse was stocked with cash, Bob would give her a few thousand more.

Bob's generosity could not compensate for his feeling that he had been too busy working to visit her as often as he'd like. "I always felt bad I didn't give her more time," Bob recalls. "Mr. Lee furnished her with company and I furnished her with money." Although he wishes he spent more time with her, Bob admits, "I've always been a worker. I don't go anywhere but to work. I'm in love with work."

With the death of his father in 1963 and now his mother, Bob was left without both his parents. One year later, Billie Jean's mother, Essie Tolliver, died on June 28, 1987, leaving her without a living parent as well. It's often a defining moment in people's lives. But in many ways, Bob had spent his life taking care of his parents, leading them into the modern world that he was now striding through as a man with a powerful vision.

BY 1987, BOB, BUDDY AND THEIR TRUSTED TEAM had grown Merrifield Garden Center into a bustling center of activity in that part of Fairfax County. What had been mostly industrial land, auto body shops, gas stations and a few fast-food restaurants serving the growing I-495 and I-66 interstate highways was now a retail magnet for families wanting to spruce up the yards of the new suburban homes that were popping up all over that part of the county.

That year Merrifield Garden Center was named Fairfax County Small Business Retailer of the Year by the Fairfax County Chamber of Commerce. Bob and Buddy were honored by the Fairfax County Board of Supervisors at an awards ceremony at the government center. "It was a great honor," Bob says. "We had been in business for a little over 15 years and it was really nice to be recognized like that. We appreciated it very much." Merrifield Garden Center went on to receive many more awards and accolades over the years and has been featured on a number of television segments and in magazine and newspaper articles.

But Bob was not ready to rest on his laurels. The 1988 holiday season was approaching, and he was eager to have a second store where he could sell Christmas trees and other holiday decorations. Merrifield owned a 33-acre site in a Fair Oaks neighborhood on Lee Highway near the Fairfax County Parkway. "I wanted to open a temporary garden center to get people used to us being out there," Bob says.

That site had been purchased in 1979, but had not been fully cleared. It was too late to transform the land into a retail center in time for Christmas, so he improvised and decided to open a temporary home across the street on the eight-acre site that he and Buddy bought earlier that year. It had an old building on it that had previously been converted into a store and had commercial zoning. Having commercial zoning already in place saved lots of time and money. Without it, the temporary store could not have been opened in time for Christmas, and Bob's hopes for a holiday retail center would have been dashed.

The staff quickly fixed up the unsightly building and made it ready to be a garden center. They scraped and cleaned the hardwood floors, painted walls, repaired broken windows and installed new light fixtures. Merrifield had a reputation as the place to go for holiday decorations and Christmas trees so Bob did not want to disappoint his loyal customers. There were no shelves or tables, but they managed with folding tables. They picked up some Christmas decorations from the original Merrifield store and spread them out on the tables instead of hanging them from Christmas trees, as was their custom. Merrifield Plant and Design Specialist Peg Bier made some of her signature Merrifield bows, and fresh-cut trees and greens were sold.

"That's how we started," Peg recalled. "Believe it or not, we had some customers. It was fun. There were no restrooms. You had to go to the nearest gas station. Now we can look back and smile on it."

The little-building-that-could started to draw a lot of customers, and business grew every year while the big nursery across the street was being constructed.

CHAPTER TEN

THE PLANT WHISPERER

Merrifield Garden Center's Fair Oaks store started out in 1988 as a makeshift holiday location to bring in customers from that fast-growing area of Fairfax County. While other businesses were focusing on more densely populated areas around the beltway, Bob had the foresight to see that much more growth for his garden center would come to the west, where more development was likely to occur.

Another benefit of that area was lower land prices. By building in Fair Oaks instead of some other areas, Bob could afford to buy more land. He needed a big footprint for the types of buildings, display beds, retail spaces and parking areas that he envisioned. Land parcels of any significant size located near population centers were costly and hard to find, especially for commercial zoning. The Northern Virginia area was experiencing rapid growth, and Bob knew it was only a matter of time before even those prices went up.

Because the nearby Springfield Bypass road—the precursor to the Fairfax County Parkway—had not yet linked up with the massive I-66 federal highway, which stretched from the Shenandoah Mountains through Fairfax and Arlington counties, property values in Fairfax were lower than in more crowded and expensive places such as Tyson's Corner, Virginia. What's more, Tyson's Corner was attracting more office building construction than the single-family houses that would need the services of a large garden center.

But before Bob's dream of a second garden center could be realized, an important question needed to be asked. After all the work was done building up the first store in Merrifield, was the company prepared to take on such a big expansion project, especially one that was going to need a lot of money and labor to complete?

The years developing the first Merrifield store were challenging, but its growth from a small parking lot with a few shrubs and flowers to a full-service garden center was gradual and manageable with family members and a growing number of outside hires. Bob started with less than an acre of land, but over the years he amassed about 10 acres for the original garden center site and another four acres for the landscape lot across the street from the garden center.

Bob's vision for Fair Oaks was beyond the scope of anything the family and the organization had ever done. The 33 acres he was holding were in no shape to become a retail destination. This would be a monumental undertaking.

"You can't let your doubts creep in," Bob says.

In his mind, Bob saw a modern facility with a large greenhouse, enclosed annual and perennial houses and a pond for colorful koi fish. It had the potential for storage of landscape materials beyond the original store and it would all be new, including more space for managers and office workers. The site was zoned residential, but Bob got a special exemption to operate a nursery. But there was just one problem: the site was a tangle of old trees, muddy creeks with cattails, thorny brush and terrible drainage. To prepare the property for development, the land had to be cleared, leveled and compacted.

"It was a real scary thing," recalled Howard Saunders, Merrifield's first general manager. "It was hard to visualize. We had 33 acres, but there was water everywhere. Bob had a vision of what he wanted to do with it."

Not only did the land need a major overhaul, but Merrifield's employees were already stretched thin in their current jobs. Merrifield Plant Specialist Tim Guy said only Bob and Manager David Watkins weren't worried.

"A lot of us were like, 'What are we doing? How are we going to take care of it?'" Tim recalled. "I'm not as risky as he is."

David said people don't realize how far ahead of the game Bob is so much of the time. "I've heard people say 'Bob is crazy!' hundreds of times," David said. "In all these years, I can't remember a time when I wish he'd done something differently. He's seeing something I can't begin to understand. It might take me three months, then I understand where he's coming from."

Bob's thriftiness and faith in his ability as the "Plant Whisperer" to nurse plants back to health came into play. He rescued magnolias, hollies, pines, boxwoods and other plants that were headed to the dumpster at the original Merrifield store and planted them on the property boundaries at Fair Oaks to comply with county requirements for a noise and visual barrier between the site and neighboring houses. "Bob never, ever wanted a plant to die," Peg Bier said. For instance, a wisteria that was in danger of death was revived with Bob's touch and today it is back at the original Merrifield store, draped over a pergola in the shrub section, where its gorgeous blooms are a delight to all.

Plants are considered orphans when a new addition or other home improvement project makes them unwanted or without a proper place to prosper. Bob was an unabashed advocate of preserving those plants, too. One success story is a gorgeous Japanese lace leaf maple in a display bed at the Fair Oaks store. The maple appeared to be doomed after being dug out during a landscape renovation. Its roots were growing around old roofing tiles left in the soil and no matter how hard they tried, Bob's team couldn't get a solid root ball together. They didn't have high hopes for its survival. But Bob didn't give up. He told them to plant the maple "bare root," and much to everyone's surprise, the maple not only survived but thrived in its new environment.

As the construction continued for the Fair Oaks store, the surrounding neighborhood began to gradually fill in with residential housing. Bob was concerned that the racket and traffic from the store project might be bothering the new families moving into homes on adjacent Marymead Drive, east of the new store. To avoid any hard feelings, he had his crews snowplow Marymead Drive after storms as a goodwill gesture that he still follows today.

Bob was happy and excited while building the new nursery. He was firmly in his element, driving a bulldozer or wielding a chainsaw instead of sitting behind a desk in a stuffy office. The long, exhausting hours were tough and stressful for others but not for him. For Bob, work is not a chore. It is an opportunity to achieve something—to rise above his humble beginnings in Alabama, where he was a family breadwinner at the age of seven when others his age were playing children's games. Work meant food on the table, coal in the stove and clothes on their backs. Bob knew that to have work was to have security and the assurance that he could go into a store and buy what he needed. When the bare essentials were secured, he could buy what he really wanted: a beautiful horse and later a fast car, a piece of land and an opportunity for the family to earn a living for generations to come.

"I just love working," Bob says. "It beats going to the movies. It beats playing golf. I love it, love it, love it."

But for his family, Bob's love of work wasn't always fun for them.

"It was terrible when we were younger," recalled Rob, Bob's oldest son. "He would start a project late, like five or six o'clock, after the customers were gone. He would say, 'I've got to run that water line,' or 'I've got an asphalt project.' You're ready to leave and he'd be in the ditch, digging. You couldn't just leave him there. You would be there until 10 at night. He's a hard worker, a workaholic. I hate to say that word. It has a negative connotation. I'm sure he enjoys work better than being at home."

Bob's daughter Debbie agreed. "I like to have my weekends free," she said. "But when you work in a retail business, working weekends is part of the job. And for Dad, it's a 24/7 labor of love. We always made business decisions over the dinner table, especially in the early days of the nursery. You never left work."

It is the nature of the gardening and landscape business to work long hours and days during the busy seasons. The Warhurst and Williams families along with many of the company's managers work six days a week in the spring, fall and Christmas seasons to handle the large crowds.

Bob's hard work allowed him to afford all the things he wanted in life. Although he and his family lived in a modest house, he bought Billie Jean new clothes and beautiful jewelry, including a 3.5 carat diamond ring and diamond wedding band to replace the tiny one he gave her when they got married. He purchased a new camper, a new boat and a new Corvette for his sons. And he bought the family a new baby grand piano. Bob chose the piano because two of his children, Debbie and Donny, had learned to play and Billie Jean and Debbie loved to sing.

A few years later, Bob started taking piano lessons himself. If the idea of his large, work-callused hands tickling the ivories sounds improbable, consider that Bob's entire life has been a series of improbable tasks that he has conquered. It is Bob's essential nature to have no qualms about using the same hands that were pricked bloody while picking cotton to also play classical music composed by silk-and-lace Europeans with perfumed handkerchiefs tucked in their sleeves. Bob even went on to play the piano at the White House when he was invited there for an event. Never one to shy away from an opportunity, Bob sat down at the large, ornate piano and began playing "Amazing Grace" and "Fur Elise" while a U.S. secret service agent snapped his photo.

Eventually, the good life and good times that seemed to have gone on forever began to show some signs of wear and tear. The national economy began to downshift. The average family's disposable income and business investment began to dry up.

Bob's investment group did very well throughout most of the 1980s on the strength of the "Reagan boom" and its robust growth, modest unemployment and low inflation. Land values had been increasing and Bob and his partners made solid investments in areas with healthy growth. But toward the end of the decade, the foundations of the United States and Northern Virginia economies were faltering.

On October 19, 1987, dubbed "Black Monday," stock markets around the world took a nose dive. In the United States, the Dow Jones Industrial Average dropped about 22 percent of its value because of worries about inflation brought on by large federal budget deficits. The housing market slipped, and many savings and loans associations (private banks that specialized in home mortgages) went bankrupt.

Iraq invaded oil-rich Kuwait in the summer of 1990, driving up the price of oil and gasoline. U.S. consumers were hit in their pocketbooks and at work as the unemployment rate skyrocketed to almost 8 percent. U.S. President George H.W. Bush sent in U.S. troops to liberate the Persian Gulf nation, setting off decades of American involvement in that region.

The official recession lasted only eight months, but its effects were felt much longer by the investment group. "In the late 1980s, they bought a lot of land," David Watkins said. "They would rent it out. Six months later, the market dropped because of the recession, but they still had to make all of the payments. And if a partner couldn't pay, the investment group had to pay that, too."

Bob and Buddy had two competing worries. Not only were they on the hook for the investment group, but they had a gardening business to keep going in a recession. Employees feared for their jobs. Bob assured them that "we just need to work harder and take care of our customers, and we'll get through this." He was not going to veer from course and cut prices or reduce inventory. Instead, Bob stressed focusing even more on the things that made them successful in the first place: quality plants and accessories, enormous selection and outstanding customer service.

Although he couldn't control the economy and consumer confidence, Bob could control the type of experience that customers would have when visiting his garden center. Now more than ever, Bob knew it was important to greet customers with a warm smile and say hello, carry their plants and products to their cars, thank them for their business and remind them to tell all their friends about Merrifield Garden Center.

For five or six years, Bob and Buddy took huge pay cuts to help keep their business and their investments afloat. "We were able to do it," Bob recalls. "It was just hard. You had to watch everything so close and be as innovative as possible."

Investment group partner Guy Lewis said, "Bob and all of us had been carried away with how well we had been doing. We had to work through it. It almost broke all of us. The banks we borrowed from had trouble, too. All of a sudden, they wanted their money back.

"Time cures everything, but for a while it looked like we made a real mess of things. We had to get through it, and we did. We had a couple of meetings where people said, 'I can't pay any more. I can't contribute.' It hurt Bob, too. He didn't have that much money in those days."

But the investment group survived.

BOB MAY HAVE LOST MONEY in the Black Monday recession, but he never lost his sense of humor, especially about people's names. Christened as Bobby Rea, Bob changed his last name to Warhurst in 1955 when he followed brother Lee to Virginia. As a result, Bob only considers a name permanent when it's carved on a gravestone.

Consider the case of Malcolm Andrew McVean, the younger brother of Kevin's best friend Tommy McVean. Malcolm had become friends with Kevin and his older brother Donny and was spending more and more time at the Warhurst house. Malcolm was working for his uncle, cleaning airplanes at Washington Dulles International Airport in Dulles, Virginia, and Washington National Airport, now called Ronald Reagan Washington National Airport, in Arlington, Virginia.

But Malcolm preferred to work outside and put his talents to better use. So one day he mustered the courage to go to the Merrifield store and ask Bob for a job. Bob grabbed a nearby shovel and put it in his hands, saying, "Here boy, help me!"

Bob told Malcolm to dig post poles for a new azalea house. "This will be easy," Malcolm thought. "I'm working with this old man." But it turned out to be a difficult job, especially at Bob's pace. "I'm the one sweating and dying," Malcolm recalled. "Bob never stops. He's like a machine."

Later that day, Bob—out of the blue—asked Malcolm if he liked the name "Malcolm."

Malcolm replied, "No!" Bob asked what he wanted to be called. "My middle name is Andrew," he replied. "I'd like to be called Andy."

Bob paused a bit and then said, like King Arthur dubbing a knave a knight with the touch of a royal sword on his shoulder, "OK, from this point on, your name is Andy."

Kevin thought it was kind of crazy. You can't just change someone's name. But that's exactly what Bob did. Old habits were hard to break and some workers forgot Bob's decree that Malcolm was now Andy.

Whenever a forgetful worker would say, "Hey, Malcolm," Bob would chime in and say, "What did you say? His name is Andy."

In the Kingdom of Merrifield, he would always be Andy. And he would always be Andy to his friends, even those he had known since childhood. But at home with his family, he was simply Malcolm.

Andy became Bob's trusted driver of his luxury motorhome on his annual pilgrimage to Russellville, Alabama. Andy's great sense of humor and love of life delighted Bob and his friends endlessly.

Kevin, the youngest of Bob and Billie Jean's five children, would soon find out that while his family name gave him many opportunities, it also came with some tough decisions about making a life of his own. In May 1989, Kevin graduated from Virginia Tech and entered a world of possibilities. He was armed with a quick mind and a college education from one of Virginia's best schools. But it didn't take long for the strong gravity of the family business to exert a familiar pull. When Kevin received a briefcase as a graduation gift, brother Rob joked, "That's great! You can carry your delivery tickets in that!" Kevin was prepared for the ribbing, but he also realized that decisions about his future were now his to make. "Working all those years at the nursery was great," he said. "I never thought I was better than Merrifield. There was a big world out there, and I just wanted to experience it."

Bob made it clear what he wanted, suggesting that Kevin work at the garden center. That summer Kevin went back to work at the garden center and then the fall season came and soon winter arrived. But one winter day, Kevin recalled, "I put on my blue jeans and work boots and I remember thinking, 'This is not the end for me. I need more challenges.'" The turning point came when Bob told him, "At this time of year, you're basically a cashier." Kevin said that triggered his determination to chart his own course after spending almost a year back at Merrifield. Kevin had a heart-to-heart talk with Bob, who was sitting in a recliner chair flipping TV channels as Kevin spoke. Kevin told his father that he appreciated the work at Merrifield but that he wanted to see what was out there in the world. "He was certainly respectful of whatever decision I would make," Kevin remembered. "But I think he owed it to himself to tell me the benefits of staying on at Merrifield. He's passionate and he means every word he's saying." Bob told his youngest son, "Merrifield is a great place to work and you can make a nice living here. You can work outside with plants and people. And you're a real people person."

In June 1990, a big door opened for Kevin when he got a job on

Capitol Hill working for Virginia's much-respected and powerful U.S. Senator John Warner of Virginia. Kevin started in Warner's office as a staff assistant. One night a week, he served as the Senator's aide-de-camp, chauffeuring the very distinguished, silver-maned senator, who was the sixth husband of Elizabeth Taylor, one of the most glamorous actresses in film history. "Assisting the senator once a week was a great opportunity," Kevin said. "We really bonded, and it gave me a chance to really get to know him. I'd go with him to receptions on Capitol Hill, dinners in downtown D.C. and TV appearances on shows such as "Larry King Live." I was only making $14,000 a year when I started, but for me it was an investment in my future. I thought it was the opportunity of a lifetime."

On Capitol Hill, Kevin was in a world far removed from the garden center. As an aide to the mighty Senator Warner, every day on "The Hill" was an opportunity to meet movers and shakers and see how the government really worked. "We were very proud of him," said Billie Jean. "He's always been real smart and had a gift for talking. He loved it. It was his kind of thing. He always wanted to do something in politics."

After working as a staff assistant for nine months, the deputy press secretary position became available. Kevin applied for and was given that job. This was the perfect fit for someone who had majored in political science with a minor in communications. In that role, he coordinated media interviews, wrote press releases and served as one of the senator's two spokespersons. Then two years later, at the age of 25, Kevin served as Senator Warner's acting press secretary for six months. "I felt really proud of myself," Kevin recalled. "I'm young and I'm working on the Hill, wearing a suit and tie and now making $30,000."

His access to the inner workings of politics was intimate, even visiting the West Wing of the White House during the Persian Gulf War as General Colin Powell, chairman of the Joint Chiefs of Staff, conferred with Warner, U.S. Senator Sam Nunn of Georgia and

Secretary of State James Baker III. On Capitol Hill, Kevin got an up-close view at how laws are crafted. He now looked to move from the business of making laws to possibly becoming a lawyer himself. Kevin applied to several law schools in Virginia and Washington, D.C. Although his grades were good and he now had great work experience, Kevin had a tough time scoring better than average on the Law School Aptitude Test (LSAT). So getting accepted into a top school in such a competitive environment was difficult. But with the help of a phone call from Senator Warner to the school president, Kevin was accepted into a one-month preparatory class at George Mason School of Law School in Arlington, Virginia, to see if he could gain admittance for the fall semester. He left Capitol Hill and enrolled in the class.

After finishing the course, Kevin married Chris Vaughan, a University of Virginia graduate who was also working on Senator Warner's staff as a legislative assistant, handling Energy and Environmental issues. Two weeks after they returned from their honeymoon on the Caribbean Island of St. Martin, Kevin received a letter from George Mason saying he was not one of the limited number of students from the class to be offered admission into their law program. "That was a hard letter to read," Kevin recalled. "I was so confident I would get in. I thought I did really well. After three years on Capitol Hill, I wanted more. I thought law school was the next step. I could always apply again next year. But I thought, 'I'm married now. This obviously wasn't meant to be.' So it was time to make another career decision."

Kevin talked to his father about returning to Merrifield. They discussed the job, the pay, the benefits, the challenges and the opportunities. Bob told Kevin that "this is a business where you work hard six days a week, but then you can also take time off when you need to." They agreed on a salary and Kevin returned full time to the family business. Kevin came back as a manager. That catch-all title is part of Bob's dislike for formal job titles. Everyone is expected to do their job plus whatever else needs doing at any time. So Kevin became a manager, focusing primarily on marketing, sales and special projects. A few months after they married, Chris also decided to leave Capitol Hill to join the family business, where she worked in the human resources department.

AS HE BEGAN HIS RISE IN THE BUSINESS WORLD, Bob came into contact with many bankers. As was the case with all of his business dealings, his mind soaked up those experiences for use at a later time.

In 1986, Riggs Bank purchased Guaranty Bank and Trust Company in Merrifield. Bob knew many of the board members of Guaranty Bank and Trust Company, including Dick Smith.

One day while he was shopping at Merrifield Garden Center, Dick mentioned to Bob that he missed having a local community bank in Merrifield.

"Why don't we just start our own bank?" Bob asked.

In the weeks to come, Bob and Dick continued talking about the possibility of a new bank as Dick met with potential investors. A decision was made to create a new bank and Bob was invited to serve on the board. Without hesitation, he accepted.

To the so-called experts, this was not a great time to start a bank, as the recession of the early 1990s wreaked havoc in the savings-and-loan business. But one of Bob's great strengths is seeing the potential in business opportunities, whether trying to turn an overgrown lot into a modern garden center or starting a bank at the bottom of the market aiming for future profits.

Owning a bank would be more than an investment. Becoming a banker would also be a remarkable achievement for a poor man's son from the back roads of Alabama.

So that's what Bob and other board members set out to do. In October 1990, they founded Horizon Bank of Virginia. "It was kind of neat," Bob says. "I thought it'd be fun to do." Horizon Bank was an investment, but also a remarkable achievement that reflected his personal reputation and exceptional record of successfully managing Merrifield Garden Center.

Ten years later, the bank was so profitable that Southern Financial Bank bought it. Bob was one of only three Horizon Bank board members to be asked to serve on the board of Southern Financial. At the time of the sale, Southern Financial Bank was worth $260 million and Horizon $140 million. Bob and the board of Southern Financial Bank grew that institution to a $1.5 billion bank.

History repeated itself in 2004 when Provident Bank bought Southern Financial. And keeping with the bank consolidation trend in the 1990s, M&T Bank out of Baltimore, Maryland, bought Provident.

In 2005, Bob and a different group of investors founded yet another bank, Virginia Heritage Bank. It came about when a mutual friend introduced Bob to Rich Buckner, who wanted to start a bank, and asked Bob if he would be interested in investing in it and serving as one of the founding board members. Bob was definitely interested and he and Rich set out to find other investors and board members. There was a lot of interest in the new bank and momentum grew. Rich eventually decided to step down as the chairman of the board but stayed on as an investor. They raised enough money to open their first branch in 2005.

When he believes in something, Bob actively promotes it to others. After Bob decided to invest in the new bank, he took every opportunity to tell others about it. Whether it was family, friends, customers, business associates or total strangers, Bob was a passionate ambassador for Virginia Heritage Bank. Even if people chose not to invest, Bob still wanted to get the word out.

"I remember years ago telling Bob that if he ever started another bank to let me know because I'd like to get in on the ground floor," said Doug Wallace, Merrifield Garden Center's insurance agent since 1984. "Then just about the time I got to a point in my life where I had some extra finances to invest with, Bob called me up one day and said, 'Doug, we're starting another bank. Do you want to invest in it?' I immediately drove over to the Fair Oaks location to meet him and gave him a check for $100,000."

A few years after the bank started, there was an opening on the board of directors. Bob nominated Doug, thinking he would be a perfect fit because he was a hard worker and a people person. The board agreed.

Bob became a member of the bank's committee that must review and decide on loan requests of $1 million or more. He's not one to focus entirely on numbers and data, but he's very good at using his natural instincts to make a judgment. "Bob is very unassuming, but you can tell very quickly that he knows how to get things done and he's very hands-on, which impressed me," said David P. Summers, CEO and chairman of the board of Virginia Heritage.

The growth of Virginia Heritage was remarkable, with $955 million in assets through June 30, 2014. The bank had six branches in Virginia: Tyson's Corner, Fairfax, Chantilly, Gainesville, Dulles Town Center and Arlington. On June 9, 2014, the Board of Directors of Virginia Heritage agreed to sell the bank to Bethesda-based Eagle Bancorp, Inc. for $182.9 million. "When we debated whether this was the right time, I think (Bob) was one of the most insightful people," David Summers said.

Selling the bank made for a nice return for Bob and the other investors.

While it may seem that everything Bob touches turns to gold, his success in banking shows that he knows how to build on past successes and trusting relationships. "Some people can do no wrong and some can do no right," Bob's son Larry said. "You would swear it wouldn't work, but it has always worked. People would line up to get it."

In his never-ending search for new opportunities, Bob realized the emerging medium of cable television could be an effective way to reach customers.

He decided to launch a television show to provide viewers with an opportunity to learn about gardening and landscaping. He also saw cable television as a way to draw customers to his stores, where they could see an enormous selection of beautiful plants and meet the experts they watched on the show.

CHAPTER ELEVEN

SHOWTIME

Over the years, hundreds of thousands of people have discovered Merrifield Garden Center by driving by the stores. And many others have found the wonders of Merrifield by watching the Saturday morning broadcasts of "Merrifield's Gardening Advisor" television show.

Merrifield's show was possible thanks to a series of events that began in 1962 when the Federal Communications Commission (FCC) began regulating the cable television industry. That coincided with the successful launch of Telstar, the first satellite that could receive and transmit television signals from different spots around the globe. Instead of relying on land-based transmissions from tall TV towers and home antennas, television programming was uploaded from an event on Earth to Telstar and bounced back to another place on Earth at the speed of light.

Real-time television went global in 1975 when "The Thrilla in Manila" championship boxing match between Muhammad Ali and Joe Frazier was shown live as a "pay-per-view" satellite event on the Home Box Office (HBO) cable channel. Cable subscribers were willing to pay money to see the event live while regular TV viewers had to wait a day to see a taped version. That boxing match proved that showing television on a cable network was financially viable, and soon the cable TV industry was expanding everywhere but did not arrive in all of Fairfax County until the early 1990s, according to the Fairfax County Development Authority.

This new technology was good business for Bob. The cable companies purchased truckload after truckload of sod, compost, topsoil and straw from Merrifield Garden Center to fix customers' yards after they dug them up to install the cable. What's more, the cable companies needed to rent space in industrial areas to park their trucks and equipment. Bob's investment group, which owned a sizable amount of industrial property in Merrifield, made a nice profit.

"When I got cable, I discovered Channel 8," Bob says. "It was a local news channel, which was rare at the time. It was right between the ABC and CBS affiliates on Channel 7 and 9, so it was easy to find. It's not like Channel 364 or something. I thought I would talk to the station about having a TV show."

In April 1990—less than a month after coming up with the idea—Merrifield had a live show called "The Gardening Advisor," with "Dr. John" Buckreis, the horticulturist who came to Merrifield Garden Center after years as a garden supply salesman and who doubled as Santa during the holidays. "I remember when I told him we were getting our own show," Bob says. "John jumped up in the air and clapped his heels together."

The show was designed to provide viewers with inspiring ideas, timely tips and expert advice about gardening, landscaping and decorating. There would be special guests and even viewer call-in questions.

On the first day when Dr. John arrived at the Media General studio near the Merrifield store to begin the show, the station's general manager asked to read the script. "I don't have a script," Dr. John replied.

The general manager explained, "We need to put it on the teleprompter. I can't do a show without a script. Do you think the newscasters memorize the news? Or the weathermen? No! They need a teleprompter!"

But Dr. John did the first rehearsal off the top of his head without a teleprompter. Eventually he attached a sheet of notes beneath the camera lens to help him remember the order of the show.

After about one and a half years, Allbritton Communications Company purchased the station and greatly expanded the show's reach beyond Fairfax County to the entire Washington, D.C., metropolitan area. The station became NewsChannel 8, a 24-hour local news channel. The time slot for "The Gardening Advisor" has changed over the years. Now it airs live from 8 a.m. to 9 a.m. on Saturdays. The station is now owned by Sinclair Broadcast Group.

Bob later told Dr. John that he wanted his daughter Debbie to be involved with the show, and Dr. John was glad to have the help. "Dad was the executive producer," Debbie recalled. "He helped our director determine the shots and the length of time to keep the camera on something. I did behind-the-scenes stuff, helped with calls, arranged the set, took notes on what was talked about."

The first half of the show was a presentation about a gardening topic and the second half was a question-and-answer period. There were also special guests, such as orchid growers, rosarians and beekeepers. Dr. John brought products and plants to the set so viewers could have visual cues.

To help viewers find success in their gardens, Dr. John took live phone calls. Want to know when to fertilize your lawn? How to prevent black spot in your rose bushes? How much to water your houseplants? Call in and ask Dr. John your question.

Initially, they were prepared to have friends call in with questions in case there were no viewer calls, but they didn't need them. On the first broadcast, Bob says "we actually got 47 calls."

Because it was a live show, Merrifield Garden Center went to great lengths to circumvent crank calls. Behind the scenes, Billie Jean, Doris and Debbie answered the phones and took the names and phone numbers of the people calling. That way, they could ring them back to make sure the calls were legitimate.

One time, a viewer called in and asked, "How do you grow a coconut?"

Merrifield Garden Center did not sell coconut trees because they are tropical plants that are not hardy in the Washington, D.C., area. But Dr. John was not flustered and responded, "I don't know, but watch next week and I'll have the answer. And if anyone knows, please call me!"

The key to taking viewer questions, he said, "is having fun and being honest."

Even the set was a Merrifield production, built by Bob's brother Carl and Bob's son Donny from Dr. John's design. Their names were included in the credits at the end of every show.

In 1998, Dr. John retired. His place on the show was taken by Merrifield Plant Specialists Peg Bier and David Yost. Bob moved Debbie from the control booth to center stage as the show's host. "I was nervous and excited!" she said. At the time, the show was renamed "Merrifield's Gardening Advisor." The set was upgraded with decorations created by Peg, giving the set a more attractive and modern look.

From time to time, Bob makes an appearance on the show. Like most of his projects, the TV show continues to thrive. It's been going strong now for 24 years, with just two or three missed episodes because of severe weather.

AS CONSTRUCTION OF THE FAIR OAKS GREENHOUSE and store continued, the nation was in a recession.

"Every time we open a new store it seems the economy is in a recession," said Larry, Bob's son. "When we were getting it ready, people told us, 'You really ought to be waiting.'"

Getting the company's second store up and running in bad economic times was certainly a challenge.

"It was hard," Larry recalled. "Money wasn't coming into the nursery, and people were getting laid off."

Other companies were laying off workers, too. "There just wasn't any work," Larry said. "Jobs just disappeared."

That was a result of what economists call a "jobless recovery." The conditions that caused the 1991 recession eased in most sectors of the U.S. economy, but cautious employers held off on hiring new workers. As a result, unemployment rose through June 1992. Every day, unemployed construction workers came to the Fair Oaks site looking for jobs. But Bob didn't want to add to his payroll during those difficult times, even if it meant the store site would take longer to build.

There were other pressures. His once-booming real estate investment group struggled to stay solvent as their holdings diminished in market value. To keep the Fair Oaks project going, Bob, his family and a few Merrifield employees handled the lion's share of the work, building roads, laying brick, digging ditches, putting down topsoil, constructing the buildings and installing the plumbing, electricity and water and sprinkler systems. Bob was concerned, but he knew the show must go on.

Even employee family members contributed. Carl's brother-in-law, Bob Beckwith, installed the boiler system in the greenhouse and the plumbing in the main store building. Peg's sons, Matthew and Mark Bier, were called to help. The Bier brothers, who went to school with Bob and Buddy's children, had their own construction business. Bob had called on them a few years back to help finish the loading dock at the original Merrifield store because Carl had broken his leg while working on the project.

The Warhursts' belief in hard work was seasoned whenever possible with lots of fun. So when the Fair Oaks greenhouse was being constructed, the family took advantage of the new concrete flooring to do a little country line dancing, which was the rage in those days.

Rob Capp said former Merrifield staffer Wayne Boyland was a competitive line dancer and taught everyone the dance moves. "None of us was very good," recalled Rob, Debbie's husband, "but we had fun."

Fair Oaks officially opened in December 1993, five years after Bob took some Christmas trees and decorations to the makeshift store across Lee Highway and envisioned a modern, prosperous store. Once again, Bob's instincts were right about opening the store despite the recession. No matter how bad the economy, shoppers seldom cut back on holiday spending. The glittering new store quickly became a success.

When Fair Oaks first opened, the cash registers, products and chemicals were housed in the greenhouse while the main store building was being built. The main store was much more detailed than the other buildings, so completion took longer. Bob and his can-do team built a wholesale building, warehouse and garage while they were finalizing the plans and collecting the permits for the main store. By 1995, the main store was finished and connected to the greenhouse by a breezeway with a brick floor laid down by Bob, his son Larry and his brothers Lee, Tracy and Carl.

The new store had some modern touches, such as a pneumatic air-pressure system that pushed plastic tubes from the wholesale building to the breezeway, much like the tubes used in drive-up bank systems, only instead of just cash and checks, these tubes delivered planting and delivery tickets and even small products, such as hand pruners.

"When construction was finished on the main store and we were about ready to open, I remember Dad coming home and saying we were going to have a party," Bob's son Kevin said. "And I thought, 'Great! We're going to have a party!' But Dad went on to clarify that we were going to have a painting party. So that night about 25 of us spent all evening at Fair Oaks painting the interior walls of the new store. Thanks for the invite."

Not long after the painting party and before the main store building opened, Bob hosted a wedding reception for Andy McVean and Sonia VandeGoor. Andy, who worked at the original Merrifield store, and Sonia were already officially married, but they were planning another wedding ceremony in Umbria, Italy, where Sonia's parents lived. Because none of Andy's local family and friends could fly to Italy for the ceremony, Bob threw the party for the newlyweds at the main store building, which was under construction and just a large, open room with walls, a ceiling and a floor. There was music and dancing for about 60 people who came to wish the new couple good luck.

BOB HAS ALWAYS HAD A FASCINATION FOR FAST and flashy cars. There were two cars that Bob always wanted: a 1957 Chevy and a Rolls Royce. Since he was a young man, Bob admired, but never owned, a '57 Chevy. For a man who loved to drive, was there any car more fabulous than a classic '57 Chevy? Yes, a mint-condition, fully restored, baby blue, '57 Chevy convertible. He bought his dream car in 1987.

Bob and his Chevy—with the custom license plate BILLI JN to honor his wife—were even featured in a local newspaper with a photo. Bob proudly told the newspaper, "This car is my baby. I do everything but burp it." The only modification to the car was changing the old "three on the tree" manual gear shift that was mounted on the steering column to a clutchless automatic that made the blue beauty easier to drive.

To this day, Bob likes to take it out for a Sunday drive or after work on a warm summer evening with the top down and the radio playing rock-and-roll, just like in the "Happy Days" era. It reminds him of simpler times.

In 1991, Bob bought a used, black Rolls Royce. It was five years old and Bob thought it was one of the nicest cars he had ever seen. A Rolls Royce is a very expensive, handmade car with a shiny, distinctive front grille topped with a small statue of a woman with a flowing cape. Even when stopped, the car appeared to be moving. The little statue comes with a story. Known as either the "Flying Lady" or the "Spirit of Ecstasy," the statue was believed to represent the secret love of auto pioneer Lord Montagu. They could not marry because she was of a lower class in status-conscious England.

Bob's rise to riches and the fabulous Rolls Royce are a wonderful American counterpoint to the sad "Flying Lady" story. Bob says he was the recipient of lots of looks, waves and thumbs up as he drove the car. "It was fun to drive and fun to get attention," he says. Once, at the stop light in front of the Fair Oaks store, a woman rolled down her window and asked Bob, "Is that a Rolls Royce?" When Bob answered, "Yes!" she turned to her child and said, "That's the most expensive car you'll ever see in your lifetime!"

But Bob's eyes later landed on another luxury car. "One day I drove a Mercedes," he says. "It was a more wonderful ride than the Rolls Royce. It's lighter and more agile. It was more responsive and easier to drive. Rolls Royces are so heavy. You're not even supposed to park them on the same spot every day on the asphalt."

So Bob bought a brand-new, black Mercedes-Benz S500. Bob now had what he lacked as a young boy growing up in a poor family where work was a necessary part of daily life and feeding the family was more important than having a toy box filled with play cars and trucks. Now he had real horses, fancy cars, trucks, motorcycles, an airplane, a helicopter and even a fire truck and two ambulances to help fill a void he felt as a child. "It's because he didn't have toys when he was young," said Lynn Warhurst, Bob's daughter-in-law and the company controller. "So now he buys real ones. He always tells me that."

BOB LIKES TO KNOW HOW OTHER BUSINESSES WORK. He doesn't like book learning, but he's naturally curious and learns by doing, talking to others and watching.

When he heard about an opportunity to attend a gardening trade show and visit nurseries in England, Bob didn't hesitate, even though he had never been overseas. In September 1996, Bob, Billie Jean, their sons Rob and Kevin, and seven Merrifield managers flew across the Atlantic to England, the world leader in gardening.

The trip was organized by Garden Centers of America and the tour guide was Englishman Ian Baldwin, a well-respected garden center consultant. Buddy and Doris's youngest daughter, Kim, represented the Williamses. Buddy and Doris stayed home because Doris doesn't like to fly.

The three-day show, known as the Garden and Leisure Exhibition (Glee), is the United Kingdom's top garden trade show and was bigger than any show the Merrifield Garden Center delegation had ever seen. "It was MANTS on steroids," Kevin recalled. "They say that's where all the big gardening trends start." MANTS is the Mid-Atlantic Nursery Trade Show, a popular East Coast show for the nursery and landscaping industry that draws thousands of people every year, including dozens of Merrifield employees.

Glee was held in the industrial city of Birmingham. The Merrifield group was surprised to find their hotel was in a red-light district. "It was a wonderful show, but I couldn't sleep very well," Peg joked. "We bought a lot of neat things. They had gorgeous statuary, containers and pots. It was difficult, though, to put together a sea container and ship it back over here." Bob still talks about the metal patio furniture they purchased at the show. "It was very well made," he says. "We've never been able to find anything like it again. It was the best furniture we've ever had."

After the show, the group visited the famous Kew Gardens with acre after acre of spectacular gardens to delight the eye. They also visited about a dozen retail garden centers, where they took away some important new ideas while also realizing that they were doing most things right. "We were pretty forward thinking," Peg said. "The trip reinforced some things we were already doing. Sometimes to learn you are doing something right is as important as learning something new."

The group toured many garden centers that billed themselves as destinations instead of simply garden centers. In addition to their remarkable plants, they offered tasty cafes, adorable petting farms and other fun activities. But as the return flight loomed, a glitch was discovered. Their return tickets were for Friday the 13th! Bob is superstitious and would not fly on that day. That turned out to be lucky for everyone. They spent three extra days in England. Bob rented a bus and driver and the Merrifield delegation visited popular tourist destinations such as Canterbury, Westminster Abbey, St. Paul's Cathedral, Buckingham Palace, Brighton beach, the White Cliffs of Dover and Big Ben, the famous clock tower in London. They flew back on Monday, full of ideas and inspiration to make Merrifield Garden Center an even better destination garden center.

IT'S ABOUT 635 MILES AS THE CROW FLIES from rustic Russellville, Alabama, to the Washington D.C., suburb of Fairfax, Virginia. But a popular farm animal provides an interesting connection between Bob and the Hope Park estate he was destined to one day own.

In 1950 when Bob was but 12, he was called on to butcher a hog to help feed his family. Eighty-eight years earlier in 1862 and states apart, another child and pig were part of what would become yet another interesting part of the Warhurst family history.

During the Civil War, a Union patrol stopped at Hope Park and confiscated what they could, including a pig owned and treated as a pet by Nettie Barnes, the 10-year-old daughter of Jack and Mary Barnes. According to Barnes' family lore, Nettie was so distraught at the loss of her beloved pig that her mother told one of the family's slaves to take Nettie to the Union camp to demand its return. Sentries intercepted them and took Nettie and the slave to their commander, who listened to little Nettie sob about her pig and what it meant to her.

The commander asked Nettie if she could identify the soldier who had taken her pig. She confidently said she could point out the scoundrel. He ordered the troops to assemble in front of Nettie and she quickly pointed to the thief. The soldier was forced to return the pet pig and carried it back to Hope Park with a happy Nettie and the slave following behind him.

One hundred and thirty-five years later in 1997, Bob Warhurst was looking for a place to build his dream house in that same Fairfax County area—Hope Park—where Nettie saved her pig. He had been looking for the perfect place for more than 20 years. "I knew what I wanted, but I never could find it," Bob says.

Then one day Bob and his son Larry delivered a pallet of stone to a house in Fairfax County.

"Who owns the place at the fork in the road where the grass is cut so neat?" Bob asked.

"My father-in-law," replied Kathy Phillipson, who had ordered the stone.

Bob told her of his search for a place to build his dream home.

"Give me your number," she said. "He's 83. We're trying to get him to move in with his youngest daughter. It might be for sale."

Two weeks later, Bob received a call about the place. He had forgotten about it because they were in the midst of the busy spring season at the nursery. Bob took his daughter Debbie with him to see the place because wife Billie Jean was away on her annual vacation with her two sisters.

"I fell in love with it," Bob recalls. "It was very close to work, but it felt like living in the country."

The owner's name was Lloyd Flint, who agreed to sell the property to Bob for $250,000.

Bob went home thinking, "Usually if I want something, everyone wants it. I didn't want everyone to start bidding. I had my attorney make up a contract." Bob's brother Lee took the contract to the owner to sign. "It was a nice feeling knowing we owned it," Bob recalls.

When Bob told Billie Jean that he bought the land for their dream house, her first thought was, "Can we afford it?"

Bob assured her that they could.

The deal was closed on August 27, 1997. Kathy Phillipson gave Bob a book about Hope Park called "Hope Park and the Hope Park Mill" that detailed the history of the property since before the birth of the nation.

What Bob now owned was a very important part of Virginia and U.S. history. Hope Park was a section of the original 1,200-acre plantation founded in the mid-1700s by Edward Payne, who was elected to the vestry of Truro Parish, an Anglican church organization that governed the Hope Park area in colonial Virginia, with some of the major founders of the United States: George Washington and George Mason. President Washington and wife Martha stayed with Edward and wife Ann Payne at Hope Park from time to time.

In 1785, the Paynes moved to Kentucky, but the Washingtons kept visiting Hope Park because of a connection to its new owner, Dr. David Stuart. The doctor married Eleanor (Nelly) Calvert Custis, the widow of John Parke Custis. John was Martha Washington's son from her first marriage.

"We're so lucky to have this land," Bob says. "You can look down the road and imagine George Washington coming up on his horse."

The Hope Park Mill and Miller's House are on both the Virginia Landmarks Register and the National Register of Historic Places.

THE WARHURST FAMILY NEVER SEEMS TO SIT STILL. There's always something new to discover. That's what led Bob, Billie Jean and Debbie to take the Metro train, the rapid transit system serving Washington, D.C., and the suburbs of Virginia and Maryland, for the first time on Saturday night, January 31, 1998 to the new MCI Center—now named the Verizon Center—in Washington, D.C.'s trendy Penn Quarter neighborhood near Chinatown.

Built above the Metro's Gallery Place/Chinatown station, the building had been open for just a month, but it promised to bring new sports excitement as the home of the NBA's Washington Wizards, the NHL's Washington Capitals and the famed Georgetown Hoyas of the NCAA, as well as the biggest names in entertainment. Bob was curious to see how it all worked.

The Warhursts were going there to see Yanni, the long-haired global performer and composer. The day after the concert, Bob wasn't feeling too chipper, but he decided not to call the doctor because he had an upcoming doctor's appointment.

"I woke up at two in the morning and felt like I had a 50-pound bag of topsoil on my chest," he remembers. "I stumbled to the bathroom and fell down on my way back to bed."

Bob suffered a major heart attack. Billie Jean called for an ambulance. Bob being Bob, when the ambulance arrived, he walked out and greeted the rescue workers. Then Billie Jean put in a frantic call to Debbie, who called her four brothers before speeding over to Fairfax Hospital. It was terrifying moment for Bob's children. For the first time, their father seemed mortal.

"It was shocking," Rob said. "He was white as a ghost."

Three years earlier, Bob's oldest brother Charles had died at the age of 69 while undergoing chemotherapy treatments. The Warhursts were fearful it would be Bob's turn next. After a lifetime of hard work, Bob was now living a full and happy life in Virginia that seemed light years from his humble beginnings in Russellville, Alabama. But he was no longer a young man after the effort and fortitude it took to found and build Merrifield Garden Center into a Washington institution. Dr. Joseph Kiernan found that the main artery to Bob's heart was totally blocked. He put in a stent to allow blood to flow again. The procedure went well, but Bob's heart was partially damaged before the cardiologist could reach the blockage.

At the hospital, Bob did what he always does. He promoted Merrifield Garden Center. He kept telling all the doctors and nurses to be sure to shop at Merrifield. He gave them his business card and wrote a note on the back saying they were to get a discount on plants.

"A few weeks later, he was digging a ditch," Rob said. "You just can't stop him."

There was a time before Bob's heart attack that he didn't have much energy. "I got tired and I didn't know why," he said. "I thought it was because I was getting older. I would stay home on Sundays and lie in bed all day. I called it, 'Let my body catch up day.'"

Rob recalled "it was so odd to see him lying around." What Bob didn't realize was that he had a blockage. Finding the cause was easy: too much stress and too much food laden with fatty calories.

"The problem was eating sausage and bacon and lard all those years and loving it," Bob says. "We eat too much bad food. I definitely changed for a while. But I went back to biscuits and gravy, hamburgers and grilled cheese sandwiches."

Now he tries to balance his old ways with new, but bland dishes.

"You can't hardly beat egg whites," Bob says.

Changing his diet wasn't easy for Bob because of his childhood history. Food was about survival, not just flavor. Animals were not raised as pets but as a food source.

The heart attack was a warning that his relentless pursuit of building Merrifield Garden Center was taking its toll. He was afraid he might not see his new home.

As he recovered, Bob started working in earnest to make his dream house a reality. He wanted something big and grand to treat his wife, children and grandchildren. What he was after was a show house—a place that made a statement and was comfortable and special for the family. After visiting several custom homes and looking at dozens of books and magazines for ideas, Bob found a magnificent design that captured his imagination.

Bob worked with an architect to modify that design to reflect both the historic nature of the area and to allow the family to finally have a place where everyone could gather in good times and sad times, holidays and holy days, graduations, showers, swim parties and Super Bowl Sundays.

Digging for the home's foundation started on July 15, 1998. Bob's next big project had begun.

CHAPTER TWELVE

GEORGE WASHINGTON WAS HERE

Owning property and a nice house have always been priorities for the Warhurst family, even in the days when Bob's father sold nearly all of their 15 cows and a few goats to buy a $60, one-acre parcel of land at the corner of Marlin Street and Harrison Avenue in Russellville, Alabama. After Bob moved to Northern Virginia and met Billie Jean, fell in love and got married, he and his young bride lived in a crowded apartment and rented an old home before eventually buying a three-bedroom, one-bath house on Byrd Road in suburban Vienna, Virginia. Bob, Billie Jean and their five kids lived there for 27 years while Bob built his gardening empire. Through the years, they added several rooms and bathrooms. Bob wanted to leave their Vienna home earlier and certainly had the means to own a larger and more contemporary home, but Bob says, "The kids wouldn't hear of it, so we gave up on that idea."

But in 1997, when the opportunity came to buy land and build a home at Hope Park, where George Washington used to visit, Bob did not hesitate. A home built on that land had to be as magnificent as its history, a representation of the ideas of America and the belief that anyone with courage, strength and determination could make such a home for himself and his family. While reading about the history of the estate, Bob learned that it was called "Hope Parke" with an "e" in an 1815 real estate advertisement. So he decided to rename the estate "Hope Parke" to honor its heritage.

Bob's Hope Parke home meets his goal and goes far beyond the wildest dreams of not only the Founding Fathers but even 21st century builders. Although Bob, his sons Larry and Donny, his brother Carl and a few Merrifield Garden Center employees helped build the impressive home, the main contractors were once again the Bier brothers. "Mark and Matt are like machines," Bob says. "They are so talented and work 10- to 12-hour days, six days a week. Their craftsmanship and attention to detail are second to none."

Built on 7.5 acres of land, the home has 23,500 square feet of finished interior space, more than the surface of two Olympic-size swimming pools, and includes nine bedrooms, 15 bathrooms (including two in the pool house) and a movie room with a 136-inch projection television set and 15 home theater, leather recliner seats, plus smaller TVs scattered throughout the house. Master Plumber Bob Beckwith installed an amazing, on-demand hot water system with more than 10,000 feet of large-width, all-copper pipe and a pump connected to a large volume water heater. The water is constantly heated by a sophisticated manifold system that Beckwith says looks like the systems used in ships. The hot-water pipes are connected to every faucet in the huge house, drawing hot water almost instantly. There is virtually no wait, because all faucets are only three feet from the nearest hot water pipe.

The house also includes a gym and a game room with pinball machines, video games, a ping pong table, a pool table, miniature basketball and more. Bob considered building a bowling alley in the basement, but it would have been beneath his bedroom. Counting bowling pins wouldn't be as restful as counting sheep. "You know, maybe I better not do that," he thought. "It works out just fine as an exercise room." The house has central geothermal heating and cooling, which is supplied by fluid piped from 14 outside water wells that are 225-feet deep. It has a natural gas backup system and an 80-kilowatt natural gas generator to provide electricity when severe weather interrupts regular service. Outside are a swimming pool, a jacuzzi, a pool house with a kitchen, a basketball court and a tennis court.

The house is so enormous that it has an elevator and six fireplaces. Billie Jean's state-of-the-art kitchen is bigger than many restaurant kitchens, and her large dining room can seat 30 hungry people. On top of the home's chimney, Bob inscribed the names of Billie Jean and daughter Debbie into the mortar work, just as he used to do every time he finished a chimney as a young bricklayer.

Bob built a heated, five-car garage to store his 1957 Chevy, a Model T, a Maserati, a Chevrolet Corvette, four motorcycles, Billie Jean's Chevy Suburban, a few Segways and two golf carts that Bob uses to drive around the estate and visit sons Larry and Donny, who live within shouting distance, and neighbors.

Even with the enormous garage, Bob prefers to park his big Ford F-250 pickup truck outside. The garage has 10-foot-wide doors and an indoor washing bay. Northern Virginia can have hard winters, so the front steps, walkways and parking areas are heated to melt snow and ice.

When he admires the home, Bob says "I think of working hard and making the right decisions. You have to have a positive outlook and you have to believe in yourself. Nothing is impossible. You can take on anything." Bob is proud of his success in business and family life but hesitant to examine the impact of what he has accomplished. "I didn't dwell on the fact that I was poor," he says. "It was a part of my life I came through." The beautiful home at Hope Parke is the physical manifestation of his achievements. His generosity in sharing the place with so many people is at the core of Bob's personality. Having his children, grandchildren and friends close by—at home and work—is perhaps his greatest personal accomplishment. From that perspective, Bob and Billie Jean have it all.

Bob and Billie Jean moved into their dream home on November 15, 2000. Not long after, they threw a housewarming party for about 150 guests. The visitors were astonished at the size of the house and the wonderful way all the rooms were decorated by Billie Jean and Merrifield Designer Joyce (Eisenman) Watkins.

Less than two months later on their first New Year's Eve at the new house, Bob and Billie Jean's kids—Debbie, Rob, Larry, Donny and Kevin—and their families slept over. On the second floor, there are bedrooms for each of them painted in green, purple, yellow, pink and safari colors.

For Bob, the best part of having such a magnificent home is that he can always have family and friends around him, sharing laughs and meals and sporting events on the big-screen television set.

"He will call me up sometimes and say, 'You want to come over for dinner?'" Donny said. "I'll say, 'Sure, what are we having?' And he'll say, 'I don't know. We'll work it out. I'll pick something up.'

"When I get there, I'll see these people that I've never seen before and found out he has just met them at a car show, at the airport or anywhere, just random people and they struck up a conversation and now they're in his house for dinner."

Bob's not one for formal education, but he does like stimulating conversation and learning from people who have interesting experiences and occupations. His mind is like a sponge, soaking up knowledge. He has a knack for getting people to talk about themselves.

Gail Crocker is a longtime customer who became a friend. "They are just an incredible family," she said. "The home is beautiful and beautifully decorated. And the garden is truly magnificent. Everything about it is very regal, but very warm and loving. They make you feel at home."

Bob and Billie Jean's children all live within five miles of their big house. In good times and bad, the Warhursts are rarely more than 15 minutes apart. "Bob cherishes his family," Bob's youngest brother Carl said. "Bob always says he built the house for his kids and grandkids. He says, 'I don't need this big house just for us.'"

Bob's sister Margene will never forget the time her brother invited her to visit. "I had been in the hospital and had gained weight," she said. "I didn't want to come. But he said, 'Bring your heart.' I called him back the next day and I came." On the pantry door, there is a calendar for family members to reserve the mansion for team parties, bridal showers, Christmas parties, birthday parties and graduation celebrations. "I love going there!" said Danny Capp, Debbie's son. "It sounds a little braggy, but I've always loved taking my girlfriends and friends there, just to see the look of awe on their faces."

That's exactly what Bob and Billie Jean were hoping for.

"It's so wonderful that they love coming over," Billie Jean said. "It's not like, 'Oh, I have to go to Grandma and Grandpa's house.'"

Billie Jean says she knows of some children who don't want to visit their grandparents because they're not allowed to touch anything or they're afraid of getting the house dirty.

"I'm never going to be like that," Billie Jean said. "They can tear it up as long as they don't get hurt. They can play or run or dance or whatever they want to do."

Hope Parke isn't just for the Warhurst family to enjoy. Bob has opened the extensive property for many Fourth of July, New Year's Eve and company parties for hundreds of employees, neighbors and friends.

It is a spectacle that can't be topped.

Hope Parke glistens at Christmas with a 15-foot Fraser Fir tree, a sparkling constellation of 5,600 lights and thousands of ornaments, in the cavernous living room. Debbie's husband, Rob Capp, spends four days decorating the tree, which he has done every year since he met Debbie. Karen Velehoski, a Merrifield plant and design specialist, and Roseanne Blaine, a Merrifield designer, are responsible for decorating the rest of the house. Their team gives the mansion's main floor and lower level a holiday makeover with Billie Jean's treasured Christmas decorations that she has collected over many holiday seasons, telling a family history of joyful times together. Karen, whose cheerfulness and enthusiasm are boundless, also takes care of Bob's beloved vegetable garden and his landscaping, including the creation of dozens of colorful container gardens that grace Hope Parke's front porch, veranda and pool area.

Events at Hope Parke usually include a scrumptious spread of pork barbecue with lip-smacking sauces, sizzling hot dogs blackened on the grill and slathered with all the fixings. Of course, there are hamburgers being flipped and several wash tubs filled with soft drinks and bottled and canned beer.

When he throws a party, Bob provides the main meal and all the drinks, but he likes his guests to bring a side dish or dessert to share.

"That's the way to eat," he says. "It's fun when you get a wide selection to choose from and everyone gets to try everyone else's dishes."

At the annual company picnic, Bob combines traditional American fare with cuisine from the countries of his Spanish-speaking employees. There's lots of crossover eating with hamburgers sharing space on a plate with pupusas. Under the big shade trees, workers who ride together in the big red Merrifield trucks get a chance to know each other as friends, as well as co-workers, with a Mexican cerveza (beer) or good ol' Bud Light.

There are pony rides, a moon bounce, a giant inflatable slide, a climbing wall, horse-drawn hayrides, a zip line and swimming in the beautiful blue pool while the DJ spins tunes from pop to rock to R&B with a big helping of Bob's favorite country tunes. Karaoke is also popular, and there are lots of singers, including Billie Jean and Debbie, entertaining the crowd and making the most of their opportunity to get up on the stage and shine.

"All his parties include kids," Matt Bier said. "That's kind of a Deep South thing. All the fun includes the kids. The fun starts early, finishes late and everybody is at the party."

Family, friends and employees love the whole scene, with Bob holding court and Billie Jean making sure all the the guests are having the best time of their lives, until the next event rolls around.

If George Washington was alive today, he would probably be part of the gathering.

"It'll be sad when we're gone and they sell the house," Bob says. "But that's part of life."

Having access to a garden has always been a must for Bob. Growing up in Alabama, Bob always seemed to have his hands in the ground. When he wasn't working at Miss Hendrix's store or helping J.C. Steinecipher cut pipe, he was wrist-deep in the family garden. Bob loved growing vegetables and watching them move from the garden to the big dinner table, where there was always thanks for God's bounty.

When the family bought the house on Byrd Road, there was barely room for all the kids and none for a garden. Bob looked around and found a small plot next to a church just off Gallows Road, about a mile from Merrifield Garden Center. Bob convinced the landowner to let him put in a garden in exchange for tidying up the grounds. Bob filled the space with corn, bush beans, pole beans, squash, peas and other vegetables to feed his family. After a few years, Bob was ready to expand his garden. He and Buddy rented a two-acre piece of land across the street from the Williamses's house in Vienna to grow their vegetables. And when Bob built his dream house at Hope Parke, he created a large garden at his friend and neighbor Maurice Katoen's home.

One of Bob's greatest pleasures is teaching customers how to grow vegetable gardens. As he speaks to them about the steps that must be taken to properly prepare the soil and plant the seeds, he is reminded of his own education in the family garden in Alabama.

Fresh eggs are a farm delight, and Bob brought some of that rural tradition to Hope Parke when he acquired some chickens. Always thinking, Bob created a mobile chicken cage with wheels so he could move the chickens around his large property and they could always eat fresh grass. He even built a small house on one end of the cage so the birds could take shelter from the elements. After work, he would let them out to roam free-range for a while in the evening, then put them back in their chicken-mobile for the night.

One night, Bob became distracted when there was a birthday party at Hope Parke. When he went to put the chickens back in their coop, he didn't notice that two birds had wandered off behind the historic house where George Washington used to stay. The next morning, he found nothing but feathers. "I felt really bad," Bob says. "I thought a lot of those chickens."

After six months, Bob took the remaining chickens to his third store in Gainesville, Virginia, where he kept them in a large pen near other animals, such as goats, turkeys and guinea hens. Children loved seeing the farm animals, but the land wasn't zoned for that use so the animals were taken to an area farm.

WHEN THE FAIR OAKS STORE OPENED for business back in 1993, the back of the property was relatively undeveloped. While others worked on the retail side, Bob devoted himself to expanding the store. "It was very important to him that it was done right," said Manager Peter Hogarth, who joined the Merrifield Garden Center team in 1997 after working at three other garden centers and family-owned Hogarth Nursery and Landscape in Jarrettsville, Maryland, where he grew up. "The Merrifield Way is to provide the best."

Bob was always available for consultation, but he counted on his well-trained sales staff to assist customers while he spent most of his time making sure the Fair Oaks expansion was innovative and exciting for customers and at the same time making a profit for the company. One way Bob did that was by adding two shade structures in the courtyard that became the annual and perennial houses in 2000. These structures, made by Cravo in Canada, had retractable roofs, a unique design in the retail environment.

"Retractable roofs have always been a dream of mine," Bob says. "I had been talking to greenhouse suppliers for years looking for this type of roof. I was thrilled when I found out that it was available."

Retractable roofs were usually used by suppliers to grow their plants before they were delivered to retail outlets. Bob saw that retractable roofs would also be a big plus for retail customers, who could keep shopping during inclement weather. When the weather changed, the roofs could be opened and closed in just a few minutes. "To be able to push a button and they closed up?" Merrifield Plant and Design Specialist Peg Bier said. "You better believe it was a big deal."

The retractable roof was particularly helpful with annuals, plants that aren't as hardy as perennials and are susceptible to damage in early spring when the weather can have frequent and dramatic temperature fluctuations. Bob also had a hand in many other innovations that were created at Fair Oaks, such as pricing products in an onsite warehouse instead of on the sales floor.

By this time, the crippling recession was over. It was now happy times. The country, the economy and Merrifield Garden Center were booming, and the sheer quantity of products was so enormous that it was overtaking the store and the salespeople. With the new system, the salespeople could spend their time assisting customers instead of getting bogged down in the time-consuming process of pricing each product.

Other changes included the creation of plant holding areas. During busy spring weekends, the staff couldn't fit enough plants into the shopping area, so they created close-in areas that allowed them to store extra plants to meet customer demand.

After much study and consultation, Bob determined that Merrifield could save money if the company used its own employees and trucks to pick up some popular products, such as compost, ice melt, gravel and sand, from suppliers, thereby avoiding expensive delivery charges. The company's fleet of big red trucks is a common sight for drivers on the crowded Washington, D.C., area highways, so the trucks themselves also serve as mobile advertisements for the company, another way Bob stretches every dollar.

Merrifield also branched out into making products themselves that had previously been previously purchased from suppliers. Topsoil is a great example of Bob's large-scale, do-it-yourself policy. The company was buying so much of it that Bob decided to purchase not only a screening machine that would sift the soil but also wheel loaders to move the soil to a canopied holding bin so it wouldn't get wet.

Wet dirt may not be a problem if you are making mud pies, but wet topsoil gets lumpy and can't be sold. Employees were trained in the art of making topsoil. "We sell so much topsoil this equipment paid for itself in no time," Peter Hogarth said.

It is Bob's nature, maybe even part of his DNA, to want to improve the world around him so that it is more beautiful and organized. Some people were born to create masterpieces and others to paint walls. Bob is one of the few who can do both. He is also a lifelong learner who knows how to listen to good advice and learn from the experts in other endeavors. That includes how to run a successful business.

Bob's first exposure to business management was at the Hendrix Grocery Store in Russellville, Alabama, where Miss Annie Mae Hendrix gave him lessons in how to communicate effectively with customers. Bob could see that a person who could please customers while also making a profit would always be successful. His journey from Miss Annie Mae's little country store to the bustling suburbs of Washington, D.C., and his trash hauling business led to The Tradin' Post's success in turning other people's trash into cash in his own pocket.

That success led to the first Merrifield Garden Center and the need to organize his business in a more formal way. The Warhurst and Williams families needed to develop a business plan and work with banks, as well as effectively handle all the other demands of managing money and manpower. And Bob did it all with just an eighth-grade education. While other would-be managers had their noses stuck in management books, Bob created a thriving business and personal financial success by sticking to the old-fashioned values of hard work, honesty and knowing the value of both money and time.

Bob doesn't have a favorite business leader but says "I admire anyone who works hard to better themselves to be successful." His relaxed management style is all about making sure that every employee knows how to treat customers with respect and patience, taking the time not just to sell a product, but to give knowledge to customers so they receive value for the time and money they spend at a Merrifield store and want to come back time and time again.

"Bob's committed to serving the customer," Peter Hogarth said. "He never sways from it. His five most important things for an employee to do are customer service, customer service, customer service, customer service and when you're not with a customer you're a worker."

A Merrifield Garden Center worker does whatever is needed at the time. Chores could range from sweeping the floors and answering the phone to stocking the shelves and watering the plants. Even managers—especially managers—should never be idle. Bob is not a fan of company meetings or year-end employee performance reviews. He prefers to communicate with his employees one-to-one or in small groups, reminding them that customers are always top priority and that there is no substitute for quality. Because his company earns most of its money outdoors selling plants, products and services, Bob doesn't want to waste precious work time talking in a conference room. He will typically meet with his managers only when it's raining or snowing.

Bob has his own, more casual way of brainstorming in which he solicits opinions and builds consensus. Howard Saunders, a longtime Merrifield manager, describes the process as "asking everybody what they think, from someone on the loading dock to top-level management." Bob's not above asking neighbors, friends and customers for their opinions. After all, they are the people who keep the business thriving. "It takes time, but the sense of belonging is important to us," Peter Hogarth said.

Bob is constantly working because work is not a bad thing in his world. Work is his world. And his business beliefs are clear:
- Hire good people and teach them how to work hard and take care of customers.
- Get the most out of your people every day. You don't have to work them to death, but when they go home at night, they should be tired and have the satisfaction of knowing they did their best that day and did an honest day's work.
- Treat people the way you want to be treated.
- Be very thrifty with your money. Pinch and save where you can. Try to fix things instead of buying new things.
- Maintain excellent credit and always pay your bills on time.
- Never lose sight of the big picture. Look for the things that matter, such as having enough cash registers open so customers don't have to stand in long lines.
- Be honest. If someone is doing a great job, praise them. If someone is not doing their best, tell them how to improve.
- Never speak negatively about the company, our competitors or your fellow workers. It's not professional and reflects badly on you and our company.
- Teach people how to do different jobs. If we need help in a different area, they'll be able to jump in and do that job, too.
- Everyone is a salesperson, no matter what his or her job is.

Bob says there are many smart people in the world, but a lot of them don't know how to work. "If someone is going to work for me, they need to work hard," Bob says. "It's my job to teach them how to be a good worker. No job should be beneath you. Toilets need to be cleaned, streets need to be swept and holes need to be dug. Once they learn how to work, that's something that will serve them well for the rest of their lives."

While he was growing up, Bob's son Donny heard some employees grumble about his father. "It was because he was driven," Donny said. "'Work hard. Work hard.' As you get older and more mature, you saw that those were lessons about the importance of hard work and doing whatever is necessary to get the job done. So now, even if you're in a position of power, you're still gonna jump in and do whatever needs to be done, even if it's some nasty job. I do that all the time and other workers will say, 'Wow, I never thought he would do that.' And it's because of what he taught you to do, to make it work. Once you think you're beyond that, I think that's when it all collapses because nobody has any respect for you."

When learning how to do a job, Bob believes that experience is the best teacher. He would rather tell someone how to do a job, or better yet, show them how to do a job, and then let them do it instead of using training manuals or tutorials to teach them. Being hands-on is Bob's trademark.

Bob is a big believer in strong personal relationships in everything he does. Much of this is because he was born and raised in the South but also because he knows that bonds of friendship and trust are the glue of business. Bringing business friends into the Merrifield family has been a success for all. Bob and his company have had the same building contractors, Mark and Matt Bier, for 36 years; the same accountant, Roy Alexander, for 33 years; the same Fairfax County land use attorney, Frank McDermott, for 32 years; and the same insurance agent, Doug Wallace, for 30 years. These and many other long-lasting relationships are remarkable in any type of business. Bob's advice to Doug early on in their business relationship—the importance of "face time with your clients"—helped him become more successful in his career.

"I was just starting out in the insurance business and I came to call on Bob to see if I could write Merrifield Garden Center's insurance," Doug said. "Now generally speaking, insurance people aren't business people's favorite people. Rather than something to help them make money, insurance is just something you have to have. So after I would write a policy, I would generally go away for a while. Well, I stopped back in the garden center a few weeks later and saw Bob. He said, 'Where have you been? When we do business with someone, we expect them to come by and say hi and make sure everything is okay—a lot.'"

In 1996, Bob was proactive when reductions in both state and county budgets led to the elimination of the Virginia Cooperative Extension horticulture programs in Fairfax County. Even though Fairfax County is a booming suburban center, it is home to many recreational gardeners who rely on the county extension programs for advice.

When Kevin heard about the budget cuts, he called David Yost, an extension agent who was about to lose his job, to see if there was anything Merrifield Garden Center could do to help. David met with Bob and Kevin that summer and he told them his greatest concern was the future of the Master Gardener program, a volunteer development program established in 1976 with more than 120 members who were now without a home. "Bob immediately offered use of the meeting room at Fair Oaks for training classes and asked if there was anything else he could do," David recalled.

David told Bob and Kevin about the Master Gardeners Plant Diagnostic Lab and Bob said he would make some room for the lab in Merrifield's wholesale building. "We think they play an important role," Bob said.

David presented Bob's offer to the Master Gardeners Advisory Board and he said they unanimously and gratefully accepted. "Bob is like Santa Claus and the Easter Bunny wrapped into one," said Senior Extension Agent Adria Bordas. "He treats us really good."

Bob always has an eye open for talented workers and offered David a job that would include continuing coordination of the Master Gardener program. David joined the Merrifield Garden Center team in September 1996.

"I was excited about the opportunity to continue with my extension work, diagnosing plant problems, teaching seminars and the challenge of doing a TV show," David said. "Since that time, everything has worked out better than expected and 18-plus years later, I'm still here."

The Master Gardener program is one of many ways Bob has tried to support the community and the gardening industry. In 2000, Bob was honored by the Northern Virginia Nursery and Landscape Association as the recipient of the annual Byron E. Wates Award, which recognizes outstanding contributors to the association and the industry at large. Kevin went on to win the award in 2006.

OF THE EIGHT CHILDREN BORN TO CLAUDE AND MARY Warhurst, Bob and Lee were the most alike. Lee was the instigator of bringing family members to Virginia after he finished his stint in the U.S. Army at the end of World War II.

Lee was part of the post-war boom that saw Washington, D.C., and Northern Virginia become a magnet for employees seeking work in the fast-growing federal government. Those workers needed both housing and office buildings, so Lee decided a good bricklayer could make a lot of money. He started his own bricklaying business in 1949, and it was so profitable that he convinced his brothers Charles, Jim, Bob and Tracy to leave their home in Alabama and come out and work for him. Their father, Claude, later joined them.

When he was 55, Lee shut down his bricklaying business, saying "I was down to a shoestring. I just gave it up." He went to work for Bob at the original Merrifield Garden Center, where he did some bush-hogging and odd jobs. It was a reversal of their roles from the family's migration to Virginia when Bob worked for Lee.

Lee affectionately became known as "Mr. Lee" in the Southern tradition of respecting elders. When the Fair Oaks store opened, he became the greeter at the new store. As soon as a customer walked in the store, Mr. Lee would appear, offering coffee or tea. "I love it so much here I can't call it work," Mr. Lee said.

Bob recalls how Mr. Lee loved making people happy: "He was a natural at it. He had a good memory and he knew what to say, whether it was asking someone about their kids or their dog or their sports car. Most people aren't that way. He didn't give away money. He gave away kindness."

Christmas has always been a special time at Merrifield Garden Center with a tradition of giving free bags of popcorn to customers as a special treat. The popcorn was always warm and delicious and the aroma filled the greenhouse.

After the 2001 holiday season, Lee lobbied Bob and the store managers to hand out popcorn throughout the year. He knew how valuable a simple bag of popcorn could be in drawing customers into the store. He campaigned to be the popcorn man.

"Everyone was against the idea," Peg recalled. "It seemed like every time you turned around there was popcorn on the floor. No one liked the mess." But in the end, "he made popcorn believers out of all of us," she said. "It was one of the best things we ever did. It just took some convincing."

Bob had a small, round table placed in the breezeway, near the popcorn and coffee machines, where Mr. Lee could sit.

"I talk and make popcorn," Mr. Lee said. "They call it public relations."

A sharp dresser, Mr. Lee preferred to wear black, which emphasized his lanky frame. He wore stylish western hats tilted at a jaunty angle.

Mr. Lee also had the enviable job of giving away free tickets to professional sporting events and concerts in and around the nation's capital at the Verizon Center, FedExField, Wolf Trap and Nationals Park. Lucky customers often shared the Merrifield box seats with Bob and Billie Jean, who liked to see the big stars, such as

Michael Jackson, Celine Dion, Madonna, Bruce Springsteen, Cher and many others who came to town.

One day, Mr. Lee introduced Bob to a customer who was a well-built, strong Black man. "Bob, you know who this is, don't you? This is Mr. Clarence Thomas."

Bob looked the man up and down and asked, "The football player?"

Lee laughed and said, "No! This is Supreme Court Justice Clarence Thomas!"

Bob quickly shook his head and apologized for not recognizing Justice Thomas right away.

The Justice handled Bob's miscue deftly and the two broad-shouldered men laughed about it and began talking. They found they had many things in common, and they developed a friendship that continues to this day. With humble beginnings, both men learned early on the value of work and perseverance and that life only gives you what you grab with your own two hands. Hard times make strong people and these two men have overcome many obstacles in their paths to success at the highest levels of business and government.

"He reminded me a lot of people who worked hard," Justice Thomas said. "Here's a guy with an eighth-grade education who has to learn horticulture. He has to learn how to be able to talk to people about plants and about soil and about moisture and weather. Who's the genius? The guy who has been coddled all his life and sent to prep school? Or the guy with less than an eighth-grade education who builds a business around something he had to learn?"

Justice Thomas learned that Bob owned a recreational vehicle, and he asked a lot of questions about it because he was interested in getting one. When Bob bought his new Prevost motorcoach a year later, he called Justice Thomas and invited him to see it. Prevost is considered the top of the line for motorcoaches. Justice Thomas eventually bought one himself, a used 40-foot coach. "I've had that coach 14 years, and it's one of the best decisions I ever made," Justice Thomas said. Prevost owners have a club, called the Marathon Coach Club. Bob worked so much that he never had time for the annual owners' gathering. But one year it was held in nearby College Park, Maryland, and Justice Thomas invited Bob to be his guest. Bob drove his Mercedes-Benz to the event and spent a wonderful day with Justice Thomas and his wife, Virginia.

"Bob is what America was and the way it should be," Justice Thomas said. "It is the America we all knew. We all had a shot, maybe not the same shot, maybe one more difficult than the other. But we all had a shot. Somehow, to some people, that's not good enough. But to Bob Warhurst, it was more than good enough. I feel the exact same way."

Justice Thomas and Virginia have been to Hope Parke on several occasions, including Bob's annual Fourth of July and Christmas parties. Merrifield Garden Center has planted many trees and shrubs at the Thomas home. Justice Thomas and his wife named the first tree that Bob planted there the "Merri Tree" for Merrifield Garden Center.

Many celebrities from the worlds of government, diplomacy, Hollywood and journalism have shopped at Merrifield. One year, U.S. Senator John Warner, a frequent customer of Merrifield and Kevin's former boss, used a reproduction of his original oil painting, Our Spring Garden, as the cover of his Christmas card. The painting was inspired by tulips from Merrifield.

IN 2002, BOB WAS DIAGNOSED with prostate cancer, the second most common type of cancer in American men behind skin cancer, according to the American Cancer Society. The type of cancer that Bob had was considered "aggressive," so he had to make quick decisions about his treatment options. After talking with his urologist, Dr. Simon Chung, the decision was made to remove his prostate.

"I was devastated," Bob says. But with his stoic persona, Bob kept his emotions in check.

Dr. Chung performed the surgery. Afterward, he went into the waiting room to tell the family the surgery was successful and that the cancer appeared to have been contained to the prostate gland and had not spread to surrounding tissue. Bob insisted that he wanted to keep working, but he eventually agreed to recover at Hope Parke rather than go to his garden centers. Unlike the placement of a stent in his heart from his earlier heart attack, this surgery was more taxing and he needed more time to recover. He stayed at home for about a month but still did business on the phone and met with managers at his house.

At a follow-up examination five years later, doctors biopsied some of Bob's cells and found cancer. After consulting with his doctors, it was recommended that Bob receive radiation treatment to destroy all the cancerous cells. Dr. Glenn Tonnesen administered 39 radiation treatments. Bob worked throughout the treatments without slowing down a bit.

BOB WAS INTO RECYCLING BEFORE THAT WORD became a national movement and a part of our daily lives. As a poor boy in Alabama, he learned that everything from a hog to a house could be used to its maximum potential with as little waste as possible. Young Bobby built a small hut out of discarded wood and crooked nails that he hammered straight. That hut was where he thought about his future.

Later when he moved to Northern Virginia and became a garbage man, he found plenty of chairs, tables, beds and other household items that had been discarded simply because they needed a coat of paint or a minor repair. He was exposed to the wanton waste that society dumped every day without a thought of what that would mean for the environment. One look around the huge Fairfax

County Landfill opened his eyes to the need to reuse as much of the world's waste as possible. Much of the inventory of The Tradin' Post, the precursor to Merrifield Garden Center, came from Bob's trash pickups in Northern Virginia.

"For years and years and years, I've been recycling," Bob says. "I see recycling as a way to use old stuff and give it value instead of throwing it away."

Bob saw no reason to let all the landscape debris go to waste, either. He started recycling soil at the original Merrifield store. Old soil from Merrifield's landscape jobs and from contractors was dumped in a big pile. Many times a day, Bob would drive a front-end loader with a bucket that he would drag across the top layer of topsoil to loosen it up and let the sun and air get in.

When the Fair Oaks store opened, Bob had a lot more room and he quickly bought a $350,000 tree grinder. "Once we got that machine, we started making mulch," Bob says. He accumulated the brush and tree limbs from landscape jobs and from contractors. If a tree died at the garden center, it would go into the mulch-making machine. "In the old days, we took it to the landfill," Bob says. "It broke our hearts to do it, but that was really the only option we had." Dumping it at a landfill also required a payment. Recycling brush and soil was good for both the environment and the garden center's bottom line.

Within a few years of operating his recycling facility out of his Merrifield and Fair Oaks stores, Bob was ready to take the recycling operation up a notch. But he needed a place to do it. And to do it right, he needed the space to house all the heavy equipment that was required to do the job and the zoning to be able to store and process the materials. "We were making mulch out of brush, trees, leaves, anything we could," Bob says. "It was time to grow, but we ran out of room."

Bob thought the perfect place to do the recycling was a piece of property that he and Buddy owned with their investment group of

Guy Lewis, Otis Poole, Ray August and W.R. Owens. They had bought the property west of Washington, D.C., and Fairfax County in 1985. It was a 40-acre parcel in the Gainesville area of Prince William County, with good road frontage and industrial zoning. A few years after owning the property, the partners sold two acres on the corner of Wellington Road and Balls Ford Road to the Southland Corporation to build a 7-Eleven convenience store. The partners thought that having a 7-Eleven would make the rest of their property easier to sell. "We wanted that 7-Eleven desperately," Bob recalled. "Buddy and I knew that having a 7-Eleven near our store in Merrifield for all those years was wonderful." They also sold an additional five acres to BMG Metals, Inc.

The partners originally bought the land for $1.25 per square foot and had it rezoned to M-T, Industrial/Transportation, to offer buyers greater flexibility in developing the property. According to the Prince William County Zoning Administration Division, M-T zoning is "intended to provide for areas and encourage development of heavy industrial uses, particularly those that generate considerable truck and/or heavy equipment traffic, or which require access to more than one mode of transportation."

"The investment group bought it to sell lots and make money," Bob says. "But it was bad times then, so we couldn't get anyone to buy it."

The more Bob thought about it, the more he thought it would be a win-win situation if he and Buddy bought out the other partners and developed the land themselves to operate their recycling business. And as he thought about it even more, Bob thought it would be an ideal place for their third garden center location.

"We needed a home to go to if we ever sell the original Merrifield property," Bob says. "Our land in Merrifield is very valuable, probably worth $50 million or more. Then we'd have a place to back up to."

Bob and Buddy discussed all of this with their family members and top managers. Everyone agreed that this would be a good move, accomplishing two goals at the same time. For most of them, following the instincts of a man who had been right most of the time wasn't that hard of a decision. "Everybody usually goes along with what I want to do," Bob says.

But the Merrifield team also did their due diligence and didn't take the decision lightly. Expanding always came with risks and they wanted to make sure this was a good move for the future direction of the company. Bob and his Merrifield team studied the area, walked the property, staked out where various buildings and parking lots might go and planned the overall flow of the garden center. They wanted to make sure the land and area were suitable for a large garden center and could generate a profit for many years to come.

In the end, they decided this is where they would build their new recycling operation and third garden center. Bob and Buddy bought the property from their investment group at a price of $1.50 per square foot, roughly $2.6 million.

"Gainesville is close to Interstate 66, only 14 miles from Fair Oaks," Bob says. "I'd rather be on Lee Highway, but to get 40 acres on Lee Highway would be way too much. We're in an industrial zone, but they're building more houses out here."

At the Gainesville property, Bob started recycling concrete. He knew it was a hard job, but it was possible with the right amount of space and the right equipment.

Bob's recycling statistics are now impressive. He estimates that now he recycles about 35,000 cubic yards of brush, 10,000 cubic yards of soil and 50,000 tons of concrete a year. The recycling effort requires a lot of manpower, space and heavy equipment. Four employees handle the recycling, working six days a week, often up to 10 hours a day. Three acres are devoted to recycling, and the machinery cost more than $2 million. Using the latest technology, the soil from landscape jobs is transported to the garden center, where it is screened, processed and enriched with organic compost. Brush and tree limbs are ground up, processed and allowed to break down into mulch.

Concrete may sound like a tough thing to recycle, but it makes an excellent base for new patios, sidewalks and driveways. "We keep it clean," Bob says. "Our concrete doesn't have any dirt, metal or other foreign substances in it, so it makes a nice base."

The equipment used in the recycling program is not only expensive, it's a marvel of technology. In addition to the many trucks, tractors and loaders that are essential to the operation, Bob has invested in some amazing machines, such as the CEC Road Runner 6X16 to screen soil coming off landscape jobs. A front-end loader puts the soil into the machine, which then mechanically separates out rocks, sticks and other debris, allowing only soil to pass through to the finished pile. The soil is then enriched with organic matter so it can be reused in the landscape. Some of the equipment sounds like it comes from a Japanese science-fiction monster movie. The Komatsu Jaw Crusher BR380JG-1 processes concrete from landscape jobs. As its name implies, the Jaw Crusher is loaded with concrete pieces that are crushed into tiny granules that can then be reused as a base.

Merrifield Garden Center is unique for its high volume and high level of recycling. Bob is most proud of the quality of his recycled products. "I think of recycling as a landfill that never fills up," Bob says.

This is the way Bob has always lived his life, converting the mundane and overlooked into things of utility and lasting beauty.

Merrifield is committed to planting trees, using water wisely and protecting natural resources. The company plants thousands of trees every year. Those trees not only beautify homes, businesses and parks, and increase property values but also absorb pollutants, lower energy costs, diminish noise levels and reduce erosion from water runoff. Whenever possible, the company encourages the use of native plants that are hardy and drought-tolerant. These plants offer more than just beautiful flowers and foliage, they also are critical to sustaining butterflies and birds, an important first step in restoring habitat that has been disturbed during the area's rapid growth in construction and development. That growth has also affected how the company uses water. Merrifield staffers have been taught to educate customers on using water judiciously and to encourage the use of products, such as moisture meters, gator bags, rain barrels, soaker hoses and drip irrigation systems that conserve water while minimizing damaging runoff.

Bob's obsession with work and benign control over his environment and those around him have made him who he is today, but another force was also at work, trying to disrupt his plans. It has a name: triskaidekaphobia. It is the fear of the number 13.

CHAPTER FOURTEEN

SUPERSTITIOUS NATURE

Bob Warhurst's life in rural Alabama exposed him to many superstitions and folk tales that are still a part of his life. Judging by his success and large family, there may be some merit in following these country habits and traditions passed down through generations of Warhursts.

Bob is most cautious about the number 13. He won't stay on the 13th floor of a hotel, won't stay in a hotel room with the number 13 in it and won't travel on the 13th day of a month. And there is no Chapter 13 in this book.

At an out-of-town trade show, Howard Saunders recalled that Bob was given keys to Room 513 while Howard and Merrifield Plant Specialist Tim Guy were assigned to Room 519. Howard, Merrifield's first general manager, said that they had to give up their room because Bob couldn't stay in Room 513.

"It was always a bit of an inside joke with our family," Bob's son Kevin said. "If we were planning a party or some other event and the choices were September 3, 10 or 13, we would all say, 'Well, we know we can't do the 13th.'"

Merrifield Manager Peter Guy, the younger brother of Tim Guy, said Bob is the most superstitious person he has ever met. Bob has a habit of blocking potential bad luck by not allowing talk about good luck. The curse can only be erased by knocking on wood. "You can't say anything unless you knock on wood," Peter said. "If I say, 'We've had a great year so far.' He'll give you that look like, 'Really?' Then he'll say, 'Peter, go find some wood.' I would say, 'It looks like great weather this weekend' or 'We haven't had an accident in three months.' Anything like that."

Knock on wood. Bob always leaves a building through the same door he entered and he won't walk under a ladder. But he says sometimes you just can't help certain situations. "If a black cat dashes in front of you, you just stop, take your right foot and make an X on the ground," he says. "And then take your left foot and make an X on the ground, and then you are good."

That happened one time when Larry was riding in the car with his father. "When I was a kid, a black cat ran out in front of us while he was driving," Larry recalled. "He pulled the car over and he did something. Then we turned around and took another route."

When she has driven her father to doctor's appointments in recent years, Debbie said "he always has to drive the same route and go into the building the same way." Howard said if Bob hands you his pocket knife open, "you have to hand it back to him open."

Some people might scoff at Bob's superstitious nature, but it's not uncommon for successful people to not want to jinx their good fortune. According to ESPN, Alabama head football coach Nick Saban has a couple of football-related superstitions. Before every game, Saban receives a lucky penny from his daughter, Kristen. In 2009, Saban wore the same straw hat at every practice. That season Alabama defeated Texas 37-21 in the BCS National Championship Game. Add up the individual digits in the score (3+7+2+1): The sum is 13. Bad luck for Texas.

If superstition works for Alabama, Nick Saban and Bob Warhurst, it must be magic.

IN 2001, MERRIFIELD GARDEN CENTER had been in business for 30 years, an accomplishment that was achieved by the magic of more than 10,000 days of hard work. Bob had every reason to be proud. What started with a humble little red barn at the corner of Lee Highway and Gallows Road in the Washington, D.C., suburb of Merrifield, Virginia, had grown to become one of the largest independently owned and operated garden centers in the nation, with two nurseries and more than 50 acres of property. Expansion plans were being made for an even bigger store at a 40-acre site in the far western suburb of Gainesville, Virginia.

"Now we see the American story as a bunch of dot.com geniuses and Silicon Valley, when instead the American story is a bunch of guys who started doing whatever they had to do to survive and turn it into a business," Supreme Court Justice Clarence Thomas said. "(Bob) is Exhibit A. It's what defined this country. It's what defined what we thought this country was all about."

Merrifield Garden Center was now a modern, multi-faceted operation with three divisions: retail, landscaping and wholesale. As the company spread its wings, Bob and Buddy never lost sight of their mission as a beauty business whose goal was helping customers fulfill their dreams, and they never wavered in their efforts to provide the best quality, service and selection possible.

Byron Wates, Jr. said Merrifield's reputation for stocking an enormous selection of plants is legendary. "If you need something, a specific variety—something new and special—they will most likely have it," said Byron, owner of Area Landscaping and historian of the Northern Virginia Nursery and Landscape Association. "Other nurseries tend to stay away from that. I use them that way. When I need a very special plant, I'll call them up. Ninety-nine percent of the time they'll have it."

Because its focus is on the needs of customers in Northern Virginia and the Washington, D.C., metropolitan area, Merrifield Garden Center developed its own brand of private-label grass seeds, planting mixes and lawn and plant fertilizers to match the growing conditions of the area.

The landscaping division takes on a variety of jobs, from million-dollar commercial projects to modest installations costing just a couple hundred dollars. Merrifield has a team of more than 25 landscape designers and consultants whose visions come to life thanks to more than 65 installation crews supported with a fleet of more than 170 trucks and specialized rigs that range from tree spades to cranes to high-tech concrete trucks. The Merrifield motto: "If you can imagine it, we can build it."

The Merrifield army is always on the march, taking on jobs not usually associated with a landscape company, such as handyman services, plowing snow for large commercial properties and the rental and haul away of "roll-off " trash and debris containers. They even repaired and restored the X-wing fighter from the original Star Wars movie trilogy. "They try to do everything," Byron said. "I think good business people do. If you make money at it, you keep going with it. If you don't, you get out of it."

With its wholesale business, Merrifield sells great volumes of plants and materials to landscape contractors. Unlike most wholesalers, Merrifield doesn't grow its own plants. That's because Bob learned early in his career as the "Plant Whisperer" that there is great risk in growing plants because of the threat of frost, drought and disease. He prefers to visit nurseries around the country, picking only the best plants. Merrifield buys in bulk, so contractors can get a discount on their purchases, but they don't receive the comprehensive plant replacement policy that retail customers enjoy. For a modest fee, contractors can also dump their landscape debris at Merrifield's facilities. Of course, thrifty Bob processes that debris into valuable landscape products that he can sell.

THERE ARE MANY WAYS TO TRAVEL, across time, across geography and across cultures, to name a few. Bob was willing and eager to take on another kind of traveling: across a language barrier. The growing number of Spanish-speaking employees at Merrifield Garden Center sparked Bob's interest in learning how to speak Spanish. Bob was constantly asking Spanish-speaking employees how to say various words, and he purchased a few books to learn the language, but he could not get past "Hola, como esta?" Bob was convinced that with the right teacher he could learn to speak the language. "I wanted to improve my ability to communicate with our Spanish-speaking employees and customers," Bob says.

In March 2003, Bob started Spanish classes at the garden center. A Merrifield employee had a close friend who taught Spanish in high school, and she agreed to serve as their first instructor. The initial class drew a large crowd of about 25 employees and was held in the conference room at the Fair Oaks store. "It's hard to learn Spanish," Bob says. "But it's fun to learn new things. It's a challenge. I'm not going to stop learning Spanish because it's hard. Work is hard, too."

The next week, about 15 people arrived for class. The following week, about 12. As attendance was shrinking, Bob encouraged his neighbors to attend and began hosting dinner before class. Eventually there was a group of about six who became regulars. Merrifield Manager Peter Hogarth remembered that "Bob was so bad at speaking Spanish it was almost hopeless. But his tenacity is just incredible. I can't imagine it was enjoyable for him, but it was important for him to learn."

Like everything else in his life, Bob dedicated himself to the task. Whenever he spoke to a Hispanic employee, he only talked Spanish. "We would be driving and he'd say, 'Let me tell you about all the words I learned this week,'" Peter said.

After years of practice, Bob is able to converse with others in Spanish. He can also recite the Spanish alphabet (forwards and backwards) and has mastered the U.S. Pledge of Allegiance in Spanish.

"He's good at memorizing and has a large vocabulary—the biggest of anyone in the group," said David Yost, one of the plant experts featured on the "Merrifield's Gardening Advisor" television show and a member of the group learning Spanish. "But he has difficulty sometimes putting the words in sentences. You could pluck

Bob down in Mexico City and he'd get by, combined with pointing and hand signals."

Bob's efforts are greatly appreciated. "I think Mr. Bob is doing a great job to try to communicate with his Spanish-speaking employees," said Luis Gonzales, one of nearly 250 of Merrifield's 750 employees whose first language is Spanish. "We all know the effort he makes. It makes me feel like he cares for us in the Spanish-speaking community."

Over the years, several instructors have taught the class. After undergoing surgery in 2005 for a left knee replacement, Bob moved the classes to his home. The group met every Thursday night. "All of us became friends and bonded through the social hour of dinner before class," David Yost said. "Many times conversations about the day and work spilled into class time. Sometimes we didn't leave until well past 10 p.m. We would travel through rain or snow or at the end of a long day at work to be there. Very rarely did we miss a class."

One time, Bob even flew back early from a trade show in Chicago to make the start of Spanish class. Occasionally, Bob treated the class to the movies, a Washington Redskins football game or a concert at the Verizon Center, but most of the time they were trying to learn how to speak Spanish. Bob collaborated with Bridget Anderson, a master gardener and communications consultant, to produce Merrifield's first Spanish/English Handbook, which has English to Spanish and Spanish to English translations of common gardening terms. The Spanish classes continued until 2013. Bob also felt it was important for Spanish-speaking employees to learn English. For a time, he also offered English classes.

IN 2004, BOB, BILLIE JEAN AND 10 EMPLOYEES traveled to Europe on an ambitious, one-week mission to look at garden centers and Deforche greenhouses in anticipation of the construction of the third Merrifield Garden Center store, this one in Gainesville, Virginia.

After touring garden centers in Switzerland, Germany, France, The Netherlands and Belgium, they came away with some good information about store layout, merchandising and how to maximize the profit potential of a large garden center. "Those garden centers were set up as destination garden centers," Peg Bier recalled. "They were all huge and had a great variety of products nicely presented. And cafes."

These elements would later be reflected in the Gainesville store. Bob was particularly interested in the cafes. Although Merrifield already had a small outdoor cafe at their original store, Bob could see how a large, indoor cafe that served tasty food without a long wait helped bring customers into the garden center. At the end of the trip, the Merrifield group visited the Deforche factory in Kortrijk, Belgium, which is about 60 miles from Brussels. Kortrijk is a special place in Belgium because of its lovely shopping squares, international bicycle races and fantastic restaurants. And beer. Lots of beer. But Bob wasn't there to party. He was a man on a serious mission: selecting the builder for the structure that would become the new greenhouse and retail store for their newest garden center in Gainesville. Bob ultimately went with Deforche after touring their factory and fabricating plant where the steel is forged and powder coated. To truly size up the company, Bob talked extensively with people who had previously bought the structures to gauge their satisfaction. He also visited places where the structures were being used, asking tough questions about the lighting, heating, cooling, roof opening/closing processes and boiler system.

On one hand, Bob liked the look of the Deforche greenhouse and retail store structure, as well as the opening and closing system for the roof. In both aesthetics and practicality, their product would help Bob and the Merrifield team achieve their goal: make Gainesville a destination location that had the size and space to make an instant impression on customers. On the other hand, Bob was not enamored of all the garden centers they visited in Europe. Some used ultra-modern or eclectic designs or bright green and orange color schemes that just didn't match the Merrifield style. But they learned something everywhere they went and saw that Deforche always delivered a quality product.

Near the end of their visit to Kortrijk, the Merrifield entourage had a sumptuous dinner with the third generation owners of Deforche—brothers Karel, Stephen and Peter Deforche—at the home of their parents—Eric Deforche and Dina Couckaert, who live next to the factory that bears the family name. Eric and Dina were seated near Bob, Billie Jean and Peg. The Deforches didn't speak much English and the Warhursts didn't speak any Flemish or Walloon (the two languages commonly used in Belgium), but everyone spoke gardening.

"We all sat at a big, long dining room table, which looked like something out of the movies," Kevin said. They were served an elegant meal with various courses, including beef Carpaccio (raw meat, thinly sliced or pounded thin), appetizers, salads, various vegetables and quail. Uniformed servers waited on them and poured their wine and coffee. The Warhursts were a bit hesitant to try some of the local delicacies, such as the carpaccio and quail. Being country folks, they are not the type to stray far from standard cooked meat, potatoes and beans.

"It was so authentic you had to pull out small pieces of lead pellets that were used to shoot the quail," Kevin said. "It was a unique experience for us to dine with our European hosts and bring our two cultures together in one room. I remember the wife of one of the Deforche brothers telling us that when she thought of America, she thought of the beautiful scenes from the movie 'The Horse Whisperer,' and how badly she wanted to go there."

After dinner, the Merrifield entourage boarded their bus and headed back to Brussels, where they stayed in a beautiful hotel.

They visited the famous Manneken Pis, the bronze sculpture of a naked little boy peeing into a fountain in Brussels. The next day, they took the bus to France for sightseeing. In Paris, they visited the famous Notre Dame Cathedral, the immense royal majesty of Versailles and its formal gardens, went up in the iconic Eiffel Tower at night and drove to the tunnel and saw the exact spot where Princess Diana of Wales died in a car crash in 1997.

Exhausted, they flew back to Virginia. "The trip was a lot of fun, just like all the Merrifield trips," Kevin said. "We're all friends and it's great to spend time together in a different setting and a different continent. The trip solidified our desire to go with Deforche and allowed us to finalize our plans for the Gainesville store. While waiting at the airport to fly home, I remember we staked off the rough dimensions of the store we wanted to build and tried to visualize the space."

On the home front, there was sad news: Bob's youngest brother, Claude Warhurst, Jr., died of cardiovascular disease on May 9, 2005 at the age of 57. For most of his life, Claude Jr., was known as Tracy after the comic strip detective Dick Tracy because he helped Bob as a private detective in the late 1950s. For the last 17 years of his life, Tracy worked for Bob at Merrifield Garden Center. The quintessential salesman, he sold trees and shrubs and just about everything else at the garden center.

IN 2007, ANOTHER BIG PROJECT WAS UNDERWAY that would bring Bob into contact with yet another culture with a different view of the world. Seven years after the Hope Parke house was completed, Bob and son Larry started making plans for a horse barn on the property.

"For 55 years, I dreamed of having a nice barn with an indoor arena," Bob says.

A barn would give Bob an opportunity to be near the magnificent animals he loved dearly since he was a boy. His beautiful horse Goldfinger was not only a great steed but had been a flashy way for Bob to attract new customers to his trash hauling business in Northern Virginia. Who could ignore a man mounted on such a beautiful and glamorous animal?

Bob's decision to build a barn greatly pleased Larry and several other family members and friends. Larry had inherited Bob's love of horses and the Western style of riding. "Dad and I had been looking at different barn buildings for years," Larry said. "I never thought it was going to happen."

After meeting with some Amish carpenters at a farm equipment show in Harrisburg, Pennsylvania, Bob and Larry visited two barns the Amish had built in Maryland and Berryville, Virginia. Bob liked what he saw and decided to hire them to build his new barn. The Amish were eager to work and traveled long distances to build the structure.

Bob had some fun with the Amish workers, who had little contact with the modern world and its technological wonders. Bob loved flying in helicopters as much as airplanes, and he and Buddy added a Robinson 44 helicopter to the Merrifield fleet, which included a Piper Saratoga six-seater airplane that they bought used in 2007. Since then, Bob has bought a Beechcraft King Air 300, a twin-engine, turbo-prop plane that can travel 360 miles per hour with a range of 1,500 miles.

One day, when about 20 Amish workers were busy building the barn, Bob landed his helicopter near the work site. "I'm going for pizza," Bob told the astonished crew as he climbed back into the helicopter and flew off. He landed at the Fair Oaks store and drove his car to nearby Ledo Pizza, where he ordered eight pizzas. Then Bob took the pizzas back to the Fair Oaks store, transferred the pizzas into his helicopter and flew back to the horse barn. "They thought I went to the pizza place in the helicopter," Bob says. "I didn't tell them any different."

Eventually the project was completed and the handsome 90' x 210' pine wood barn was ready for riders and horses. The barn has an indoor arena, 10 stalls, a bathroom, a shower and a storage area.

For Bob, the barn and riding arena would be something beautiful to see but unfortunately not for him to use. Due to the total surgical replacement of his left knee, he could no longer ride his beloved horses. But he enjoyed watching others ride, especially Larry and other family members. A couple of years ago, Bob tried riding once more when the family acquired a quarter horse from Wyoming. He rode the horse at a walking pace around the stable for about ten minutes or so before he dismounted, not willing to risk a fall.

"I decided not to ride anymore," says Bob, who was 74 at the time. "If I couldn't ride the way I used to ride, there's no need for me to fool myself. That's what happens when you get old."

Although he would no longer ride, the big barn still gave Bob pleasure. He is always looking for ways to have fun with his staff outside the workplace. He decided a barn dance would be just the thing for employees and their families to have a good time. Everyone dressed up in cowboy hats, boots and Western wear. Bob had a large wooden dance floor framed and custom built for the event. Of course, there was scrumptious barbecue, cold beer and a multitude of great dishes that employees brought to share. Even the city slickers let their hair down to the country tunes of Black Jug Relic, a band that included Merrifield electrician JR Nelson, son-in-law of Bob's brother Carl.

The barn space also was made available to other events, including the American Farrier's Association. Their horseshoeing and forging team once used the barn in preparation for the international championships. Horseshoeing is not just the act of nailing a metal shoe to a horse's hoof. The shoe must be precisely fit to the hoof to allow the horse to use all of the gaits (walking, trotting, canter and gallop) without causing injury to the horse. When the event was held at Hope Parke, two draft horses from Mount Vernon were brought in. More than 200 spectators were on hand to see the precision fittings and enjoy Bob's beautiful barn.

WITH THEIR GREEN INITIATIVES IN PLACE and a growing population base in Prince William County, Bob and Buddy were now ready to go forward with the Gainesville retail garden center project.

In 2007, as with the Fair Oaks store, Bob opened a makeshift garden center so that customers could become accustomed to shopping there while the main store was under construction. There was a variety of plants on display, a small barn that was stocked with grass seed, fertilizer and tools and a double-wide trailer with bathrooms, a kitchen, a copy machine and a conference room.

The Prince William County Department of Transportation gave the Merrifield owners naming rights for the connecting street that runs next to the property, which they named Merrifield Garden Way.

Bob and Buddy's domain now extended about 20 miles west from the original store they opened more than 35 years earlier.

CHAPTER FIFTEEN

STILL STANDING STRONG

After their visit to Belgium to look at various greenhouses, Bob and his Merrifield team had decided to purchase a greenhouse and store structure from the Deforche company. The pieces of the buildings were shipped to the United States in sea containers from Belgium, and a small crew of Belgian workers flew over the Atlantic Ocean to put it together in fast-growing Gainesville. "They put it together like a puzzle," Bob says. "It cost an arm and a leg. With the original store, it was a much simpler process. We just built it ourselves and then slowly added on when we needed more space. And I'm proud to say that all these years later those buildings are still standing strong."

Although the Deforche crew was trained to fit the steel and glass pieces together to form the buildings, an experienced contractor was still needed to handle all the details, oversee the overall construction process and help do the exacting work required to build such a structure. Once again, Bob turned to the Bier brothers, Mark and Matt, still muscled, nimble and wiry in their fifties. The sons of Merrifield Plant and Design Specialist Peg Bier are talented and trusted friends that Bob had relied on before. It took an army of engineers, architects, Merrifield employees and Belgian workers to build the gleaming new store and greenhouse.

"I think he's a visionary," Matt Bier said of Bob. "He's got the courage to grow. I certainly admire that."

Because he was once a bricklayer and has done a little bit of everything in the construction business, Bob is particular about how he wants things done.

"He can be particular about wanting it done one way today," Matt said. "And if he changes his mind tonight, then he will be particular about changing it tomorrow."

Bob will look at Matt with a twinkle in his eye and ask, "Why did you let me do that? Why didn't you talk me out of that? You shouldn't have let me do that."

Matt said Bob can be a challenge, "but always a fun challenge."

"It requires a lot of flexibility," Matt said. "Flexibility yields a better result anyway. That's all Bob is after. A good result. I always look forward to working with Bob, particularly when he is in the right spirit, and he usually is."

In December 2008, the huge store opened in Gainesville to great fanfare. Customers raved about the beautiful, spacious new garden center and the extraordinary glass greenhouse with a retractable glass roof and a radiant-heated concrete floor. "I don't really care about the building," Merrifield Manager Peter Guy said. "It's the (employees) who make us." Nancy Wyatt, a customer who lives in Linden, Virginia, says she makes the 60-mile round trip to Gainesville because of the warmth and helpfulness of the staff. "It's literally my second home," she said. "I get plenty of hugs when I go there."

Bob says Gainesville's popularity made him happy but didn't surprise him. "We had 37 years of building a customer base," he says. "We know how to take care of customers and give them what they want."

At Gainesville, there is a lot for customers to be happy about: a 12,000 square-foot store, a 37,000 square-foot greenhouse and 350 extra-wide parking spaces so customers can open their vehicle doors to load their purchases without dinging the vehicle next to them. "I love a big parking spot," Bob says. "Instead of making our parking spaces 9' wide—which is the norm—we made our spaces 10' wide at Gainesville and even made them 10-1/2' wide right in front of the store."

From the back of the main store building at Gainesville, customers can look straight through the huge glass wall into the tree and shrub sections, which are sandwiched by the 22,600 square-foot annual house and the 15,800 square-foot perennial house. Both of these Cravo structures have roofs that open and close with the touch of a button. The Fair Oaks store also has these Canadian-made buildings. "We're thrilled with how it all worked out," Bob says. "The annual and perennial houses are a little too far apart. But we needed the middle to be open so customers could see the shrub and tree sections. Nothing's ever perfect."

But some designs at Gainesville are pretty close to perfection. Consider the restrooms. In both the men's and women's restrooms, the stalls are made of a gorgeous marble tile and the walls go straight from the floor to the ceiling with no gaps. "I wanted us to have the perfect restroom," Bob says. "I wanted everyone to have a private stall. I hate to go into a restroom and see another guy's britches down below his knees."

Peter once overheard a woman telling her friend, "You've got to see this bathroom! They're nicer than the ones in our hotel!"

The main store building offers seasonal home decor with stylish designs, a diverse selection of local and international wines, a creative floral department and a cafe with delicious food. The greenhouse is impressive in design and size. At 37,000 square-feet, it dwarfs the 10,000 square-foot greenhouse at Fair Oaks and the 1,000 square-foot greenhouse at Merrifield. The Gainesville greenhouse is so enormous that it houses a Plant Diagnostic Clinic and a 75-person capacity seminar room in addition to thousands of colorful tropical plants and lush foliage, hundreds of containers in all shapes, sizes and colors and a myriad of products to help gardens grow.

Bob's master plan includes two more buildings, but he decided to start smaller and build only two of the four planned structures. "We were going to build a Taj Mahal and it didn't make sense," he says. "We need the space outside more than inside. Of course, we spent a lot more money than we intended, but that always happens." The main store and greenhouse were already quite large so there was no rush to expand. The other two buildings can be added when more growth comes to Prince William County. Bob thought it was best to be conservative and see how business progressed.

Bob's "sense" turned out to be spot on. As the Gainesville store neared completion, the collapse of the global financial markets brought on the Great Recession of 2008 that hit the United States and much of the world. The trouble came fast and furious. Home values suddenly dropped, causing overseas markets heavily invested in United States home loans to fall. Many home buyers then owed more on their mortgages than their homes were worth and many incomes were lost or cut as the job market shrunk, and layoffs were all too common. Buyers could no longer afford to make mortgage payments and foreclosures ensued. Mortgage lenders, savings and loan companies and insurance brokers shut down. Rampant fraud was exposed, most notably the Bernard Madoff swindle of thousands of investors and billions of dollars. All in all, the Dow Jones Industrial Average lost half of its value, according to the Associated Press.

When the financial crisis hit, most of the financial commitments to the development of the Gainesville site and the actual construction process were either done or nearly completed. The immediate problem was how such bad economic news would affect consumer confidence and behavior. When people fear for their jobs and the health of the overall economy, they spend less money. In the past, Merrifield Garden Center held its own during recessions, because people would often forgo trips and big ticket items to spend more time fixing up their homes and gardens. But this was no ordinary recession. Not only did it rock financial markets, it threatened the very foundation of the global financial system.

Merrifield had already spent millions of its own money and borrowed from banks to build the site. They were in way too far to turn back. Had the recession hit before they broke ground, they would have waited and not built anything. But now they had to make the best of it and do all they could to make it work.

"Gainesville was probably the hardest venture we've ever done," said Lynn Warhurst, Bob's daughter-in-law and the company controller. "It was so large and they wanted to build the big greenhouse from Belgium. Banks tightened up. Quarterly ratios had to be met; before it was once a year. You had to hit your numbers. We deal with several banks. It was an extremely difficult time to get through."

Bob's team came together and made a plan. It wasn't easy. They would hold off on plans to build a loading dock, a warehouse and a garage at the Gainesville store. But they moved forward with the completion of the annual and perennial houses because they were needed to properly display and protect their investment in those plants. They postponed employee raises and laid off some workers.

The managers decided to look at the past before charging blindly into the future. Their mission was to look at what worked and what needed fixing and most importantly, why. The bad national economy was not the only problem. As Merrifield Garden Center had grown to three locations and more than 750 employees, it had to adapt to the new economic climate and change to remain efficient and profitable. The sheer number of employees made it impossible for Bob, Billie Jean, Buddy, Doris and the senior managers to work closely with everyone and personally explain how they wanted things done and their vision for the future.

"We felt we were losing touch," said Hal Williams, a manager and the son of Buddy and Doris. "We had to go back to what this garden center was built on: customer service and quality plants. We had to go back to teaching Merrifield 101."

The result was "The Merrifield Way," an eight-page document signed by the four owners to firmly outline and explain the company's core principles and beliefs to both new and longtime employees alike. Their goal was to build a foundation upon which all future training would be based. The document detailed the basic principles that guided Merrifield throughout its 37-year history and led them to where they were at that point: customer service, personal conduct and how the nursery should operate.

"I believe it," Hal said. "I live it. I breathe it."

The next step was to make sure managers could implement the blueprint for success. "I think a lot of people bought into it," Hal said.

No stone was left unturned with customer service. From how they answered the phones to how they treated people when they walked in the door, it was all about serving customers the best they could. Customers were offered free coffee, free popcorn, free seminars, free tickets to sporting events and free advice. They reviewed everything they did from top to bottom to make sure it was all about the customer experience.

Taking care of customers has always been Bob's mantra. "People still don't get good service at many stores," he says. "Many places I go to, I can't even get people to help me. There's no one there. And, if there is, they don't really care."

Unlike some companies in the same boat, Bob refused to slash prices or inventory. "We wanted to make sure our shelves were filled," Hal said. "We never wanted to (remind) our customers the economy was bad. It took a lot of conversations to make that happen."

The Merrifield team used technology to help them analyze sales and stock, and culled the intuition and experience of their buyers and managers to strike the right balance. Quality was another tenet of the company. In the past, they had visited the nurseries where they bought their plants, but the recession and company belt-tightening left little money for travel. But the results were apparent: a larger than ever percentage of substandard plants were arriving. They were quickly sent back to the growers, but the sheer number of bad plants was alarming. Each grower received a letter from Bob and Buddy, reminding them about the company's insistence on high quality. They demanded the best and if they didn't get it, they would find another supplier.

Merrifield plant specialists and buyers began visiting nurseries again, typically examining more than 75 nurseries in nine states to find the best trees and shrubs for their customers. There was a cost associated with that type of scrutiny, but Bob and Buddy knew their customers expected nothing but the highest quality. "We hit it hard," Bob's son Rob said. "We saw a lot of places. We had a quality issue we had to straighten out." The buying teams didn't just visit growers to inspect their inventory. They spent hours walking through growers' fields hand tagging specific trees and shrubs that they wanted delivered to Merrifield. Whether it was crape myrtles in North Carolina, shade trees in Tennessee or Hinoki cypress in Oregon, the team hand tagged between 5,000 and 6,000 plants a year. The buying team even had their own lock tags with the Merrifield Garden Center logo to ensure that the growers sent the exact plants they had specified.

Recessions and expansions are tides in the natural cycle of the economy. Hard times force businesses to refocus, trim excess, work harder, be smarter and become an overall better business.

"In the end, it made us a better company and allowed us to learn from our mistakes," Kevin said. "We are so thankful to all our customers for supporting us, and we are proud that we were able to adapt."

An important part of that adaptation was making the Merrifield stores exciting and fun places to shop. That idea blossomed into Ladies Night Out, a new holiday tradition that started in November 2010 and has proved to be an overwhelming success at all three stores, even filling the huge Gainesville parking lot all four years it has been held.

Merrifield Garden Center customer Nancy Wyatt said she always look forward to Ladies Night Out. "(The employees) have mascara and makeup instead of gardening clothes," she said. "Between the chocolate wine and dressed up gardening people, it's all very lovely."

Although Merrifield Garden Center has always put on a traditional Holiday Open House event, Ladies Night Out is extra special with wine tasting, hors d'oeuvres, music and more. As darkness descends, the stores sparkle and glisten with thousands of twinkling lights and glorious ornaments. Merrifield's talented designers work all fall to make sure their gorgeous holiday decorations are finished in time for the big show. The parking lots quickly fill. As guests arrive, a squad of quick-fingered hors d'oeuvres makers assemble a delicious array of cheeses and other mouthwatering treats on platters held high as they walk through the various holiday displays offering their creations.

Ladies Night Out works because research shows that women shopping with their friends are the biggest shoppers. The excitement puts everyone in a holiday mood as they look for that special ornament or tree while the sound of seasonal music fills the air.

Gainesville, the store with the smallest population base, has outsold the Merrifield and Fair Oaks stores three of the four years Ladies Night Out has been held. "They love it," Peter Guy said. "They LOVE it. Our customers say it's the greatest thing in the world."

Another way Merrifield Garden Center dealt with the recession was trying new ways to attract customers, especially younger shoppers who are more apt to utilize technology to help determine where to spend their money. After looking at several options, Merrifield decided to experiment with Groupon. Merrifield offered an amazing deal of $50 worth of plants and gardening supplies for just $25. Although Merrifield is not a discount nursery, Bob, Buddy and their team felt it was important to try this new promotion and see if it might draw new customers to the garden center. Merrifield offered its first deal in the spring, a second in the fall and a third the following spring. All were home runs. In fact, they sold more than 42,000 in their third deal, breaking the record for all Groupon sales in the Washington, D.C., area.

But the Merrifield team felt Groupon wasn't the perfect fit for their business model. "We gave it a try," Bob says. "But too many people were waiting for the next Groupon to come out before coming back, and that was never the intention. That's not to say we won't ever do things like that again, but we just feel it's better to stick to our normal way of doing business."

With the opening of the new Gainesville store, Merrifield Garden Center now had three locations to serve their growing base of customers throughout Northern Virginia and the Washington, D.C., area. Although the three stores primarily draw their customers from people who live or work near a particular location, Bob and his staff have noticed that some people have their favorite store and are willing to travel farther to shop there. Some customers shop at all three stores, enjoying the same wide selection in each unique venue.

"I was talking to a couple the other day who were shopping at Gainesville and I asked what area they live in, and she said Bethesda, Maryland," Bob says. "I asked if she knew we had a store in Merrifield, which was much closer, and she said, 'Yes, we shop there, too, but we love coming out to this store.' We have people who come down from places like Pennsylvania, Delaware and New Jersey or come up from North Carolina or Tennessee. I asked them why they come all the way to Virginia and they say things like 'We just love this place' or 'We don't have anything like this where we live.' I'm so proud. You never plan for anything like this. Every year you just try to do better."

Merrifield Garden Center was a clear success when it came to attracting customers, but managing that growth required that they update their antiquated computer system to keep up with technology. The turning point came when their system crashed during peak business activity. With 60 percent of their income generated in four months in the spring, the old way of connecting to the Internet through T-1 lines strung throughout their offices and connected to a server crammed in a closet had to go. To wrangle all that data, they decided to upgrade to the robust SAP system that allowed them to use a wide range of applications, such as point of sale, inventory management and finance, with an overall goal of adding applications for wholesale, landscaping and customer relationship management.

Lynn Warhurst had seen the SAP product at trade shows and thought it would be a good fit for Merrifield. "All the big guys were using it," she said. "Best Buy, Zappos, Home Depot. People we could relate to."

Merrifield began to use the SAP system on the Amazon Web Services cloud to improve reliability and security, cut back costs and eliminate the burden on the IT staff so the company could focus on customers while also receiving detailed information about how the company was functioning. When stores close, managers receive a text message with that day's sales numbers. The company that once ran wires across hallways and through windows is now being promoted by giant Amazon as an example of how a small company can thrive using its cloud-hosting services.

FOOTBALL IS BIG IN NORTHERN VIRGINIA. In 2011, the Fairfax County Youth Football League had more than 6,000 players, making it one of the largest leagues of its kind in the United States. Approximately 20 organizations in the Northern Virginia region comprised the Fairfax league, but the biggest was the Gainesville-Haymarket Grizzlies, with about 600 kids in tackle football, 700 in flag football and 250 cheerleaders.

The popular Grizzlies needed a new place to play their home games. Their field at George G. Tyler Elementary School in Gainesville was regularly damaged by overuse and poor drainage.

A coalition of public and private organizations provided financial support and a 35-year land lease on a 17-acre parcel for the Grizzly Sports Complex in Prince William County. But the Grizzlies needed more help to make their dream a reality.

While driving home one day, Dean Mathews, vice commissioner of the Grizzlies, saw Merrifield's new Gainesville store and thought, "Let's hit Merrifield Garden Center" because he vaguely knew of Bob.

Not long after, Dean and Laura Landrum, who was doing marketing and fundraising for the Grizzlies, walked into the store. They asked for Bob, who appeared on his motorized scooter. They asked for a few minutes of his time and he led them back to the wine tasting area. Their goal was to get Bob to donate sod for their two fields.

"Before you even start," Bob told them, "our economy is in the tank. Merrifield Garden Center is working hard to make ends meet. We already love our community." He listed the Boy Scouts and several charitable causes the company was supporting.

As Laura started her presentation, Bob asked Dean what he did for a living. When he said he worked for the Arlington County Police Department, the conversation took a different track. "He and I hit it off," Dean recalled. "It was a fantastic conversation."

With the amount of use those fields would get, Bob let them know that grass fields could not possibly hold up. "You need to turf these," he said. Dean had already priced two artificial turf fields at $1.2 million, making it cost prohibitive. Bob insisted that the two fields be outfitted with artificial turf. "I started a bank down the road," he said. "We just financed a turf field in Herndon. We'll give you the money. We'll make it work."

Dean thought: Who is this man? "He was driving around in his scooter," Dean recalled. "He looked like a down-to-Earth, hardworking guy. Then all of a sudden he's talking in a way that is hard to believe. Your bank is going to give us $1.2 million because you say so?"

Dean said he and Laura drove to his house to do an Internet search and see if Bob really was a founder of Virginia Heritage Bank and a member of their board of directors. Dean was already thinking that a loan wouldn't work because they had tried. The roadblock was their lack of collateral. They didn't own the land. They had several hundred thousand dollars, but that wasn't enough to get a bank to bite.

The Grizzlies' request ultimately was not approved by Virginia Heritage Bank. Bob told Dean that he could try to influence the board, but he wanted to avoid controversy. "The bad news," Bob said, "is the bank is not going to finance your loan. The good news is, 'I'll give you the money.'"

Dean wasn't sure what it all meant. Bob arranged a meeting at his Fair Oaks store that was attended by some of his children and top managers and Dean, Laura and Gary Skeens, the commissioner of the Gainesville-Haymarket Youth Football League (GHYFL).

"He just wanted us to explain to his kids what we are and what we do," Dean said. "We did that. They left us with the impression of 'We'll look into this and see if we want to do this.' (On the way out) Bob patted me on the back and said, 'Don't worry, you're going to get the money.'"

The Grizzlies group heard back several times from the Warhursts, asking for more information. Bob later called Dean and said it was a done deal. Merrifield Garden Center would loan the Grizzlies $850,000 as an investment for the company's retirement trust at 7 percent interest. "Understanding that it could have taken many more years of fundraising to raise enough money to install turf at the complex, we are humbled by the generosity of Merrifield Garden Center," the GHYFL commissioner was quoted as saying in a press release announcing the Grizzly Sports Complex. "Their commitment to the youth in our community has allowed this organization to immediately provide a quality product engineered for the safety of young athletes."

Several years later, the Grizzlies were able to refinance their loan with a bank because of the collateral they accrued while making payments to Merrifield.

BEFORE THEY CO-FOUNDED Merrifield Garden Center, Bob Warhurst and Buddy Williams were friends and neighbors in Vienna, Virginia. Their families spent much time together sharing a love of horses and camping together under the stars as the sparks from their campfire rose into the deep night sky, climbing as high as their shared dreams.

Bob and Buddy loved horses, and despite living in Virginia—where the usual riding style was thoroughbred and very English with velvet riding jackets and knee-high black boots—they were happiest on quarter horses with big Western saddles, cowboy boots and cowboy hats.

"It was the original thread," said Wanda Flanagan, Buddy's oldest daughter. "They loved to be around horses and horse people." Or, as the old saying goes, "There is nothing as good for the inside of a man as the outside of a horse."

Buddy owned as many as 12 horses at one time at Hampton Hill, his private barn at his home in the village of Waterford in Loudoun County. He opened his property to riders from the Tri-State Riding Club for Western lessons. Later he brought in English-style riders, too.

"He wanted to support Tri-State and their endeavor to find a safe place to ride and better their horsemanship," Wanda remembered. "He wanted them to be good to their horses. In his opinion, good horsemanship in any discipline is the same. Good is good."

Buddy's love of horses carried on even after he could no longer ride and care for them. After a lengthy illness, Buddy died on July 20, 2011. "Buddy Williams was Merrifield Garden Center," his son Hal said. "He was so proud of what the two families built. It was his life." At the funeral, Bob honored his longtime friend and business partner with his most touching musical performance, playing "Amazing Grace" on the piano with the help of a musical accompaniment. "Buddy was a wonderful friend to me for 50 years," Bob says. "The last few years of his life weren't easy for him. I don't think God would want to keep someone sick for so long and make them suffer. It's a natural thing in life for people to pass away. Buddy's in a better place now with no pain and I'm sure he's enjoying his horses."

Doris took over as Bob's new business partner.

"I am so thankful to have been partners with Buddy and Doris all these years," Bob says. "They are great people. We stuck together and made it all work. I can never thank them enough for the role they played in making our dream of Merrifield Garden Center come true."

Another sad development happened in June 2012. After months of tests showing his prostate-specific antigen (PSA) levels going up, Bob found out that his cancer had returned and started to spread to other parts of his body. Dr. Robert Reid, a Fairfax, Virginia, oncologist, told him they could treat him with chemotherapy and drugs to buy some time, but there was no cure.

"It was very hard news to swallow," Kevin said. "All my life I have looked up to my father and thought of him as a man who could do anything. He was almost invincible. He is big and strong and had survived the Great Depression, growing up poor, being struck by lightning, suffering a heart attack and having his prostate removed. But now we faced the realization that he was facing something that even he couldn't conquer—cancer."

The doctor told Bob it was hard to say exactly how much time he had left since each case is different, but the normal range was anywhere from six months to five years. The good news was that he was still strong and not feeling any pain.

"So, do I think you have more than six months?" Bob recalls the doctor saying to him. "Yes. Do I think you have five years? No. Probably not."

The doctor went on to say that Bob probably had one to three years, but that it was hard to say. Bob was stoic. He took the news with a resigned calmness. He's not the type to cry or punch his fist through a wall.

"You have to face reality," Bob says. "What can I do about it? It is what it is."

As sad as death is, Bob always says, "It's a part of life." He had buried his father and mother and saw the passing of his brothers Charles, Jim and Tracy and Buddy Williams.

Bob didn't share the bad news with many people other than family members because he didn't want employees to stop working and come up to his office and ask him how he was.

In May 2013, Bob was admitted into Fairfax Hospital with breathing difficulties. It turned out that he had a serious problem: blood clots in his lungs that were restricting his breathing and reducing the oxygen in his blood. Bob overcame the scare. Doctors inserted a trap in the veins in his abdomen to stop the clots from traveling up his body and lodging in his lungs. After about a week in the hospital, Bob was discharged and went back to work.

Later that year, Bob was having discomfort and bleeding as the cancer continued to slowly grow inside him. He spent 22 days at Fairfax Hospital, where he underwent surgery. This was a precarious situation because of his age, the clots and the tumors. He wondered at times if he was going to make it out alive.

Before the surgery, Billie Jean and all their children visited him at the hospital. Kevin bent over and kissed his father's forehead just before he went into surgery. It was the first and only time Kevin remembered kissing his father. Being tough in a tough situation is a Warhurst family trait, but this was a time for tenderness.

The surgery was successful. Two months later, when he turned 75 on December 8, 2013, Bob said, "If someone had told me all those years ago that I could live to be 75, I'd say, 'I'll take it!' I've done just about everything I wanted to do in my life. I overcame all obstacles. I've really had a great life."

Bob had talked to his family from time to time about how they should proceed after he was gone, but many years had passed since they addressed it head on. He recognized that this was now the time. Despite his innate reluctance to talk about his own passing, Bob knew it needed to be done. He started a dialogue with family members about the future. The topics ranged from personal family matters to the future direction of the company. He expressed his thoughts, asked their opinions and made certain that everything was properly addressed.

"As delicate a conversation like this can be, I think it was a really healthy, respectful, honest and important discussion," Kevin said. "In a way that's hard to explain, I have never been more proud of my dad, my mom and my family than I was during this time. No matter how much time our father has left, which we hope and pray is a lot, I know we'll cherish every day and continue to learn from him. As I said in a poem that I wrote for his 65th birthday, *'Needless to say we are proud of this man, and all that he has accomplished since his birth, and are thankful to our Father in Heaven for making him our father on Earth.'*"

While family members and managers take care of most of the daily operations and decision making, Bob is still the boss and the leader of Merrifield Garden Center. He plans the future and makes all the big decisions based on the long-term best interests of the garden center.

When Bob's grim diagnosis arrived, Lee Warhurst, Bob's older brother, took it upon himself to do what he could to help Bob. Although he was rickety, Mr. Lee doted on Bob. Mr. Lee, who had encouraged Bob to leave home in Russellville, Alabama, when he was just 16 and come work for him as a bricklayer in Northern Virginia, often said he loved Bob like a son.

Next to Bob, Mr. Lee was arguably the most popular and recognizable person at Merrifield Garden Center's Fair Oaks store. He greeted tens of thousands of customers every year with a bag of fresh-popped popcorn or a hot cup of coffee.

Slim and trim and always stylishly dressed, Mr. Lee was in near perfect health until he was diagnosed with cancer at the age of 82. Thirty radiation treatments couldn't dull his spirit or slow his step.

A year later, Mr. Lee fell while walking out of a restaurant and suffered a painful herniated disk in his spine. "The doctors said it was the worst case they'd ever seen, too bad for surgery," he said. "They gave me a belt and said, 'Good luck.'" Mr. Lee wore the belt around his waist whenever he was at work, which was six days a week during the busy seasons, just like store managers. The back injury limited his mobility, and he didn't stray far from his table near the popcorn and coffee machines. He couldn't golf anymore, but he still lived alone in his condominium near the Fair Oaks store and drove himself to work in either his Ford Escape SUV or snazzy, red Chevy Corvette.

In 2013, Mr. Lee underwent gallbladder surgery. A dedicated worker just like Bob, Mr. Lee returned to work the day after he left the hospital. "He and I were the most alike of anyone in our family," Bob says. "The next week, Mr. Lee wasn't feeling well and left work early. I don't know why he didn't go to the doctor. He always went to the doctor when he didn't feel good."

Mr. Lee did not come in to work the next morning. After several calls went unanswered, Bob sent two Merrifield employees to his condo to check on him. They found him dead. He was 86.

"His mind was still young, but his body was falling apart," Bob says. "The last three or four months of his life, you could see he didn't have much strength. He was so stiff, he was walking sideways."

Mr. Lee's funeral was held on July 17, 2013, at the National Funeral Home in Falls Church, Virginia. Mr. Lee's Merrifield Garden

Center name badge, which recognized his 25 years of service, was pinned to his suit lapel and his favorite cowboy hat adorned the coffin. Bob prepared a speech about his beloved brother, but in a rare display of emotion, he broke down and was too emotional to read it. Bob handed his notes to Rob, his oldest son, who delivered the eulogy for him.

Before the casket was closed, Mr. Lee's youngest brother, Carl, put a bag of popcorn in Mr. Lee's hands for eternity. "That was his thing," Carl said. "If there was something wrong with the popcorn machine, he would call me. It was like we couldn't go a day without popcorn."

Mr. Lee's casket was buried above his brother Tracy's casket and next to his mother, father and brother Charles. During the burial ceremony, Bob noticed that some of the family plots were now very close to Lee Highway after a Virginia Department of Transportation road expansion project. Bob's folding chair vibrated as large trucks passed the cemetery. He also noticed that the land was low, making the caskets susceptible to water damage.

Bob decided that wasn't good, so he spent $70,000 to put 14 plots together for himself, wife Billie Jean, their five children and their children's spouses, plus two extra plots. The plots are all within 6 to 8 feet of each other on a hill. "It dries well," Bob says.

"Buddy and Doris's plots are just down the hill from us," Bob says. "Carl and his family will be near us. I hate leaving Mother, Daddy, Lee and my other brothers, but I don't want to be over there. During a rainy season, the water would probably seep right into the coffin. But that's just where the bodies are kept. We'll all be up in heaven together."

AS THE GREAT RECESSION GOUGED into the U.S. economy, Bob thought he would try another way to make money. Given that the stock market had taken such a hit in the financial crisis, Bob felt there was a golden opportunity for great returns. He started buying and selling stocks on a daily basis. He was not a true "day trader," who closes out his accounts at the end of the trading day but more like a patient eagle soaring above a river looking for fat trout in the rolling waters below. Only now his perch was overlooking three large computer screens in his office.

While he could no longer continue his labor of love spent over a shovel, a garden hoe or the steering wheel of a tractor, Bob could keep an eye on his trades from the comfort of his office.

"The thing I miss the most is not being able to do the things I could 15 years ago," Bob says. "Even three years ago I was doing real hard manual labor. When I had a tree to plant, I could do it. When I needed to unload a truck, I could do it. Fun stuff."

But Bob found stock trading to be a formidable new test.

"He has always thrived on challenges," Peg Bier said. "It's what keeps him going."

Bank stocks were hit hard by the aftershock of the financial crisis, but the $700 billion federal government bailout provided a huge psychological boost in consumer confidence. A year or two later, the once-roiling waters of Wall Street were calmed, but unemployment was still high. Bob took in the view and decided that big banks, like Bank of America, which hit a high of $50 a share before the crash and traded under $5 afterward, had only one direction to go and that was up.

Bob had dabbled in stocks over the years, but would always go through stock brokers. Now that he was becoming more fascinated with the process and following stocks more closely, Bob wanted the ability to execute trades himself so he opened a TD Ameritrade account and consulted with a few financial experts.

To learn all he could about investing, Bob attended a seminar held in the ballroom of a local hotel. Bob was dressed in his typical cowboy boots, blue jeans and Western vest. Bob asked a question about a particular stock and the "expert" leading the discussion looked up and down at Bob's outfit and asked how much money Bob had in a particular stock.

"Oh, six hundred," Bob replied.

The expert assumed Bob meant $600. And then the expert made a comment to the effect that if that was all the money Bob had to invest, he shouldn't be day-trading stocks.

Bob corrected him. "Six hundred thousand dollars."

The expert's face turned red in embarrassment. He didn't follow one of Bob's golden rules: Treat everyone no matter how they're dressed the way you want to be treated. The expert picked up a little newfound knowledge of his own.

Bob began searching for opportunities with other undervalued companies and began investing in them. Now that he was able to execute trades with the flick of his calloused fingertips, Bob was soon placing buy and sell orders within seconds. Because he was able to make trades for large amounts of money, he could earn big profits from small increases in his portfolios. He continues to listen to brokers, but he doesn't always follow their advice. Typically, they are too conservative for his liking.

Bob so believes in himself that he sometimes bucks traditional thinking.

With his stock earnings, Bob treated himself to a 2011 Maserati convertible, a white beauty with a blue top. As in his younger days hot-rodding in Arlington, Bob liked it because "everyone looks at you big time."

At one point, Bob owned 800,000 shares of Bank of America stock. Some of Bob's high-flying financial deals created concern from his family members. "The kids got all afraid," Bob says. "That's normal. If something did happen, it would really hurt. I could make more if I wasn't trying to please them."

Overall, Bob says he has been successful and made a profit in his two years of trading stock. Bob admits to often wondering if he had the chance to devote himself to it full time could he have made more money trading stocks than dealing with all the complications and regulations involved with running a group of garden centers.

In general, Bob believes in buying good solid companies that are undervalued and that have either good management or good products or services. He likes picking stocks that are not too expensive, say under $20 a share, so he can have more buying power with which to work. Although it's true that it's the same return whether you buy one share for $1,000 or 1,000 shares for $1, he likes the cheaper stocks because you can afford more shares without putting out so much money at a higher share price. Bob is okay with losing money on a stock, as long as he is able to glean some insight to make him a better trader in the future.

That search for the "magic" of knowing when to buy and sell is exciting for him. In the same way he picked the brains of experts to build and operate his garden centers, he studies the stock market.

BOB HAS ALWAYS HAD A GREAT VISION of the future, combined with a sharp mind for the value of property. Consider the evolution of the original Merrifield Garden Center at the intersection of Gallows Road and Lee Highway.

He had the foresight to see the unremarkable industrial-commercial strip for what it could become instead of what it was. What it became was an urban area that included high-density development and a new town center called the Mosaic District, a nexus of commerce and high-density housing just three miles from the always-booming Tyson's Corner area.

"All these years we've been getting offers to buy our land," Bob says. "Most of the time, they don't tell you what they want to build. There's not a year that goes by that we don't get 10 to 15 offers. It's such a hot corner."

Although it has soared in value, Bob has resisted the temptation to sell the "hot corner" because keeping the property allows him to operate his business and make a profit while also paying down the debt on the property as it continues to increase in value. Between his corporate, personal and LLC holdings, Bob owns more than 130 acres of land in Northern Virginia.

Selecting the site for the first store in Merrifield was not dumb luck. Bob's intuition told him that the Merrifield crossroads had potential for bigger and better things. Over the years, he did everything he could to buy other parcels of land around it.

A key move in the development of the Merrifield area came in 1986 when the Dunn Loring-Merrifield Metro Station opened. The station is less than a 10-minute walk north of Merrifield Garden Center. Immediately, the land in the area became much more valuable, because people want to buy property near mass transit. In 1999, Fairfax County decided to amend the comprehensive plan for the area, including the land in and around the Metro station, extending south toward the area where the Mosaic District is now located. The area was a strong location for commercial and industrial land, but with the Metro station so close, it was important to increase density to utilize mass transit. Kevin served on a task force to study the area and make recommendations to the Fairfax County Planning Commission and Board of Supervisors. The task force recommended the most intense development at two main anchor areas—the area near the Metro station and a new town center that was envisioned south of Lee Highway. But they also saw the need to keep many of the service-oriented businesses, such as heating and air conditioning companies, flooring stores and plumbing companies, for which the area was known.

The first phase of the town center was built with both retail and apartments, but the Great Recession arrived and development was slowed. Several years passed with little growth until the recession started to abate, and new developers broke ground on what would become the hip Mosaic District. It is a sophisticated mix of retail, restaurant and entertainment businesses that includes large apartment buildings and townhouses, 40 stores and restaurants and a state-of-the-art Angelika multiplex cinema. Large garages were built to keep parked cars off the surface streets.

What was once a place where dump trucks and cement mixers ruled the roads had changed into something far different than what Bob Warhurst and Buddy Williams could have imagined back in 1971 when they paid $325 a month to rent the land that would become the first Merrifield Garden Center.

The Virginia Department of Transportation (VDOT) bought about 20,000 square feet from Merrifield Garden Center for road widening. Now Bob is left with a nine-acre treasure chest at the original Merrifield Garden Center site, about 4.5 acres at the landscape lot, which is located near the Metro site, and a few smaller parcels scattered in the area. With his partnership group and another investor, Bob also owns a 60-year land lease on the property where Home Depot operates in Merrifield, Virginia.

While the Merrifield area was always good for business, it's even better now because highway access is vastly improved at the once congested intersection of Lee Highway and Gallows Road. A half-mile stretch of Lee Highway was widened from two to three through lanes and dual left-turn lanes were added. What's more, a 3/4 mile stretch of Gallows Road was widened from two to three through lanes. The rise of the Mosaic District as an entertainment destination is introducing Merrifield Garden Center to a new generation who seek the beauty of colorful flowers and abundant greenery, just as the generations before them.

One of the challenges for the family is to determine when, if ever, will be the optimal time to sell. Million-dollar townhouses and high-rise apartments are poised to take over the spot in the shiny new neighborhood where a simple plant store that was going to be named Bob and Buddy's Garden Center became Merrifield Garden Center. It's almost certain that as soon as the original Merrifield Garden Center store is sold, bulldozers will tear down the wood structures that Bob built more than 40 years ago to make way for glitzy new development.

No one can predict with certainty what the future holds.

But the time is coming when the next generation will take the reins.

CHAPTER SIXTEEN

FAMILY IS EVERYTHING

Since he was a young boy growing up in rural Russellville, Alabama, during the Great Depression, Bob Warhurst's life has been defined by his burning will to not only survive, but to thrive as the leader of his family.

From being a young boy entrusted to slaughter a hog so his family could survive a bitter winter to becoming the owner and founder of Merrifield Garden Center, one of the most successful independent garden centers in the nation, Bob has always put family first. Family is what his life has been all about.

"What I'm most proud of is my wonderful wife and our kids," he says.

Bob Warhurst made his mark on this Earth. He wasn't born to build pyramids or skyscrapers, but his monuments are our memories: a picnic beneath a beautiful oak tree in a suburban backyard, the rustle of autumn leaves on a sunny day in Georgetown, forsythia framing an Easter egg hunt in Middleburg and a Christmas tree laden with precious ornaments and a Merrifield bow.

"I'm very honored to call myself his granddaughter and to be a Warhurst," said Madison Warhurst, who has visited Alabama with her grandparents and her father, Kevin. "We've heard stories about Russellville, but to actually see it first hand was so interesting. Spending time with the people he grew up with showed me how special he is and really how amazing his story is. He took on the world at such a young age."

Bob will always be with us because his achievements are as timeless and diverse as the four seasons and as beautiful as a woman named Billie Jean.

"I'm nearly 50," Bob's son Larry said. "I don't consider myself a man. I'm a grown-up. My Dad is a man. Look at all my Dad has accomplished with literally nothing. I don't think I'll ever make it to that point."

Family is at the core of Bob's life, both at work and play. When customers visit any of the three Merrifield Garden Center stores, they are bound to bump into a Warhurst. After 43 years, Bob and Billie Jean still work and are joined by 22 family members, many in key positions with the company. In the list below, their five children are in bold:

Debbie Warhurst Capp – *Advertising Director*
Rob Capp (Husband) – *Plant Specialist*
Danny Capp (Son) – *Sales, Marketing and IT Associate*
Sarah Capp (Daughter) - *Warehouse Associate*

Rob Warhurst – *Manager*
Lynn Warhurst (Wife) - *Controller*
Lyndsey Warhurst (Daughter) - *Works outside the family business*
Ashley Warhurst (Daughter) - *Accounting Associate*
Robert III (Son) - *Works outside the family business*
Dave Ostroski (Lynn's brother) – *Landscape Designer*

Larry Warhurst – *Construction and Operations Manager*
Leslie Warhurst (Wife) - *Housewife*
Chance Warhurst (Son) – *Chef at Gainesville Café*
Jake Warhurst (Son) – *Landscaping and Construction Associate*
Whitney Warhurst (Daughter) – *Sales Associate*
Harley Warhurst (Daughter) - *Student*

Donny Warhurst – *Construction and Operations Manager*
Single

Kevin Warhurst – *Manager*
Chris Warhurst (Wife) – *Human Resources Director*

Madison (Daughter) - *Student*
Grace Warhurst (Daughter) - *Student*

Additionally, Bob's youngest brother, Carl, and most of his family work at Merrifield Garden Center. Carl serves as the company's facilities manager. Carl's wife, Sheila, works in accounting with their daughters, Melissa and Jennifer. Their son, Chris, is a sales associate and his wife, Emily (Merrifield) Warhurst, is a plant specialist. Jennifer's husband, JR Nelson, is a master electrician. JR's father, Donnie Nelson, worked for the Warhurst Trash Company and Merrifield Garden Center before moving out of state.

"For the most part, Bob has tried to treat all the family who work here like employees," Merrifield Manager David Watkins said. "They have to work. Certainly Bob is swayed by family. You can't not be. Bob hates conflict. A big role I've had is to talk to family members when something's not right."

The Warhurst name comes with great responsibilities.

"There is a certain level of behavior that is expected of you," said Lyndsey Warhurst, Rob and Lynn's oldest daughter. "You are not just reflecting on yourself, but on your entire family and the family business."

Growing up in a retail work environment where excellent customer service is part of your world, the Warhurst kids and grandkids have been immersed in a culture of politeness and responsibility. While other kids were learning their A-B-C's, the Warhursts were interacting with customers and learning to become people pleasers, problem solvers and critical thinkers.

The togetherness of family life is the glue that holds the business together.

"We are all so close," Lyndsey said. "Being together all the time, we got to see how you're supposed to act."

At some point, the third generation of Merrifield Garden Center will have to take responsibility for what their grandparents and parents created for them. For many businesses, that make-or-break scenario depends on the willingness of that generation to work as hard and long to maintain success as the previous generations did to create it.

If Merrifield Garden Center was a professional sports team, analysts would say it has a "very deep bench," meaning that it has a strong supply of replacements for starting players now leaving the game.

"I've got a lot of cousins who are starting to come into the fold," said Chance Warhurst, Bob's first grandchild. "They're feeling the urge to come back and contribute and keep going what Granddad has worked his whole life to build. As a kid, I always wanted to work at Merrifield. It was always a treat to see Dad at work. If you were lucky, Granddad would be there and he would buy you an ice cream cone.

"It has always been a positive environment. That's the way we do it. Granddad has created a positive environment and a family environment for our customers and our employees. You feel like you're at home except you don't have to clean up! I want Merrifield to remain this way. I'm going to do my best to keep it going in a positive direction and to make customers happy and want to be here."

Chance has had several roles with the company since he started working at the age of 15 on the Fair Oaks loading dock. The loading dock is no place for the weak. It's all about lifting and carrying, like a Gold's Gym, only with dirt, mulch and plants instead of barbells. After high school, he began working full time. He tried his hand at many different outside jobs, trying to find his niche. After an injury, he started working in the Gainesville Cafe. He found he enjoyed it and has a knack for cooking. When the cafe manager left, Bob picked Chance to take the reins.

"I've always enjoyed cooking," Chance said. "It's more fun and mentally stimulating. It allows me to be creative." He's hesitant to say he's excelling at the job but will admit, "I was dropped in and told I could either sink or swim. As of now, I'm still swimming."

Chance credits Bob with letting him be just another worker.

"Working your way up makes you appreciate it more than if you were born into it," he said.

Danny, Bob's third grandchild, also "grew up with Merrifield." After graduating from James Madison University in Harrisonburg, Virginia, with a communications degree, he pursued his interest in the wine industry. He never felt pressured to join the family business.

Debbie has always told son Danny that working at Merrifield is a wonderful life, but it's not for everyone. "As a member of a family business, you are held to a different standard," she said. "You have to work harder, put in more hours and be ready to go in whenever you are needed and to do whatever is needed. But the rewards are incredible. You feel like you are part of something really important and something that really means something to you. From a young age, I always felt like my opinions and suggestions really mattered."

Now Danny wants to bring back to Merrifield what he has learned.

"I want to be there to continue it on," Danny said. "Merrifield provides jobs for more than 500 people. I want to keep it going. It's part of our legacy."

Danny said his mother's generation "will all have to fill Granddad's shoes eventually. Then it'll be me, Chance, Jake and the others. It'll be fun. I'm excited to see what the future holds."

Lyndsey, Bob's fourth grandchild and first granddaughter, has decided to work outside the family business as a senior account executive at Capstrat, a marketing and communications firm in Raleigh, North Carolina. She graduated as a valedictorian from North Carolina State University with a degree in business administration, majoring in marketing with minors in art and design.

"I wanted to learn from as many people as possible before coming back," she said. "I always say, 'The day I stop learning and stop being challenged is the day I'll move on.' This has been a great place for me to get my feet wet."

The magnetic pull of Merrifield Garden Center was always there, but she resisted. "I knew that if I was going to try working away from the family business, I had to do it right away," she said. Her younger sister Ashley went away briefly but is now at Merrifield. "My sister says, 'I love it! I'm never leaving!'"

Bob gave Lyndsey some advice that she has not forgotten.

"If you want something, you have to work hard to get it," she said. "Will I ever come back? I feel like I will. It's in my bloodstream. I can see it coming out that way."

Of course, there is no replacement for Bob. The grandchildren can follow his lead, but the world has vastly changed since the days when Bob and Buddy Williams started Merrifield Garden Center. Will the grandchildren have the same hunger and drive for hard work, sacrifice and working together as a family?

Bob thinks for a moment and says, "You would hope so. We'd like to keep it going through the grandchildren. You never know who might step up to the plate. The nursery will certainly be here."

When work is done, the Warhurst family comes together. One of the unique aspects of the large Warhurst clan is the fact that they really like being together. Many families think of themselves as close, but the Warhursts live it. They work hard and they play harder, always with lots of friends to share the fun.

Hope Parke is the epicenter of the family. There is no better or more convenient location. There is so much going on that a schedule board must be maintained to avoid overlap. The family has many traditions and is always adding new reasons to come together.

Bob's children have a tradition of singing songs, writing poems and creating videos for Bob and Billie Jean to celebrate special occasions, such as birthdays and anniversaries. Billie Jean sang "If My Heart Had Windows" by Patty Loveless to Bob at their 50th wedding anniversary.

George Washington never had it so good.

BOB IS SINGLE-MINDED AND GETS WHAT HE WANTS. He is clear in his vision and explains in detail so others can see where he wants to go. He knows that he needs the expertise of others when he ventures into areas where he doesn't have a lot of experience.

In both size and personality, Bob is a big man. He remembers his roots but does not trip over them. He asks common sense questions when analyzing complex problems, often to the chagrin of self-proclaimed experts.

Bob sees the big picture and the horizon beyond it, anticipating action and reaction. Thanks to his days of hard manual work, he believes the devil is in the details, whether it's knowing how one brick is stacked on another and held together by mortar or knowing the tax implications of a multi-million dollar bank loan.

If Bob has a special power, it is the power to see the future of a prospective employee, someone who will join what Bob likes to affectionately call the "Merrifield family," which encompasses all of his workers.

"He knows right off if they're going to be a good worker or not," Billie Jean said. "It's a sixth sense, a gift for knowing people and feeling their vibes. He got a lot of that from his dad."

Bob's sixth sense is verified by looking at some of the people he has brought on: Sam Aylestock, Howard Saunders, Tim Guy, David Watkins and Peg Bier. Sam left to become a minister, but Howard has now worked at Merrifield Garden Center for 40 years, Tim for 39 years and David and Peg 38 years. Excluding family members, 45 people have worked at Merrifield Garden Center for 20 years or more, including 12 who have worked for 25 years or more. For their 25th anniversaries with the company, employees receive a watch, ring or other piece of jewelry.

There are some gifts that money can't buy, at any cost. What would compel a person to work the long, hot summer hours and the chilly, winter days for so many years? What motivation would it take to maintain Bob's exacting standards day after day?

If there is one episode in Bob's life that shows what the "Merrifield family" is all about, it would be the series of events that began on December 27, 1987.

Merrifield employees David Watkins and Joyce Eisenman were married that day at their small townhouse in the Washington Beltway suburb of Annandale. They are one of at least eight couples who married after meeting at Merrifield Garden Center.

At the Watkins' wedding celebration, a piano and dozens of guests, most of them fellow Merrifield workers, were squeezed in the tiny space. The guests listened to Bob's daughter Debbie sing "The Rose," a romantic ballad that was one of Bette Midler's biggest hits.

Not long after the ceremony, Bob looked at this watch and said, "All right, we've got to get on the road." The road was Interstate 95 South. Bob and Billie Jean and family members Rob, his wife Lynn, Donny and Kevin climbed into Bob's Travelcraft camper. Larry followed in his station wagon with his wife and two children.

The Warhurst caravan drove straight through the long, dark winter night to Jacksonville, Florida, for the funeral of Tim and Peter Guy's mother, who died after a lengthy illness. Tim began at Merrifield Garden Center in 1975 when he was 16 years old and his brother Peter started in 1987 after graduating from the University of Florida.

The caravan continued south on I-95 in the darkness. After 15 hours, they arrived in Jacksonville, where the group of wedding guests transformed themselves into mourners, changing clothes, putting on neckties and brushing their teeth before walking into the funeral home.

Tim was deep in thought about his beloved mother when the doors swung open.

"I turned around and there was Rob and Lynn and Bob and Billie Jean," Tim said. "They drove the entire night. Straight through. All of them. Larry. Donny. Kevin. It was unbelievable. I turned around and said, 'Mom, guess who's here?' Then I realized Mom isn't here."

It was Bob's idea to drive to Florida. "We all said, 'Yes!'" Rob recalled. "There was no convincing. Dad thought Tim was a good guy. He has been with us since he was 16 and now Peter started working here, too. Dad knew their mom and dad back in the early days of picking up their trash at Stonewall Manor."

If you ask Tim Guy why he has worked for Bob for 39 years, he'll tell you about Bob's generosity and thousands of acts of kindness over the years. And, if you ask Bob, he'll tell you about the look on Tim's face when the doors opened at the funeral home.

Thousands of people have been employed at Merrifield Garden Center through the years. Many were teenagers working their first jobs as cashiers or loaders. "From the lowest one to the highest one, he treats everyone like family," Billie Jean said.

Merrifield is large, with more than 750 employees working during the busiest seasons at the three stores and at various landscape job sites in Northern Virginia and the Washington, D.C., area. Despite that large number of workers, Bob the "Plant Whisperer" is also the "People Listener." If a worker has an idea, they can go straight to the boss without navigating the many layers of bureaucracy found in many other companies or government and academic institutions.

Bob sets the tone for the company. He's warm, friendly and caring, with high expectations that employees be productive, committed, take pride in their work and, above all, help customers. He has created a nurturing environment, more like a small town instead of the high-voltage atmosphere of the nation's capital. "He loves people," said Luis Gonzales, who has worked 25 years for the man he calls Mr. Bob. "The English-speaking people and the Spanish-speaking people."

When you talk to Bob, you really talk to Bob. He pays attention and asks good questions. His strong affinity for getting to know people makes him more than just a good manager. It also makes him an excellent judge of human nature. He knows what motivates his employees, whether it's family, money, a fancy car or a new home. His ability to find the buttons that trigger a worker's efficiency and enthusiasm must be in his DNA.

"Bob takes good care of the people who take good care of him," Howard said.

That's why Jean Myers, who has worked 28 years in the accounting department, drives 100 miles round trip every day from her Madison County home when she could work closer to home at a different job.

"He'd give you the shirt off his back," Jean said. "He's just a very good person. He cares. It's not just about him."

Bob noticed that Jean was self-conscious about a missing front tooth, which kept her from smiling. He bought her a whole new set of beautiful teeth.

"He's done other things for me over the years," Jean said. "I know he's done things for other people. I'm sure you would run out of space with all the good things he has done for people."

Many people claim to be a "people person," but Bob can rightfully say he is one.

"Bob is such a great guy and does so much for people," said Doug Wallace, Merrifield Garden Center's insurance agent. "But it is tough to do something for Bob. He doesn't like to go out to dinner. He doesn't like to go out to lunch. He just wants you to be there. He'll say, 'Come by the house' and he means it. He always says to bring your wife and family."

BOB IS NOT THE KIND OF GUY to toot his own horn or boast about his incredible lifetime of accomplishments. But his achievements and contributions have not gone unnoticed. At the MANTS horticulture industry trade show in Baltimore, Maryland, in January 2014, Bob was honored by his peers, some of the biggest buyers and sellers of plants in the nation, for his four decades of hard work and innovation in the beauty industry.

At a special breakfast meeting of the Virginia Nursery and Landscape Association (VNLA), with more than 100 of his horticulture friends in attendance, Bob was named 2013 VNLA Professional of the Year.

Decked out in a suit and tie and his signature cowboy hat and boots, Bob received a standing ovation from the people who know and admire what he's done for the industry.

"Under Bob's hands-on direction, Merrifield Garden Centers are among the premier garden centers in the eastern United States," wrote Robert Saunders when he nominated Bob for the honor. Robert Saunders is president of Saunders Brothers Inc., a family owned and operated wholesale nursery, orchard and farm market in the foothills of Virginia's Blue Ridge Mountains. He also wrote, "Bob's innovation and entrepreneurship not only in garden center design but also in the reuse and recycling of debris and construction materials is unique and admirable. Merrifield is a leader in our industry."

Bob never went to marketing school or business school. But he has a special skill for using these principles in his business. "You don't need to go to school," he says. "You just need to go to work and learn how to do it."

Bob's special skill includes the ability to find and hire the best people to fill the technical and artistic needs of his complex organization and integrate them into the Merrifield culture. That blend of high tech and high touch is evident in the beauty of his garden centers as well as the brute force of the massive machines that power his extensive recycling operations. He may call himself a humble "Plant Whisperer," but it is his ability to orchestrate all the components of his businesses that truly make him much more than that.

"Bob really pushed for professionalism in the industry, and for training and education," said Adria Bordas, a Fairfax County agricultural extension agent. "He's brought a lot of vision to the industry and a lot of drive. Our industry needs to work on professionalism and how to run their business and Merrifield is a great model. He's instilled it in his children and employees."

Bob Warhurst is many things to many people in the world of gardening. His innovations, his foresight and his ability to focus on a situation with blinding intensity is legendary. He has changed an entire industry with his ideas. Perhaps his most lasting contribution is his passion for hard work and its redeeming values.

"I'm proud of coming from such a humble beginning where we barely had enough food to eat to building the best nursery in the country," Bob says. "There wasn't any magic in it. I just did what I thought was the next step. The secret to my success is my work ethic. Each thing I did led to the next thing. I figured out how to do everything I wanted to do. Life is such a gift. The problem is, time just flies."

IT WAS A CHILLY, SPRING AFTERNOON and Merrifield Garden Center was at full throttle, with workers quickly unloading racks of beautiful new plants from big trucks and excited customers filling the familiar Merrifield red wagons with their wants and needs.

But Bob came home to Hope Parke earlier than usual. The big house was quiet. Billie Jean was looking out from the huge expanse of windows that framed the patio, the swimming pool and the thick oak forest behind the house.

Their five children were still at work at Merrifield Garden Center, some digging, some helping customers, some ordering plants and some managing accounts on a computer screen.

Bob was dressed in one of his brightly colored Merrifield Garden Center button-down shirts with the words "Plant Whisperer" stitched on the breast pocket, his overalls and his polished cowboy boots, clean but clearly worn from years of driving his big Ford F-250 pickup from the garden center to worksites. His gait was slow, the aftermath of surgery on both knees, mended but not as strong as the legs that once clambered up walls with a full hod of bricks and mud, legs that once wrapped around a powerful horse at full gallop.

Inside his thoughts, he's still the confident kid with the slick-backed hair wooing girls in the balcony of the Roxy movie theater, the speed demon who won running races in his father's shiny black dress shoes and drag races in his own 1957 Ford Fairlane, the young man who fell in love at first sight, the private detective tracking illicit affairs, the pilot who flew over the Statue of Liberty and the piano player at the White House and at his friend and business partner's funeral.

Seeing the fatigue on his face and his slow pace, Billie Jean, the one true love of his life, watched him ease into a big, comfortable chair and handed him a bottle of water. She turned to him and touched his shoulder.

"When are you going to retire?" she asked.

"What do you mean, retire? I've got too much work to do."

About the authors: Sharon and Sal Ruibal are award-winning journalists who met at USA TODAY, where they were sportswriters covering the Olympics and adventure sports. Sharon is Director of Communications at Merrifield Garden Center.